AF693328

Law, Language, and Legal Determinacy

Law, Language, and Legal Determinacy

BRIAN BIX

CLARENDON PRESS · OXFORD

This book has been printed digitally and produced in a standard specification in order to ensure its continuing availability

OXFORD
UNIVERSITY PRESS

Great Clarendon Street, Oxford OX2 6DP

Oxford University Press is a department of the University of Oxford. It furthers the University's objective of excellence in research, scholarship, and education by publishing worldwide in

Oxford New York

Auckland Bangkok Buenos Aires Cape Town Chennai Dar es Salaam Delhi Hong Kong Istanbul Karachi Kolkata Kuala Lumpur Madrid Melbourne Mexico City Mumbai Nairobi São Paulo Shanghai Taipei Tokyo Toronto

Oxford is a registered trade mark of Oxford University Press in the UK and in certain other countries

Published in the United States by Oxford University Press Inc., New York

© Brian Bix 1993

The moral rights of the author have been asserted
Database right Oxford University Press (maker)

Reprinted 2003

All rights reserved. No part of this publication may be reproduced, stored in a retrieval system, or transmitted, in any form or by any means, without the prior permission in writing of Oxford University Press, or as expressly permitted by law, or under terms agreed with the appropriate reprographics rights organization. Enquiries concerning reproduction outside the scope of the above should be sent to the Rights Department, Oxford University Press, at the address above

You must not circulate this book in any other binding or cover and you must impose this same condition on any acquirer

ISBN 0-19-826050-4

For
Stanley Paulson

Preface

This book began life as a doctoral thesis, although I hope that it has transcended its origin in that limited genre. There are many people I would like to thank for their assistance. My greatest debts are to Joseph Raz and A. M. Honoré, who supervised the work on the thesis, and continued to offer their help at later times. I am also greatly indebted to Ronald Dworkin, Joseph Raz, and John Finnis, for the way that their writings and lectures have showed me how subtle and meticulous legal theory can be at its best; I hope that my work has improved by trying to reach those standards, though I know that substantial room for further progress remains. Finally, I would like to thank Gordon Baker, John Finnis, Ronald Dworkin, John Bell, Andrei Marmor, Simon Blackburn, Stephen Mulhall, John Tasioulas, Mark Addis, John Gardner, Alan Thomas, Sophie Botros, Kenneth Campbell, Kent Greenawalt, David Helman, and Adam Tomkins for their helpful comments on earlier drafts of various parts of this book.

Earlier versions of various parts of this book have been published elsewhere as articles: 'The Application (and Mis-Application) of Wittgenstein's Rule-Following Considerations to Legal Theory', 3 *Canadian Journal of Law and Jurisprudence* 107 (1990) (reprinted in D. Patterson, ed., *Wittgenstein and Legal Theory* (1992)); 'H. L. A. Hart and the "Open Texture" of Language', 10 *Law and Philosophy* 51 (1991); 'A. D. Woozley and the Concept of Right Answers in Law', 5 *Ratio Juris* 58 (1992); and 'Michael Moore's Realist Approach to Law', 140 *University of Pennsylvania Law Review* 1293 (1992).

Contents

Introduction

LANGUAGE AND LAW

Language is the medium through which law acts. The nature of the medium necessarily has a pervasive effect on what purposes can be achieved through the law and how well those purposes can be forwarded. Part of my present task is to consider the relationship between language and law, focusing on how the two interact within the question of legal determinacy. In looking at the question of legal determinacy, I use examples from three different approaches to legal theory: H. L. A. Hart's legal positivism, the interpretative approach of Ronald Dworkin, and the metaphysical realism of Michael Moore. Each of these approaches appears to have a different view of the role of language within law. Roughly and generally—the details are to follow—Hart saw language as placing a limit on legal formalism and explaining the inevitability of judicial discretion; Dworkin believed that any problems created by language could be circumvented; and Moore viewed language, alternatively, as a path to finding the correct result and as a temptation towards the wrong result that must be overcome.

Like Wittgenstein's image of 'family resemblance',[1] in which a number of separate threads interweave to constitute a single rope, a number of separate but interrelated themes run through this text. First is the issue of legal determinacy: whether law always (or most of the time or never) provides unique correct answers to legal questions. Second is the role of language within law, and third is the use (or misuse) of Wittgenstein's approach to the philosophy of language within the jurisprudential debate.

One disclaimer: while aspects of my argument depend on a particular interpretation of the work of Wittgenstein (and occasionally other philosophers as well), and while on some occasions I will argue that some other legal theorist has interpreted a philosophical theory incorrectly, I do not put forward this book

[1] L. Wittgenstein, *Philosophical Investigations*, sec. 67 (New York: Macmillan, 1968).

as a text about the philosophy of language. What I do claim is that I discuss legal theory in a way that tries to be serious about philosophy (not that I am the first to do so). I believe that my claims about law and legal theory are sufficiently independent of my interpretations of various philosophers of language that one could agree with the former even while disagreeing with the latter.

Regarding in particular my reading of the later Wittgenstein, while little in that work is uncontroversial (either by way of exegesis or evaluation), the part on which most of my discussion is based, the rule-following considerations, is relatively unproblematic compared to other parts (for example, the private language argument). However, it is inevitable that occasionally I will offer an interpretation (or evaluation) of the later Wittgenstein with which some readers might disagree. To the extent that I have underestimated the difficulty of certain writings, or the controversy of certain claims, I apologize in advance.

INTERPRETATION IN CONTEXT

John Finnis has warned that an undue emphasis on legal interpretation tends to distort one's understanding of law.[2] Finnis's point is that if one is to follow H. L. A. Hart, Joseph Raz, and many other modern theorists in positing the guidance of future conduct as a principal point or function of law, then the interpretation of texts (constitutions, statutes, contracts) must be considered relatively unimportant compared to the initial creation of those texts and the deliberation which precedes that creation. This is not to imply a naïve distinction—between, say, a statute as pure object and a statute as an interpreted object—that neither he nor I intend.[3] It is a matter of considering what percentage of choices regarding the (legal) co-ordination or regulation of action are attributable primarily or entirely to the legislature or executive as against those attributable primarily or entirely to the judiciary. In Finnis's words: 'Interpretation resists being taken for the whole of practical reasoning.'[4] The initial legislative choices, which create reasons for action both for judges and for other citizens, do

[2] J. Finnis, 'On Reason and Authority in *Law's Empire*' (book review), 6 *Law and Philosophy* 357, 361–3 (1987).

[3] See ibid. 361.

[4] Ibid. 363.

not comfortably fit within the category of 'interpretation' or 'interpretation of a practice'.[5]

When the focus is judicial interpretation, there is a danger of overemphasizing the theoretical aspects of the topic. It is too easy for theorists to project their activity on to the subject of their work: for example, to see legal interpretation as being abstract and philosophical, analogous to or constituted primarily by theories of legal interpretation. Legal interpretation cannot be fully understood unless its context of institutional processes, politics, and coercion is also considered. It is not being melodramatic to conclude, with Robert Cover, that '[l]egal interpretation takes place in a field of pain and death'.[6] By its place and function, legal interpretation is inextricably linked to the signalling of or the justification for deprivations of a person's goods or the imposition of violence or forcible constraints upon a person.[7]

As interpretation, the issue of legal interpretation involves enquiries into the nature of language. However, as legal interpretation, these enquiries occur against a background of political debates and practical problems. For example, issues of judicial practice within a particular legal system often turn on how much power should be delegated to the judiciary, to what extent the judiciary should co-operate with the legislature, and how clearly the legislature must speak in order for citizens to be bound by the enactments.

'Language questions' and 'political questions' seem to occur at different levels of discourse, separable within a discussion of legal interpretation. Under this view, one would first ask what range of interpretations of a text are allowed given the nature of language, and then one would delimit that range in the name of judicial restraint, due notice, parliamentary sovereignty, and so on. However, this distinction does not in fact hold up on closer inspection. Even a superficial look at the relevant literature is enough to show that the two levels of discourse cannot be kept apart. The debate in the legal literature often occurs simultaneously on various levels: for example, to the conservative claim that judges have been acquiring too much power, some writers reply that given the nature of language and legislation judges can

[5] Ibid.

[6] R. Cover, 'Violence and the Word', 95 *Yale Law Journal* 1601, 1601 (1986).

[7] Ibid.

(should) do no less than they have done; and to the claim that judges should respect the rights of parties in hard cases, other theorists answer that given the nature of language and practical reasoning, in such cases neither party can be said to have a legal right to succeed.

Legal interpretation is (1) an interpretation, (2) in aid of practical reasoning, (3) which is both influenced by and influences the distribution of power among branches of government and between the government and the citizenry. My emphasis in this thesis will be primarily on the first aspect, with considerable attention given also to the second, but relative inattention to the third; I leave the latter to political philosophers. However, this last statement requires some clarification. The distribution of power within government would be relevant to my discussion in at least one way. A judge will have a particular conception of what role the judiciary does play and should play within the legal system and within society. That conception cannot but affect the way he or she proceeds: for example, how much deference the judge gives to the legislature when interpreting a statute. What I am disclaiming in this paper is the taking of any position on what role the judiciary *should* play in particular legal systems.

LANGUAGE AND CONTEXT

Legal philosophy, like many forms of philosophy, is a hybrid of conceptual analysis and empirical description. Many of the misunderstandings in the field—both among theorists and between theorists and their readers—can be ascribed to a failure to distinguish the two aspects. For example, a discussion of the role moral principles play in law may focus on the way judges actually act within a legal system or the way people actually use the term 'law', or it may focus on a conceptual analysis of that term. Admittedly, the two types of analysis are normally linked. The conceptual analysis is usually meant to reflect, or at least be constrained by, the empirical observations, and the empirical observations usually support, explicitly or implicitly, some conceptual point. None the less, the two types of investigation should not be confused. I see my work as primarily, though not exclusively, conceptual. Most of my conclusions are meant to turn on the nature of language (and on the interpretation of particular philosophical theories) rather than on how legal officials generally act or on how legal terms are generally used.

The extent to which problems of legal interpretation often do not turn on the nature of language was exemplified by A. W. B. Simpson's comment: 'difficulties in interpretation . . . seem to be difficulties about words [but] are really difficulties about the applicability of rules to facts.'[8] While judges and legal commentators claim to be trying to discover (and be bound by) what the words of a statute or a constitutional clause actually mean, something else entirely may be going on. In one type of situation, for which H. L. A. Hart's hypothetical applications of the rule 'no vehicles in the park'[9] were examples, there may be no answer forthcoming from language. Neither the usage nor the authoritative definitions of the term 'vehicle' may be sufficiently clear or narrow conclusively to include or exclude (say) skateboards. A decision must still be made in the relevant case, and the decision will be a binding precedent for the correct interpretation of 'vehicle' (for the purpose of that statute) in the future, but it would be misleading to attribute the decision to (or to blame it on) language.

A second type of situation is Dworkin's favourite example of *Riggs* v. *Palmer*,[10] where a murderer claimed the murdered man's estate under a simple wills statute. There was no difficulty about what the words of the statute meant; there was only an unease about the outcome the words seemed to command in that particular case, which would have allowed someone to benefit from a murder he had committed. These are the situations Frederick Schauer discussed extensively in his article 'Formalism': in extreme cases, where the clear application of a rule to particular facts seems to lead to a particularly unjust result, decision-makers are (often) authorized to decide contrary to the rule's clear meaning.[11]

The point is that while understanding language plays an

[8] A. W. B. Simpson, 'The *Ratio Decidendi* of a Case and the Doctrine of Binding Precedent', in *Oxford Essays in Jurisprudence*, 158 (A. Guest, ed., Oxford: Oxford University Press, 1961) (emphasis omitted).

[9] See H. L. A. Hart, 'Positivism and the Separation of Law and Morals', 71 *Harvard Law Review* 593, 607 (1958).

[10] *Riggs* v. *Palmer*, 115 N.Y. 506, 22 N.E. 188 (1889); see R. Dworkin, *Law's Empire*, 15–20 (Cambridge, Mass.: Harvard University Press, 1986).

[11] F. Schauer, 'Formalism', 97 *Yale Law Journal* 509, 515–20 (1988).

important role in understanding law, many other factors play significant roles in the legal process, so that even a major change in one's philosophy of language may not require a substantial shift in how one believes a legal system does—or should—work. My narrow focus on language and interpretation in law may mean that my conclusions about law will not be radical or surprising, but that does not detract from the value of the inquiry.

AN OVERVIEW

Chapter 1 offers a close reading of H. L. A. Hart's discussion in *The Concept of Law* of 'open texture', while also comparing Hart's notion of 'open texture' with similar ideas in the writings of Ludwig Wittgenstein and Friedrich Waismann. Chapter 2 summarizes Wittgenstein's rule-following considerations and criticizes the way various legal theorists have tried to apply those arguments to the problem of legal determinacy. Chapter 3 considers the paradigmatically uncontroversial 'easy cases' in law, and investigates what such cases can show us about the role of language within law and about the problem of legal determinacy. Chapter 4 discusses various aspects of Ronald Dworkin's right answer theory and his interpretative approach to law. Chapter 5 offers a critique of Michael Moore's metaphysically realist approach to law. Finally, Chapter 6 offers an overview of some of the book's ideas and themes.

I

H. L. A. Hart and the 'Open Texture' of Language

HART'S DISCUSSION OF 'OPEN TEXTURE'

In *The Concept of Law*,[1] H. L. A. Hart argued for a position on judicial interpretation half-way between formalism and rule-scepticism.[2] Hart's middle position was based on—or, at least, was justified by—a theory of the open texture of language.[3] This concept comes from the work of Friedrich Waismann,[4] which was in turn probably based on a constructivist view of language Wittgenstein put forward in the early 1930s.[5]

In a chapter in *The Concept of Law* called 'Formalism and Rule Scepticism', Hart argued that legal rules, whether promulgated by a legislature or derived as the *ratio* of a prior case, characteristically have a core of plain meaning. The decision whether a rule applies to a particular situation often turns on the meaning—on delimiting the range of meanings—of a general term. For example, the application of the rule, 'no vehicles in the park', will usually turn on whether a particular object is a 'vehicle' for the purpose of the rule (or whether a particular area is a 'park' for the purpose of the rule). In plain cases, 'the general terms seem to need no interpretation . . . the recognition of instances seems unproblematic or "automatic" . . . there is a general agreement in judgments as to the applicability of the classifying terms'.[6] However, in cases in the 'penumbra' of the term's meaning (for the purpose of the rule), it no longer seems clear whether the general term should apply or not. '[T]here are reasons both for and against our use of

[1] H. L. A. Hart, *The Concept of Law* (Oxford: Clarendon Press, 1961).
[2] Ibid. 121–44. [3] Ibid. 120–32.
[4] See ibid. 249; F. Waismann, 'Verifiability', *Proceedings of the Aristotelian Society*, suppl. vol. 19, 119–50 (1945).
[5] See G. P. Baker, 'Defeasibility and Meaning', in *Law, Morality, and Society*, 51 and n. 76 (P. M. S. Hacker and J. Raz, eds., Oxford: Clarendon Press, 1977).
[6] Hart, *The Concept of Law*, 123.

the general term, and no firm convention or general agreement dictates its use.'[7]

The tendency of rules to have 'a fringe of vagueness',[8] to become indeterminate in their application to borderline cases, Hart called the 'open texture' of rules (and of language in general).[9] Hart added that the 'open texture' of legal rules should be considered an advantage rather than a disadvantage, in that it allows rules to be interpreted reasonably when they are applied to situations and to types of problems that their authors did not foresee or could not have foreseen.[10] (Compare Anthony Quinton's discussion of Waismann's idea of the 'open texture' of concepts: '[T]he kind of linguistic indeterminacy it implies is a positive advantage. It allows for the continuous development of a language to accommodate new discoveries, as exemplified by the progressive amplification of the scope of the concept of number from the positive integers to complex numbers.')[11]

Hart was concerned with the problem of social control through law: not questions of strategy or political theory, of how social control could best be effected, but the preliminary question of how social control could even be possible. How can a government guide its population's actions on the basis of legislation and precedent, and to what extent will those means necessarily need supplementation? Hart stated: 'If it were not possible to communicate general standards of conduct, which multitudes of individuals could understand, without further direction, as requiring from them certain conduct when occasion arose, nothing that we now recognize as law could exist.'[12]

He considered two forms of guidance, corresponding to two sources of law: examples, analogous to precedent, and verbal instructions, analogous to legislation.[13] Compared to verbal instructions, examples seem far less clear and determinate. When someone tells us to do as he does, we cannot be certain what aspects of his performance must be imitated and where deviation is condoned because irrelevant. Transforming the example into a verbal rule seems to avoid these problems. Now the citizen need

[7] Hart, *The Concept of Law*, 123–4.
[8] Ibid. 120.
[9] Ibid. 124–5.
[10] Ibid. 125–6.
[11] A. Quinton, 'Introduction', in F. Waismann, *Philosophical Papers* p. xiii (B. McGuinness, ed., Holland: D. Reidel, 1977). I discuss the similarities and differences between Hart's and Waismann's ideas of 'open texture' below.
[12] Hart, *The Concept of Law*, 121.
[13] Ibid.

'only "subsume" particular facts under general classificatory heads and draw a simple syllogistic conclusion'.[14] However, Hart showed how general rules can take on both the character and the problems of guidance by example. According to him, when the rule (for example, 'no vehicles in the park') is enacted, both the legislators and the public have in mind a particular problem, particular situations that are to be brought about or avoided. In the 'no vehicles' example, the image is of excluding normal car, bus, and motorcycle traffic from the park.[15] Interpretation of the rule is thus seen as similar to reading a rule off an example, here the example being the problem the legislation was meant to meet.

Hart used a mixture of a paradigmatic and a criteriological approach to meaning. According to his analysis, our first move in defining a general term for the purpose of a rule is to invoke the image, example, or particular situation at which the rule was aimed. In interpreting the rule 'no vehicles in the park', we might begin by thinking: 'If anything is a vehicle a motor-car is one.'[16] In deciding whether, for the purpose of the rule, 'vehicle' applies to roller-skates or toy cars, one would 'consider . . . whether the present case resembles the plain case "sufficiently" in "relevant" respects'.[17] We begin with the plain case or the paradigm (the car) and then consider a list of criteria which allow us to begin to evaluate how similar a purported extension would be. For example, like a car, roller-skates make noise (but not nearly as much) and they threaten safety and order (though the threat is on a much lower scale). Further dissimilarities include the facts that roller-skates are far smaller than cars and that they do not pollute the air. There are both similarities and dissimilarities; some criteria are fulfilled, others are not. In Hart's language, 'there are reasons both for and against our use of a general term'.[18] This is the 'open texture' of rules, that particular situations arise that we are not thinking of when proffering the rule and which are different in some ways from the situation we had in mind (the paradigm) at that time.

Sometimes the extension of a general term from the original paradigm case to a different case is clear, not because there are no differences between the two cases, but because the problem of

[14] Ibid. 122.
[15] Ibid. 125–6.
[16] Ibid. 123.
[17] Ibid. 124.
[18] Ibid. 123.

extension has come up many times before, and a consensus has developed as to whether the term should apply. Hart noted: 'The plain case[s] . . . are only the familiar ones, constantly recurring in similar contexts, where there is general agreement in judgments as to the applicability of the classifying terms.'[19] For him, the problem of 'open texture' will recur regularly, because there are 'fact-situations, continually thrown up by nature or human invention, which possess only some of the features of the plain cases but others which they lack'.[20] The slow building of a consensus about whether to apply a general term to particular, relatively common, borderline cases will do little to mitigate the problem of 'open texture', for life will soon provide more uncertain borderline cases to replace those convention has transformed into 'plain cases'.

WAISMANN'S DISCUSSION OF 'OPEN TEXTURE'

I want to digress briefly to consider the intellectual origins of Hart's concept of 'open texture'. I will trace the concept back to the writings of Friedrich Waismann, and will also consider whether it can be traced one step further back to the work of Ludwig Wittgenstein.[21]

To understand Waismann's concept of 'open texture', it is useful to see it within the context of his work in general. Waismann's work was devoted largely to presenting Wittgenstein's ideas in a more accessible form; however, some of Waismann's concepts were his own extension of Wittgensteinian ideas. The concept of

19 Hart, *The Concept of Law*, 123.

20 Ibid.

21 While Hart's idea of 'open texture' derived from Waismann, his talk of 'a core of certainty and a penumbra of doubt' (Hart, *The Concept of Law*, 119) may have come from Bertrand Russell, though no attribution for those ideas was given nor was there any reference to Russell. Note the following from a 1923 Russell article: 'The fact is that all words are attributable without doubt over a certain area, but become questionable within a penumbra, outside which they are again certainly not attributable', B. Russell, 'Vagueness', in *Collected Papers of Bertrand Russell*, vol. ix. 149 (J. Slated, ed., London: Unwin Hyman 1988). I learned of the possible connection between Russell and Hart from F. Schauer, *Playing by the Rules*, 213 n. 9 (Oxford: Oxford University Press, 1991). Compare also Waismann's comment that for some concepts one could speak of 'a nucleus of meaning surrounded by a haze of indeterminacy', F. Waismann, *The Principles of Linguistic Philosophy*, 222 (R. Hare, ed., London: Macmillan 1965).

'open texture' belonged to the second group; it exemplified his particular approach to the philosophy of language.[22] Waismann, like Wittgenstein, disagreed with the metaphysically realist approach to language but also distanced himself from many of the positions that had been offered as alternatives to metaphysical realism. For example, the concept of 'open texture' was presented as an argument against the phenomenalist position that material-object statements are equivalent to (can be reduced to) some combination of sense-datum statements.[23]

'Open texture' was introduced to elucidate a particular problem for verification theory. It is because of the 'open texture' of empirical concepts, Waismann argued, that material-object statements cannot be translated into sense-datum statements and that empirical statements cannot be conclusively verified.[24] He wrote: 'a term like "gold", though its actual use may not be vague, is non-exhaustive or of an open texture in that we can never fill up all the possible gaps through which a doubt may seep in.'[25]

Like Hart, Waismann wrote about uncertainty arising from situations we have not foreseen: 'there will always remain a possibility, however faint, that we have not taken into account something or other that may be relevant to [the] usage [of terms in a statement]; and that means that we cannot foresee completely all the possible circumstances in which the statement is true or in which it is false.'[26] Elsewhere, Waismann wrote that a complete definition of a term cannot be constructed: because 'we can never eliminate the possibility of some unforeseen factor emerging', 'the process of defining and refining an idea' to meet each new factor 'will go on without ever reaching a final stage'.[27]

To try to understand Waismann's argument better, I will

[22] See Quinton, 'Introduction', pp. xii–xiii.

[23] Waismann, 'Verifiability', 120–1.

[24] Ibid. 121–3. Waismann's concept of 'open texture' should not be confused with more recent writings about vagueness, where it is argued that many concepts are 'boundaryless'. See e.g. R. M. Sainsbury, 'Is There Higher Order Vagueness?', 41 *Philosophical Quarterly* 167 (1991), and 'Tolerating Vagueness', 89 *Proceedings of the Aristotelian Society* 33 (1988–9). (I briefly discuss Sainsbury's ideas about vagueness in a later section of this chapter.) 'Boundaryless' concepts would probably also be impossible to translate into a sum of finite sense-datum statements, but for different reasons. One could think of 'open texture' as describing the potential vagueness (in extreme or unusual circumstances) of terms that are not otherwise vague.

[25] Waismann, 'Verifiability', 123.

[26] Ibid.

[27] Ibid. 125.

consider similar arguments from his other writings. Though discussions of verification are often the context for Waismann's analysis of 'open texture', the concept is not concerned exclusively with problems in that area. In fact, in *The Principles of Linguistic Philosophy*, Waismann seemed almost indifferent regarding the question of verification. He wrote: 'We were asking the question whether the assertion that a ball is lying on the table can be finally verified. The answer to this question is that this can be decided on our part by an arbitrary determination.'[28] It all depends on what we mean by 'verified', and there is no a priori reason, according to Waismann, to choose one approach over another; and under some approaches, the statement would never have final validity.[29]

Waismann argued that our language, as well as our usual approaches to verification, is organized to respond to normal background conditions and to the small-scale problems of everyday life. Our language and our grammatical rules do not serve us well if we start to imagine wildly unusual circumstances or deceptions of a Cartesian magnitude. Here Waismann's comments are quite relevant to 'open texture':

> The laws of any age are suited to the predominating characteristics, tendencies, habits and needs of that age. The idea of a closed system of laws lasting for all time, and able to solve any imaginable conflict, is a Utopian fantasy which has no foundation to stand upon. In actual fact every system of law has gaps which are, as a rule, noticed and filled out only when they are brought to light by particular events. Similarly we must admit that grammar is incomplete, and that should the circumstances arise we would make it more complete by introducing new rules to provide for such situations. No language is prepared for all possibilities. To deplore the insufficiency of language would be merely misguided.[30]

In a later chapter, he came back to a similar theme, but under the topic of definition—delimiting concepts (whether there is 'anything at all like an exhaustive definition—a definition which limits the concept in all possible directions').[31] He started by considering hypothetical strange situations: for example, a table that everyone can see but nobody can grasp, and an element that reacted chemically like gold but emitted a new kind of radiation.[32] Again, his conclusions echo his comments on 'open texture':

[28] Waismann, *The Principles of Linguistic Philosophy*, 74.
[29] Ibid. 74–5. [30] Ibid. 76. [31] Ibid. 222. [32] Ibid. 222–3.

Try as we may, no concept is outlined in such a way that there is no room for any doubt. We introduce a concept and limit it in *some* directions; we say, for example, "This is gold" in contrast to silver, platinum, etc. This suffices for most practical purposes, and we do not probe any farther. We *forget* that there are other directions in which we have not limited our concept. And if we did, we could imagine hundreds of situations which would necessitate new limitations. Are our concepts therefore incomplete, inexact? But what then would be an exact concept? One which anticipated all cases of doubt, one which is outlined with such precision that every nook and cranny is blocked against entry of doubt? But then we have to own, that *no* concept satisfies this demand; and we begin to see that there is something utopian in the demand for absolute precision. A concept is good if it fulfils the purpose for which it has been devised.[33]

Finally, in the article 'Language Strata',[34] Waismann argued that different types of statements—for example, sense-datum statements, material-object statements, aphorisms, and natural laws—must be analysed in different ways. 'Statements may be *true* in different senses, *verifiable* in different senses, *meaningful* in different senses. Therefore the attempts at defining "truth", or at drawing a sharp line between the meaningful and the meaningless, etc., are doomed to fail.'[35] It is a mistake, he argued, to try to apply the analytical tools of one language stratum to another, or to try to reduce one stratum to another, as phenomenalism and behaviourism attempt to do.[36] (Here, and throughout the article, Waismann's discussion of there being different language strata resembles Wittgenstein's discussions of there being different 'language games'.)

There are two arguments in 'Language Strata' relevant to the concept of 'open texture'. First, material-object statements cannot be reduced to a collection of sense-datum statements: 'a statement about a cat is a statement about a cat: and not a truth-function of sense-datum statements, or an infinite class of perspectives, or an infinite group of *sensibilia*, or heaven knows what.'[37] Second, the description of material objects (as contrasted with, for example, geometrical figures) is never complete:

[33] Ibid. 223.

[34] F. Waismann, 'Language Strata', in *Logic and Language*, 2nd ser. 11 (A. Flew, ed., Oxford: Basil Blackwell, 1961).

[35] Ibid. 26. [36] Ibid. 28–9. [37] Ibid. 29.

However many features I may assert of a thing, say of this chair, or however many relations I may state which hold between it and other things, or however many statements I may make about its life history, I shall never reach a point where my description can be said to be *exhaustive*, that is, such that no further increment in knowledge is possible. Any real thing is inexhaustible. My knowledge of it is always extensible. There is no maximum description.[38]

Both of these arguments fit well with arguments given in the article 'Verifiability'.

WAISMANN AND WITTGENSTEIN

Though Waismann's concept of 'open texture' is said to derive from a middle period of Wittgenstein's thought, corresponding with the material eventually published as *Philosophical Remarks* and *Philosophical Grammar*, related ideas remain in Wittgenstein's later writings as well. The following quotations are from *Philosophical Investigations* (which was published in 1953, eight years after the article which contained Waismann's primary discussion of 'open texture'):

I say 'There is a chair.' What if I go up to it, meaning to fetch it, and it suddenly disappears from sight?—'So it wasn't a chair, but some kind of illusion.'—But in a few moments we see it again and are able to touch it and so on.—'So the chair was there after all and its disappearance was some kind of illusion.'—But suppose that after a time it disappears again—or seems to disappear. What are we to say now?[39]

It is only in normal cases that the use of a word is clearly prescribed; we know, are in no doubt what to say in this or that case. The more abnormal the case, the more doubtful it becomes what we are to say.[40]

Despite these surface similarities, Gordon Baker and Peter Hacker claimed that there is actually a large conceptual distance

[38] F. Waismann, 'Language Strata' in *Logic and Language*, 27.

[39] L. Wittgenstein, *Philosophical Investigations*, sec. 80 (New York: Macmillan 1968); cf. id., *Philosophical Grammar*, 220 ff. (Oxford: Basil Blackwell, 1974).

[40] Wittgenstein, *Philosophical Investigations*, sec. 142; see generally G. P. Baker and P. M. S. Hacker, *Wittgenstein: Rules, Grammar and Necessity*, 229–32 (Oxford: Basil Blackwell, 1985).

between Waismann's concept and the ideas of the later Wittgenstein, at one point stating: 'according to the outlook of the *Investigations*' 'Waismann's concept of open texture is doubly incoherent.'[41]

Baker and Hacker argued that Waismann's concept 'presupposes a distorted conception of what it is for a set of rules to be complete (or incomplete)'.[42] They stated that the concept of 'open texture' 'is internally related to the concept of hypothesis (*Hypothese*), being the correlate of the thesis that an hypothesis can be made only more or less *probable* by any relevant evidence'.[43] The belief that material-object statements are 'hypotheses' made more or less probable—but never completely verified or falsified—by our experiences apparently intrigued Wittgenstein during his 'middle period'[44] and has some resonance with an early Waismann article, 'Hypotheses', that was not published during Waismann's lifetime.[45]

While Waismann did not elaborate, or even mention, a 'hypothesis' position in the later articles (discussed above) where the notion of 'open texture' was put forward, Gordon Baker has persuaded me that the conceptual framework of 'hypotheses' was tacitly present even in those articles. One piece of evidence for this view is the ability to trace back some parts of the article 'Verifiability' to earlier writings explicitly on the 'hypotheses' approach and to Wittgenstein's dictation on 'hypotheses'.[46] A second piece of evidence is the references in that article to evidence 'speaking for' or 'speaking against' a proposition,[47] which is the jargon of the 'hypotheses' approach.

[41] G. P. Baker and P. M. S. Hacker, *Wittgenstein: Understanding and Meaning*, 383, n. 12 (Oxford: Basil Blackwell, 1980).

[42] Ibid. 432.

[43] Ibid. 383, n. 12.

[44] Ibid. 432. Wittgenstein's ideas about 'hypotheses', and their similarities to some of Waismann's writings, can be seen by looking at F. Waismann, *Ludwig Wittgenstein and the Vienna Circle*, 99–101, 158–62, 210–11 (Oxford: Basil Blackwell, 1979)—the book contains Waismann's transcriptions of Wittgenstein's conversations with members of the Vienna Circle in 1929–32—and L. Wittgenstein, *Philosophical Remarks*, 200–1, 282–97 (Chicago: University of Chicago Press, 1975).

[45] F. Waismann, 'Hypotheses', in *Philosophical Papers*, 38–59 (Holland: D. Reidel, 1977)—this article was composed in 1936.

[46] Letters from G. P. Baker, 27 Mar. 1990 and 8 May 1990. See Waismann, 'Hypotheses', 38–59; Waismann, *Ludwig Wittgenstein and the Vienna Circle*, 99–101, 158–62, 210–11.

[47] See e.g. Waismann, 'Verifiability', 128.

I am tempted by the position that the criticisms, even if conceded, would only be a mild corrective for Waismann's approach. Waismann agreed with Wittgenstein that our concepts are not completely defined/fully delimited/completely verifiable, that this 'ideal' could not be reached, and that this 'deficiency' had no negative consequences for our use of language under normal circumstances.[48] The problem with Waismann's position from a Wittgensteinian point of view is that it does not make the distinctive Wittgensteinian continuation: if it does not make sense to speak of there being a *complete* set of rules defining and delimiting concepts, then one should not characterize concepts as being '*in*complete' or '*in*determinate'.[49] Though on this matter of characterization I find the Wittgensteinian approach generally superior (usually clearer, though in some contexts potentially misleading), I tend to see this dispute as a matter of philosophical style.[50]

However, I also understand the position of those who would claim that the differences between Waismann's position and the position of the later Wittgenstein are significant. Against the obvious structural similarities between Waismann's 'open texture' analysis and Wittgenstein's analysis in terms of defeasible 'criteria', the argument for a difference would centre on the view that the later Wittgenstein better explained that in understanding language (and in understanding our understanding of language) we must distinguish the agreements that partly constitute the meaning of particular terms and the background conditions of the natural world and social practices which are 'the framework within which our language-games are played, not part of the games themselves'.[51] Waismann's concept of 'open texture' arguably conflates the two, by claiming that changes in the background conditions

[48] See e.g. ibid. 123–6; id., *Principles of Linguistic Philosophy*, 76, 223; id., 'Language Strata', 26–8.

[49] See e.g. Baker and Hacker, *Wittgenstein: Understanding and Meaning*, 383, 432–3.

[50] There is an analogous (partly stylistic, partly substantive) argument regarding whether defeasible, criteria-based claims should be characterized as 'knowledge' in circumstances where no more certain (non-defeasible) claims are possible. See C. Wright, 'Second Thoughts about Criteria', in *Realism, Meaning and Truth*, 268–75 (Oxford: Basil Blackwell, 1987).

[51] Baker and Hacker, *Wittgenstein: Rules, Grammar and Necessity*, 228.

might cause problems for the definition or application of terms.[52]

HART ON 'OPEN TEXTURE'—REVISITED

Returning to Hart's adaptation of Waismann's analysis, what is different between the two concepts of 'open texture' is the type of unforeseeability—the type of exceptional circumstances—that was being considered. In this, Waismann's examples were far more extreme; he wrote of cats growing to gigantic sizes and people disappearing (asking how those events would affect our labelling of the objects as 'cat' and 'a friend' respectively).[53] When he referred to the 'unforeseen', he meant 'some totally new experience such as at present, I cannot even imagine' or 'some new discovery . . . which would affect our whole interpretation of certain facts'.[54] Compare this to Hart's legislators, who just happened to be thinking about cars when they promulgated their rule about access to the park, but who certainly *could* have imagined the possibility of roller-skates, skateboards, or golf carts in the park.

One could connect the two conceptions by seeing Waismann's idea of 'open texture' as Hart's idea taken to its limit. Imagine an extremely careful legislative draftsman who spent many hours listing dozens of objects that might be in a park and that might be considered vehicles, and then writing detailed classificatory clauses to clarify the original, 'no vehicles in the park'. At that point, the type of 'unforeseen' situations for Hart would begin to resemble those for Waismann, and the reasons why judicial discretion might still be necessary in applying even the most meticulously drafted statute would begin to resemble (without actually reaching) the reasons Waismann gave for our not being able to define an empirical term completely.

[52] While remaining critical of Waismann's concept of 'open texture', in recent correspondence Gordon Baker wrote that he now had 'qualms about whether the contrast between hypotheses and criteria is as sharp as I once thought it to be'. Letter from G. P. Baker, 27 Mar. 1990.

[53] Waismann, 'Verifiability', 121–2.

[54] Ibid. 127.

'OPEN TEXTURE' AND JUDICIAL DISCRETION

Hart argued from the 'irreducibly open-textured' nature of language to the need for judges in some cases to make 'a fresh choice between open alternatives'.[55] Even if the conclusion (partial indeterminacy) follows from the premiss (the 'open texture' of language), the basis for that premiss is not well established in the text; 'open texture' is more asserted than argued for. Gordon Baker claimed that Hart's argument is circular: Waismann's notion of 'open texture' derives from his argument/assumption that a term's sense is constituted by the rules governing its application and that no rule can be formulated in such a way that the rule's application is never in doubt; given that indeterminacy of application is built into the idea of 'open texture', it is not surprising to find it as one of the idea's consequences.[56] Baker went on to note: 'Although this is not generally recognized, the notion of open texture makes sense only within a particular form of semantic theory . . . As a result it might well be impossible for Hart to incorporate it into his philosophy of law.'[57] Searching for the philosophical presuppositions and consequences of Hart's concepts becomes even more complex if one believes, as I do, that his idea of 'open texture' is in fact substantially different from Waismann's idea.

I do not think that Hart's conclusion of partial indeterminacy—in my view, summarized by more than based upon the idea of 'open texture'—derived from a view of language so much as from a view of how people create and think about rules. Hart was not concerned about creating, elaborating, or defending a particular general philosophy of language. His concern was with the way that legal rules are (and should be) applied. Hart had not proven from the nature of language that judges must have discretion;[58] rather, he gave reasons why legal texts should be interpreted in a way that leaves judges discretion in applying the law.

In Hart's discussion of 'open texture', he often seemed to refer to words, sentences, and rules interchangeably. This might reflect an inexactness in transcribing an idea, not being sufficiently

[55] Hart, *The Concept of Law*, 125.
[56] Baker, 'Defeasibility and Meaning', 37.
[57] Ibid. 37 n. 46; see ibid. 50–7.
[58] Ibid. 37.

careful in describing the idea's domain or scope. It might also reflect a tension within Hart's concept, which arose because he was adapting an analysis of descriptive terms (Waismann's 'open texture') to an analysis of rules—and not just an analysis of rules as such, but analysis of the application of rules by judges in modern legal systems.

Waismann was writing about language in general; Hart was writing about language in the context of law—in particular, in the context of applying and interpreting rules—and the problems to which his ideas responded derive from that context. If, while we are walking through the park, my friend tells me about 'that vehicle' while pointing towards a toy car or a skateboard, I may find her usage strange or quaint, but I understand what she said; I can understand the use of the term 'vehicle' to refer to an object to which that label is not usually applied. Because the extension (from the usual usage of the term) is not radical or bizarre, I do not react by correcting my friend, as I might if she had used the term 'vehicle' while trying to refer to a banana or a book. A certain tolerance or laxness in the application of terms is beneficial in normal conversation; all is well as long as I think I understand roughly what my friend was trying to say (and she thinks I understood roughly what she was trying to say).[59]

The situation with commands, instructions, suggestions, and so on, is different. With such uses, because the focus is on the guidance of behaviour and because such sentences are often meant to be applied ('followed') on an indefinite number of occasions, the scope of the rule's application—determined at least in part by the scope of the rule's terms—is important. As Gerald Graff, in a slightly different context, wrote: 'the practical concerns of the law occasion the imposition of a number of artificial restrictions on interpretive procedure, restrictions that do not apply outside the legal context. These restrictions arise from practical, ethical considerations rather than epistemological ones.'[60] When language is used to guide and co-ordinate behaviour, the problems of interpretation and meaning will necessarily be different from those

[59] See e.g. D. Davidson, 'On the Very Idea of a Conceptual Scheme', in *Inquiries into Truth and Interpretation*, 196 (Oxford: Clarendon Press, 1984).

[60] G. Graff, ' "Keep off the Grass," "Drop Dead," and Other Indeterminacies: A Response to Sanford Levinson', 60 *Texas Law Review* 405, 411 (1982) (emphasis omitted).

that accompany language *qua* method of expressing one's thoughts or *qua* method of communication between persons.

On the issue of language alone, one point directly supports Hart's connection between 'open texture' and judicial discretion. According to one theorist about vagueness, R. M. Sainsbury, when a term is (intrinsically) vague it does not have any boundaries between when it must be applied and when its contrary must be applied. However, while there is no necessary place for drawing the line, it could be permissible to draw the line in any of a number of places. Consider an example from the area of colours: though there is no clear boundary between red and yellow,

> [n]o one can criticize an art materials shop for organizing its tubes of paints on various shelves, including one labelled 'red' and another 'yellow', even though there is a barely detectable, or perhaps even in normal circumstances undetectable, difference between the reddest paint on the shelf marked 'yellow' and the yellowest paint on the shelf marked 'red'.[61]

If this approach to vague terms is correct, then there is discretion (in the sense that any of a variety of responses would be equally correct) in setting the boundary lines for the application of vague terms in a statute.[62] Sainsbury also argued that the fact that the (vague) term itself does not set clear boundaries is an advantage for moral and legal claims that use the term, for an expression like 'child' can be used in expressing duties of care, 'whereas an analogous sharp predicate would draw lines in places which seem to have no moral significance'.[63]

Properly seen, Hart's approach was not based on a theory of language, at least not if that is defined as a theory about the meaning of particular terms. (The problems of focusing on particular terms as a way of understanding daily communication, let alone legal rules, was illustrated by Lon Fuller's 'improvement' example. Fuller showed that the meaning of 'improvement' in the sentence fragment 'all improvements must be promptly reported to . . .', cannot be understood outside the sentence's context—not

[61] R. M. Sainsbury, *Concepts Without Boundaries*, 16–17 (London: King's College London, 1991).

[62] Sainsbury also argued that vagueness is far more common than most theorists have supposed. See e.g. ibid. 22.

[63] Sainsbury, 'Is There Higher Order Vagueness?', 180.

only what the requirement relates to, but also who gave the order to whom, and what set of practices surrounds the situation.)[64]

While Hart at times seemed to argue that something about language makes it inevitable that judges will have discretion, he seemed at other times to concede that judges could interpret rules in such a way that they would rarely need to exercise discretion. For example, he considered and rejected a way of clarifying the meaning of terms within rules based simply on language: attaching necessary and sufficient conditions which an object or event must satisfy if it is to be subsumed under that term.[65] Hart's argument was couched as often in terms of policy as it was in terms of a meaning theory: he argued that any attempt to reduce judicial discretion significantly would have negative consequences (in particular, an inflexibility—an inability to recharacterize rules to meet changing circumstances).[66]

At this point, it is helpful to introduce a distinction between what meaning a writer (or speaker) tried to convey by his or her words, and what the words, considered by themselves, actually mean ('the well-known distinction between what a speaker means and what his words mean').[67] This distinction appears in various forms throughout the philosophical literature. It also appears, explicitly or indirectly, in many of areas of law,[68] as will become clear in later discussions.

The distinction can be used to clarify even some of the more obscure arguments in legal academic writing. For example, J. M. Balkin offered a 'deconstruction' of the idea that a text has a clearly definable 'core' of meaning independent of context, and only the text's 'peripheral' meanings are affected by context. Balkin wrote: 'If two parties have adopted a code for contracts involving livestock where "cow" means "horse", the core meaning of "cow" will shift radically . . . [I]t is the "normal" context in which we use the word "cow" that gives us its "core" meaning.'[69]

[64] L. Fuller, 'Positivism and Fidelity to Law', 71 *Harvard Law Review* 630, 664–7 (1958).

[65] Hart, *The Concept of Law*, 126–7.

[66] Ibid.

[67] M. Dummett, 'A Nice Derangement of Epitaphs: Some Comments on Davidson and Hacking', in *Truth and Interpretation*, 460 (E. LePore, ed., Oxford: Basil Blackwell, 1986).

[68] See e.g. J. W. Harris, *Law and Legal Science*, 132–43 (Oxford: Clarendon Press, 1979)—the 'will model' and the 'natural meaning model' as alternative 'models of rationality' for justifying legal decisions.

[69] J. M. Balkin, 'Deconstructive Practice and Legal Theory', 96 *Yale Law Journal* 743, 780, n. 106 (1987).

Balkin concluded that 'core' meanings, like 'peripheral' meanings, are context-dependent. The problem with this argument is soon clear. Balkin's contracting partners are not using the English word 'cow' in an 'abnormal context'; in a sense, they are not using the English word 'cow' at all. They could be described either as using the word 'cow' incorrectly, or of using a language of their own, where the word 'cow' has different rules for usage and different applications than it does in English.[70] In terms of the discussion above, we could distinguish the fact that (in English) the word 'cow' means cow from the fact that these parties used the word to mean horse. If the point of Balkin's 'deconstruction' is only that the meaning (the acontextual meaning, the 'core' meaning) of a word can change as we move from a common language to an idiolect (for example, from English to these parties' code) or from one common language to another (for example, from English to French), then his point is correct, but not surprising.

HART ON 'OPEN TEXTURE'—IN CONCLUSION

Hart's discussion of 'open texture' in *The Concept of Law* seemed to rest half-way between emphasizing speaker's meaning and emphasizing words' meaning, and half-way between a theory of meaning and a theory of statutory interpretation. The approach focused on what the speaker meant (and resembled a theory of statutory interpretation) in that Hart seemed to want the judge to focus on the problem the rule-makers had in mind. However, Hart did not have the judge try to discover the rule-makers' aim from legislative (or in the case of construing precedent, judicial) records, but rather from the rule's words alone: rule-makers' aims were equated with the 'clear examples' that fall under 'the language used in this context'.[71] Because the rule-makers formulated the rule the way they did, Hart implied, they must have had *those* cases (the 'clear examples') in mind, 'and [their] aim in legislating is so far determined because [they] have made a certain choice'.[72]

For Hart, the rule-makers' aim is embedded in the language,

[70] See Baker and Hacker, *Wittgenstein: Rules, Grammar and Necessity*, 332.
[71] Hart, *The Concept of Law*, 125.
[72] Ibid.

and where the application of the words to a particular case is no longer clear, '[the rule-makers'] aim is, in this direction, indeterminate'.[73] If Hart had been concerned only with what the rule-makers meant, or only with implementing their intentions, he would not have us reach that conclusion so quickly. He would have had us try to discover whether, the words the rule-makers chose notwithstanding, their aim might still have been determinable and determinate. He would have advised us to look through relevant records or to ask counterfactual questions (for example, 'even if the rule-makers did not consider the question of skateboards in the park, what would they have said had they thought about it?') to try to discover the rule-makers' aim. However, he did not do so.

On the other hand, Hart's approach was also not dependent solely on what the words meant. In fact, for Hart, decisions can sometimes actually contribute to meaning: '[w]hen the unenvisaged case does arise' and we make our decision ('by choosing between the competing interests in the way which best satisfies us'), we will have 'incidentally . . . settled a question as to the meaning, for the purpose of this rule, of a general word'.[74]

One matter which may explain some of the more paradoxical and counter-intuitive ideas in Hart's discussion is his use of 'we' throughout the relevant section: '*we* . . . frame some general rule of conduct', '*our* aim . . . is so far determinate', '*[w]e* shall have rendered more determinate *our* aim', and so on.[75] Hart's analysis of rule-application appeared to occur in a hypothetical context where the same person, group, or institution which had created the rule had the responsibility of applying or modifying it. Such a situation is, first, far different from the most common situation in most legal systems, and, second, far less troubling. The problems legal theorists face in the area of rule-application come largely from the fact that those who apply rules are usually applying rules written by someone else; in the American context, this means judges applying statutes and constitutional provisions or judges applying rules set down by other judges. Within such a context, one's view about how rules should be applied (interpreted, modified, supplemented) must depend in part on one's theory about the proper role of various institutions and the relationships among them. For example, those who see the role of judges as

[73] Ibid. 126. [74] Ibid. [75] Ibid. 125–6 (emphasis added).

merely implementing the will of the legislature,[76] and who believe that any judicial action that cannot be so characterized is illegitimate, would probably recommend an approach different from Hart's approach for facing an 'unenvisaged case'. (They would probably want judges only to make decisions that could reasonably be characterized as implementing the legislature's aims or values.)

Hart's discussion seems to rely on an unrealistic and distorting model, relative to the way most legal systems work most of the time. However, it may be *no more* unrealistic and distorting than the model implicit in many theories about judicial reasoning: the theories are written as if 'a single judge . . . has decided and will in the future decide all the cases in the legal system'.[77] A more accurate model (for American law) should probably take into account the facts of multi-judge panels, appellate review, and different judges (or judicial panels) having equal authority within a jurisdiction.[78]

To get the most from Hart's discussion, we must disentangle the various strands: conclusions based on the nature of language, conclusions based on the nature of rules and rule-application, general recommendations for how rules could best be applied, and recommendations for rule-application that are grounded in particular types of situations or particular views of institutional relationships.

One postscript to this section: when an earlier version of portions of this chapter appeared in an article form, H. L. A. Hart sent me a note commenting on it. While he was sympathetic to much of what I had written, he took issue with one aspect my interpretation:

> I certainly did *not* think I was saying something applicable only to the language of *statutes* or *rules* or *statutory* interpretation etc. My view was (and is) that the uses of *any* language containing empirical classificatory general terms will, in applying them, meet with borderline cases calling for fresh regulation. This is the feature of language called 'open texture'.[79]

[76] See e.g. R. Posner, *Law and Literature*, 220–47 (Cambridge, Mass.: Harvard University Press, 1988).

[77] L. Kornhauser and L. Sager, 'Unpacking the Court', 96 *Yale Law Journal* 82, 115 (1986).

[78] See ibid. 82–3, 115–17. I discuss this issue briefly in Chap. 4.

[79] Letter from H. L. A. Hart, 16 July 1991.

While I was obviously in no position to argue with Hart about what he meant when he wrote *The Concept of Law*, I continue to stand by my somewhat different reading of that text as being philosophically more defensible.

'GAPS', 'EXTRA-LEGAL SOURCES', AND DISCRETION

Hart had not been completely clear in his description of the situation in which judges must use discretion. Are there 'gaps' in the law because language, rules, or the law have 'run out' entirely, or because the meanings of the relevant materials have simply 'faded' so much at the periphery that they no longer determine a particular answer or interpretation, even though they do establish a range of permissible (and, by inference, a range of impermissible) answers and interpretations? The references to 'gaps' in the law, the law 'running out', and rules 'fading' are all, obviously, metaphors. Discovering the meaning of the metaphors would involve answering one of the central questions of legal theory: to what extent can rules, within the decision procedures of a legal system, determine unique correct answers for every—or for any—question presented to the courts.

On the subject of 'gaps' in the law, John Gardner recently offered a helpful gloss on Hart's discussion.[80] Gardner distinguished between instances where the law provides no complete answer and where it provides no required answer. In other words, there will be occasions where there are legal materials relevant to (or adequate for) the solution of a problem, yet the materials do not collectively entail a particular decision. This situation will occur, for example, where contrary legal standards of equal weight apply to the same problem or where a permissive source of law (for example, a treatise) suggests the answer to the problem.[81]

Gardner conceded that the traditional response would be that any choice between two equally valid legal options must, almost by definition, be based either on a policy choice by the judge (and thus, discretion in the strong sense),[82] or at least on extra-legal

[80] J. Gardner, 'Concerning Permissive Sources and Gaps', 8 *Oxford Journal of Legal Studies* 457 (1988). [81] Ibid. 457–60.

[82] Discretion in the 'strong sense' involves a decision not bound by standards, as contrasted with discretion in the 'weak sense', where the application of standards

standards of some sort.[83] However, he suggested that sometimes when choosing between equally viable alternatives, decision-makers may 'simply "judge", without resort to *any* further norms'.[84] (I will consider a similar analysis of decision-making when I discuss incommensurability in Chapter 4). Thus, in the kind of cases Gardner was discussing, though the law does not determine a unique correct answer, a choice is made without recourse to extra-legal standards.

It is of some importance to clarify what 'discretion' means in the context of Hart's discussion of 'open texture'. (While I have some interest in what Hart *meant* by 'discretion', I am primarily interested in which notion of discretion would be most defensible in this context, whether it is the notion Hart in fact intended or not.) There are various, mutually inconsistent ways of defining 'discretion' in this context; I will analyse 'discretion' as the negative analogue of the 'one right answer' approach. That is, judges have discretion if it is not the case that, as a matter of law, there is only one right answer to the question before them. Thus, under this approach, judicial discretion is consistent with there being for a particular case *either* a range of possible right answers (along with a range of wrong answers) *or* no justified characterization of any answer as 'right' or 'wrong' before the decision is handed down.

Under this approach, discretion is certainly not equivalent to licence. In a later essay, Hart wrote that by his notion of judicial discretion he did not mean that the judge's decision would be merely arbitrary.[85] This picks up on a passage from *The Concept of Law* where he had written that in the filling in of 'open texture', judges display 'judicial virtues' (for example, impartiality and reliance on neutral principles) in a legislative task.[86] Judicial discretion would be consistent not only with the relatively weak constraints of rationality Ronald Dworkin equated with 'strong

may involve judgement or where the decision-maker's choice is final and unreviewable: R. Dworkin, *Taking Rights Seriously*, 31–4 (London: Duckworth, 1977).

[83] Gardner, 'Concerning Permissive Sources and Gaps', 459–60.

[84] Ibid. 460.

[85] H. L. A. Hart, 'Problems in the Philosophy of Law', in *Essays in Jurisprudence and Philosophy*, 106–7 (Oxford: Clarendon Press, 1983).

[86] Hart, *The Concept of Law*, 200–1.

discretion'[87] and the 'judicial virtues' Hart discussed,[88] but also with more significant constraints (for example, that only two or three of a larger number of possible solutions would be acceptable). Discretion is a negative freedom, an absence of constraint, but not necessarily (or usually) an absolute freedom.

Even with this minimalist approach to discretion, a number of complex conceptual questions remain. When I say that law does not determine a single correct answer for a particular case, what is meant by 'law'? Though legal theorists often seem to believe that much is at stake in the question of whether a particular source, factor, or justification is 'legal' or 'extra-legal', much of the discussion on this issue is confused or question-begging. Questions are begged because what is or is not part of law is as contested as whether law is or is not a closed system (with regard to judicial interpretation), and the two issues interrelate in ways that are in part a matter of substantive theory and in part a matter of stipulation or definition. Confusion occurs because the debate often is a symptom of a more basic disagreement about purpose or methodology.

One example of this strange debate occurred when Joseph Raz argued against Ronald Dworkin that while judges may be 'legally required to follow certain moral standards', *qua* moral these standards would not be part of law.[89] In his response, Dworkin described Raz's use of the word 'law' as arbitrary, and appealed to the 'ordinary usage' of the term, which would, he said, tend to characterize as 'law' (at least) all the standards that judges had a duty to apply.[90]

The disagreement between Raz and Dworkin derives from a more basic disagreement regarding law and legal theory. As Dworkin sees law (or at least the English and American legal systems) as being primarily or paradigmatically about the justification of state coercion,[91] one can understand why his legal theory, and his division between 'legal' and 'extra-legal', focuses on judicial decisions. Raz's legal theory, by contrast, views law as

[87] Dworkin, *Taking Rights Seriously*, 33.
[88] Hart, *The Concept of Law*, 200–1.
[89] J. Raz, 'Legal Principles and the Limits of Law', in *Ronald Dworkin and Contemporary Jurisprudence*, 85 (M. Cohen, ed., London: Duckworth, 1984).
[90] R. Dworkin, 'A Reply by Ronald Dworkin', ibid. 261–3.
[91] Dworkin, *Law's Empire*, 93, 109, 127.

essentially a means of guiding and co-ordinating citizens' behaviour, and the theory divides 'legal' and 'extra-legal' along corresponding lines (for example, that standards that require further moral reasoning before a citizen knows what can and cannot be done are not—at least not yet—'legal').[92]

As one can see by the Raz–Dworkin debate outlined above, 'law' is used in two different ways by theorists: either (1) whatever standards judges are under a legal obligation to apply, or (2) a certain set of standards, usually a subset of those judges have an obligation to apply, that is derived from particular institutional criteria. The two definitions diverge in cases where judges have an obligation to apply standards whose source or whose basis for validity lies outside the legal system (for example, moral standards). Legal systems often give binding force to the rules of other institutions (for example, the internal rules of a trade union or a religious institution).[93] There is a sense in which such standards, though enforced by legal institutions, are 'extra-legal'.

However, the problem of discretion is not merely a product of where we place the 'legal/extra-legal' boundary line. Discretion would occur on the borderlines of whatever standards the legal system adopts and applies. If judicial decisions are to be based on what the legislature had decided (or would have decided had they considered the question), on the position of 'community morality', on the usual business practices in the area, or on whether an action was reasonable, there will always be borderline areas, and in these unclear borderline areas judges will have discretion.[94]

AN OVERVIEW OF THE CRITICS

> It is like saying I have to choose between giving food to a starving man and being mimsy with the borogoves.[95]

Some critics have claimed that the law has means or procedures for circumventing the problems of 'open texture'. I will briefly

[92] See e.g. J. Raz, 'The Problem about the Nature of Law', 21 *University of Western Ontario Law Review* 203, 207–16 (1983).

[93] See J. Raz, *Practical Reason and Norms*, 2nd ed., 152–4 (Princeton, NJ: Princeton University Press, 1990).

[94] The reason one cannot get around the problem by having default positions, burdens of proof, or presumptions, will be discussed in the next section.

[95] Fuller, 'Positivism and Fidelity to Law', 656.

consider comments from three such critics: Lon Fuller, Ronald Dworkin, and David Lyons.

Fuller, in response to an early formulation of Hart's theory of 'open texture',[96] offered the following criticisms. First, judges do not usually interpret words, but rather whole sections of a statute. A section does not have 'standard instances' or 'penumbras' in the same manner that words do.[97] Second, the 'core meaning' of terms in a legal rule derives from a consideration, albeit often tacit, of the rule-maker's purpose in enacting the rule.[98] Fuller characterized Hart as accepting meaning's dependence on function and context within formal systems (for example, in games and in the legal system), but missing the fact that this insight could be applied more broadly to 'the countless informal and overlapping systems that run through language as a whole'.[99] Such systematic elements in language, Fuller argued, are what allow us to understand familiar words even when they are used in a novel sense. He asserted that this point vitiates any simple derivation of an 'open texture' of law from the 'open texture' of general classifying terms: 'Professor Hart seems nowhere to recognize that a rule or statute has a structural or systematic quality that reflects itself in some measure into the meaning of every principal term.'[100]

Under my reading of *The Concept of Law*, Fuller's criticisms largely miss the mark. For example, I do not think Hart would disagree with the point of Fuller's rhetorical question: 'Is it really ever possible to interpret a word in a statute without knowing the aim of the statute?'[101] Hart would accept Fuller's position as the starting-point for judicial interpretation, but he would disagree that such resources are sufficient to avoid the need for judicial discretion.[102] Fuller wrote: 'We must . . . be sufficiently capable of putting ourselves in the position of those who drafted the rule to know what they thought "ought to be". It is in the light of this "ought" that we must decide what the rule "is".'[103] Hart's response would be that this inquiry is at least partly misguided. The rule-makers have decided 'what ought to be' regarding the 'plain cases'

96 Hart, 'Positivism and the Separation of Law and Morals', 606–15.

97 Fuller, 'Positivism and Fidelity to Law', 662–3.

98 Ibid. 663.

99 Ibid. 668 n. 40.

100 Ibid.

101 Ibid. 664.

102 See e.g. Hart, *The Concept of Law* 125–6; Hart, 'Introduction', in *Essays in Jurisprudence and Philosophy*, 7–8.

103 Fuller, 'Positivism and Fidelity to Law', 666.

before them. (This could be seen as an answer to Fuller's criticisms about 'core meaning' applying only to words. The 'plain cases', the cases the rule-makers had in mind when formulating the rule, can be seen as the 'core meaning' of those rules.) However, the rule-makers 'have not settled, because [they] have not anticipated, the question which will be raised by the unenvisaged case when it occurs'.[104]

Frederick Schauer has argued that Fuller overstated the importance of context in meaning and understanding. Words like 'cat' and 'vehicle' do have a meaning—and, if you like, a 'core meaning'—even when they are completely shorn of any context.[105] Schauer referred to an example Fuller had proffered as a rebuttal to 'core meaning': the application of the rule 'no vehicles in the park' to a war monument that included a working truck.[106] Schauer wrote, and I would agree, that the upshot of the alleged counter-example is not that trucks are not part of the 'core meaning' of 'vehicle', but that the strict application of rules sometimes produces absurd results (or, at the least, results inconsistent with the rules' purposes).[107]

Schauer did not discuss what I would consider the more difficult argument to meet: Fuller's example, discussed earlier, of the way the meaning of the word 'improvement' varies from context to context, and has little content when no context is present. Andrei Marmor has suggested that 'improvement' in Fuller's argument works as a 'family-resemblance' term, having different but related meanings in different contexts. It is not then the case, as Fuller would have it, that 'improvement' has *no* 'standard instances'. Rather, it has different, related groups of standard instances, just as for the term 'game' there would be different, related standard instances of board games, team sports, and one-person games, but no one standard instance of 'game' itself, and no attribute common to all referents of the term.[108]

Fuller's arguments were directed primarily against the positions that words can always be understood acontextually and that the application of legal rules usually turns on the acontextual meaning

104 Hart, *The Concept of Law*, 126.
105 Schauer, *Playing by the Rules*, 55–60.
106 Fuller, 'Positivism and Fidelity to Law', 663.
107 Schauer, *Playing by the Rules*, 58–9.
108 A. Marmor, *Interpretation and Legal Theory*, 133–5 (Oxford: Clarendon Press, 1992).

of particular terms. I think we are properly warned against taking such extreme positions in our legal theory or in our reading of Hart. However, as I have argued, a proper reading of Hart would not ascribe such positions to him.

Ronald Dworkin argued (in his early works) that there are procedural ways to circumvent the problems of 'open texture', that lawyers and judges have established ways of dealing with the vagueness of words within a statute or the vagueness of a statute itself. First, there are canons of statutory interpretation 'which determine what force a vague word must be taken to have on a particular occasion, or at least make its force depend upon further questions that in principle have a right answer'.[109] Secondly, a judge might be said to have a duty to choose from among the permissible interpretations of an indeterminate statute the interpretation that 'best advances the set of principles and policies that provides the best political justification for the statute at the time it was passed'.[110] Thirdly, a lawyer might argue that if a statute is indeterminate, the statute should be held to change the status quo 'only to the extent justified by the indisputable core of the language employed'.[111] (In the United States, a rule for interpretation similar to Dworkin's cutting-back-to-the-core rule appears to be mandated for criminal statutes.)[112]

I do not think that Hart need be troubled by such arguments. As for the value of canons of interpretation, he wrote: 'they cannot eliminate, though they can diminish, [the] uncertainties [of interpretation]; for these canons are themselves general rules for the use of language, and make use of general terms which themselves require interpretation.'[113] Secondly, to argue that we could interpret a statute by arbitrarily delimiting the range of some term to its clear instances is to assume—strangely—that the line between that term's clear applications and its unclear applications can be cleanly drawn even though the line between where the term applies and where it does not cannot be.[114] Such a position

[109] R. Dworkin, 'No Right Answer?', in *Law, Morality, and Society*, 68 (P. M. S. Hacker and J. Raz, eds., Oxford: Clarendon Press, 1977).

[110] Ibid.

[111] Ibid.

[112] See e.g. *McNally* v. *United States*, 483 U.S. 350, 359–60 (1987).

[113] Hart, *The Concept of Law*, 123.

[114] See J. Raz, *The Authority of Law*, 73–4 (Oxford: Clarendon Press, 1979); H. Putnam, 'The Meaning of "Meaning" ', in *Mind, Language and Reality*, 216–17 (Cambridge: Cambridge University Press, 1975).

immediately raises many difficult questions: for example, how much uncertainty and of what kind is necessary to signal the beginning of a term's penumbra/borderline cases? And what if everyone agrees that the term applies to a particular case, but not everyone agrees that the case is 'plain' or 'clear'? A better view seems to be there is a spectrum that goes from plain case to penumbra to non-application.[115]

Dworkin's challenge and the initial responses could be seen as presaging a recent development in the theory of vague concepts. R. M. Sainsbury[116] has discussed in a series of articles the nature of vagueness: in particular, the idea that vague concepts are completely boundaryless, and that such boundaryless concepts may be quite common (thereby forcing us to rethink approaches to language which are based on the assumption that most words can be defined in set-theoretical or natural-kind ways). Some theorists had treated vague concepts (like 'bald') as though they divided the world into three: positive cases (definitely bald), negative cases (definitely not bald) and borderline cases (not sure).[117] The assumption was that the problem of borderlines occurs only at this first level: that though we cannot draw sharp lines between the positive cases and the negative cases, we *could* draw sharp lines between the borderline cases and either the positive cases or the negative cases. This follows the basic approach used by Dworkin—and perhaps even by Hart—in their discussions of 'open texture'.

Sainsbury showed the difficulty in assuming that there are any sharp borderlines in vague predicates, using the example of the predicate 'child': if there were a sharp boundary between definite cases of being a child and borderline cases of being a child, 'it would remain true that there would be such a thing as the last heartbeat of my childhood, or at any rate the last hearbeat of my definite childhood, and that seems as crazy as the idea that the predicate "child" divides the universe into a set and its complement within the universal set'.[118]

[115] Dworkin seemed later to recognize the difficulty of his position; he noted in a different context that 'it can be a hard question whether the case at hand is a hard case or an easy case': Dworkin, *Law's Empire*, 354.

[116] His primary works on this subject are *Concepts Without Boundaries*; 'Is There Higher Order Vagueness?'; and 'Tolerating Vagueness'.

[117] Sainsbury, 'Is There Higher Order Vagueness?', 167–8.

[118] Ibid. 168.

Returning to Hart's critics, David Lyons offered a variation on the theme of Dworkin's critique. He drew an analogy between law and ordinary language: 'it does not follow that there are determinate facts only where our current linguistic resources enable us straightforwardly to express them'; by analogy, even if we concede that law is irreducibly 'open textured', law has further resources which allow us to determine legal conclusions even where legal formulations have indeterminate implications.[119]

Underlying the disagreement between Lyons and Hart appear to be different assumptions regarding the nature of language or the nature of law, although these assumptions go largely unstated. Hart's position was based on the position that law is constituted by rules; that is all there is. When rules are indeterminate, law is indeterminate. It is not clear what alternative vision Lyons was defending. His argument here was that particular rule-formulations are only tentative approximations of the legal truth. However, to evaluate that argument properly, we must be clearer about what this position asserts to be the nature of 'legal truth'. There are at least two possibilities: Michael Moore's metaphysically realist approach to law and Ronald Dworkin's view of law as constructive interpretation. As I will consider both of these views later in this paper, I will not consider Lyons's position extensively here. However, I will briefly discuss some considerations to keep in mind when evaluating the type of argument Lyons seemed to be invoking.

Lyons asserted that in normal language we go beyond mere words to find meaning ('reality') and, analogously, judges look beyond legal rules to find legal meaning ('the Law'). This may or may not be an argument for a distinction between a rule and its various possible formulations. However, though such a distinction would be consistent with metaphysical realism regarding rules, it does not entail that position; we can accept the distinction between a rule and its expression in one particular formulation without having to believe the rules are abstract (Platonic) entities.[120]

For example, different rule-formulations could be like the alternative interpretations of a single rule Wittgenstein discussed

[119] D. Lyons, 'Moral Aspects of Legal Theory', 7 *Midwest Studies in Philosophy* 223, 240 (1982).

[120] See Baker and Hacker, *Wittgenstein: Rules, Grammar and Necessity*, 41–2; Waismann, *The Principles of Linguistic Philosophy*, 82–3.

in his rule-following considerations. In trying to determine the application of a particular rule, Wittgenstein wrote, we sometimes begin by offering an interpretation of the rule—the same rule in a different formulation: 'in the course of our argument we give one interpretation after another.'[121] Wittgenstein's point had been that this approach would never bring us any closer to determining the correct applications of the rule than we had been to begin with. However, the various interpretations (formulations) of the rules in the example are in a sense equivalent, and they are equally powerful—and equally impotent—in determining the correct application of the rule.[122]

As Scott Landers argued, while both the distinction between rules and rule-formulations and the reasons for making the distinction seem clear, what is not clear is whether anything of philosophical interest follows from that distinction.[123] It is not grammatically correct to say either that a rule (rather than its formulation) has nine words or to say that Jones violated a rule-formulation (rather than a rule).[124] However, the fact that we can speak of a rule separately from its formulations no more forces the conclusion that rules are entities of some Platonic type than the fact that we can speak of a word's meaning separate from the definitional rules and actual applications which constitute that meaning requires us to think of meanings as abstract, Fregean entities (or the conclusion that understanding is a matter of grasping such entities), though Wittgenstein might note in both cases how we are 'tempted' towards such misleading conclusions.[125]

Even if we accept the existence of 'real rules', this may not completely solve the problem posed by the partial indeterminacy of language. For example, if there is a 'real rule' which can be formulated in a number of different ways, how would we choose one formulation over another? One formulation may seem to give

121 Wittgenstein, *Philosophical Investigations*, sec. 201; see also sec. 198.

122 See ibid., sec. 198.

123 S. Landers, 'Wittgenstein, Realism, and CLS: Undermining Rule Scepticism', 9 *Law and Philosophy* 177, 194–5 and n. 41 (1990).

124 Ibid. 194, n. 41.

125 Cf. P. M. S. Hacker, *Insight and Illusion* rev. edn., 325–6 and n. 17 (Oxford: Oxford University Press, 1986), quoting L. Wittgenstein, *Philosophical Grammar*, 123–4, in discussing the differences between a proposition and the sentence in which it is expressed.

a determinate answer to the case presented while other formulations do not, but determinacy in this case may or may not be sufficient reason to prefer one formulation over another. Substantial further arguments would be needed to develop this position.

When Lyons wrote of the law having further resources, he may have been referring to resources other than rules. Like Dworkin,[126] he might have been asserting that law contains other forms of guidance: for example, principles and policies. However, all standards—whether canonical rules, canons of interpretation, or general legal principles—must be formulated in words if they are to be of use to legal actors (assuming, as most people do, that one cannot run a legal system in a complex society entirely on something as suspiciously amorphous as an 'intuitive sense of justice'). Once we are back to dealing with language, we must worry about the 'open texture' of language and of rules, and about the indeterminacy of the borderline case.

[126] See Dworkin, *Taking Rights Seriously*, 14–45.

2

The Application (and Mis-Application) of Wittgenstein's Rule-Following Considerations to Legal Theory

> I am sitting with a philosopher in the garden; he says again and again 'I know that that's a tree', pointing to a tree that is near us. Someone else arrives and hears this, and I tell him: 'This fellow isn't insane. We are only doing philosophy.'[1]

INTRODUCTION

Wittgenstein's writings on 'rule-following' remain an important—and sharply contested—part of his later thought. The reference to 'rule' in those writings was both broader and more basic than the use of that term in most discussions of practical reasoning or legal theory. Wittgenstein's use of 'rule' refers to all normative constraints which apply over an indefinite variety of cases, to practices where our actions might be said to be guided, to situations where characterizing actions as 'correct' or 'incorrect' makes sense. However, '[h]e aimed not to write a book on rules but to examine specific problems arising out of insights into the normative nature of a language, of logic and of reasoning'.[2] He focused in particular on normative practices that on the surface do not seem troubling or difficult to understand: for example, using a word correctly, understanding a signpost, and continuing a simple mathematical series.[3] In such examples, the interesting question is not whether a particular response or continuation is right or wrong; Wittgenstein specifically chose examples where there would be consensus on that issue. Wittgenstein's question is, what

[1] L. Wittgenstein, *On Certainty*, sec. 467 (New York: Harper Torchbooks, 1972).

[2] Baker and Hacker, *Wittgenstein: Rules, Grammar and Necessity*, 39.

[3] See Wittgenstein, *Philosophical Investigations*, secs. 143–242.

is it about the rule or about ourselves which makes our responses right or wrong (or which justifies us in reaching that evaluation)?

Wittgenstein's discussions on rule-following have been brought to bear on the issue of legal determinacy primarily by those who argue that law is radically indeterminate. They offer a reading of Kripke's reading of Wittgenstein[4] to support the position that rules do not have determinate applications. The argument runs along the following lines. Wittgenstein (Kripke) has shown that there is no fact of the matter to prove that I mean the same thing by my current use of a word as I did by a former use, and no fact of the matter to prove that I am applying the word (that is, applying the rule that governs the word's usage) correctly.[5] Furthermore, 'there is [no] fact about our past use, intention, or attitude towards a word . . . that controls or restricts or limits our future uses of that word'.[6] If there is no fact of the matter that tells us how to use a word, if any way we go on can be characterized as following the rule, then, it seems, anything goes.[7] The legal indeterminacy theorists then follow Wittgenstein (Kripke) in concluding that judgments of correct and incorrect (in following a rule or in the use of a word)—that is, the whole concept of meaning—are based on (*can only be* based on) the consensus of the community. We are using a word correctly if and only if our use agrees with that of the vast majority of our peers.[8] This approach fits well with the position of many legal indeterminacy theorists. They need not, and do not, deny that there are 'easy cases' in the law. However, they attribute the easiness of these cases not to language but to a (temporary) consensus of the society (or the relevant legal subset

[4] S. Kripke, *Wittgenstein on Rules and Private Language* (Cambridge, Mass.: Harvard University Press, 1982); see e.g. C. Yablon, 'Law and Metaphysics' (book review), 96 *Yale Law Journal* 613 (1987). At one point in his book (p. 5), Kripke hedged regarding the extent to which the argument he elaborated was actually Wittgenstein's. At other places, he was more confident about the ascription (see e.g. pp. 70–1). My view is that Kripke's reading does not accurately reflect Wittgenstein's position, and that Wittgenstein's actual position is superior to the one Kripke (more or less) ascribed to him. While I will in passing offer arguments to support both of these assertions, it is not my purpose to go into these disputes in any depth.

[6] Yablon, 'Law and Metaphysics', 628.

[7] See Kripke, *Wittgenstein on Rules and Private Language*, 11–13, 77–8, 84–93; see e.g. Yablon, 'Law and Metaphysics', 632.

[8] See Kripke, *Wittgenstein on Rules and Private Language*, 90–8, 110–12; see e.g. Yablon, 'Law and Metaphysics', 632–6.

of society).[9] This consensus has a political or ideological component, and some might assert that it has been imposed by more powerful elements of the community upon the rest. If and when the society's ideology changes, which cases are considered easy will, according to this approach, also change.[10]

THE RULE-FOLLOWING CONSIDERATIONS—A SUMMARY

> Why do philosophers ask the meaning of quite ordinary words? . . . Have they forgotten it?[11]

I believe that Wittgenstein's lessons were different. However, there is always reason to be cautious when offering exegesis of the *Philosophical Investigations*. The *Investigations*, including the material on rule-following, is presented in short passages which are often aphoristic or cryptic. To read a particular argument or viewpoint into these comments requires an implicit or explicit filling out of details and clarification of ambiguities. The interpretation I present is by no means the only tenable one. Nevertheless, it does coincide generally with the interpretations offered by Peter Hacker, Gordon Baker, David Pears, John McDowell, Colin McGinn, and Simon Blackburn, among others (who, whatever their disagreements about other aspects of Wittgenstein scholarship, are in consensus or near-consensus regarding the aspects of rule-following relevant to my discussion). One can be particularly confident regarding the rejection of Kripke's reading of Wittgenstein: it is in fact very hard (if it is possible at all) to find a serious Wittgenstein scholar who is in substantial agreement with Kripke's reading.

Kripke was right in reading Wittgenstein as asserting that there is no fact of the matter (no 'superlative fact')[12] which justifies the

[9] See e.g. Yablon, 'Law and Metaphysics', 632–6; id., 'The Indeterminacy of the Law: Critical Legal Studies and the Problem of Legal Explanation', 6 *Cardozo Law Review* 917, 918–20, 929–45 (1985); M. Tushnet, *Red, White, and Blue*, 54–6, 60–9 (Cambridge, Mass.: Harvard University Press, 1988).

[10] See e.g. Yablon, 'Law and Metaphysics', 632–6.

[11] Wittgenstein, quoted in T. Redpath, *Ludwig Wittgenstein: A Student's Memoir*, 82 (London: Duckworth, 1990).

[12] See Wittgenstein, *Philosophical Investigations*, sec. 192.

way we understand rules. (Simon Blackburn noted that Wittgenstein would not have expressed the point in those terms. As an alternative more congenial to Wittgenstein's approach, Blackburn offered: 'taking a term in a certain way is something different from *presenting* anything as an aid to understanding it, or from *accepting* anything as aids to understanding it.')[13] Kripke was wrong, however, in portraying this as a 'sceptical problem' which requires a 'sceptical solution'.[14] Crispin Wright has pointed out that Kripke's reading of Wittgenstein inverts the focus of Wittgenstein's discussions. Kripke's sceptic has us wondering how we could know what rule we are or had been following, wondering, in fact, about 'the very existence of rules and rule-following'. By contrast, Wittgenstein was actually concerned with 'the nature and epistemology of rule-following'—that is, how we can know what a rule requires of us in a particular situation.[15] If the signs and symbols of the rule were somehow insufficient to allow us to know whether a certain action was or was not in accordance with the rule, how could the addition of further signs and symbols in our minds (or in the Platonic realm of Ideas) remedy this insufficiency? If we 'restrict the term "interpretation" to the substitution of one expression of the rule for another', '[w]hat this shows is that there is a way of grasping a rule which is *not* an *interpretation*, but which is exhibited in what we call "obeying a rule" and "going against it" in actual cases'.[16] The idea of a 'sceptical problem' comes from the philosopher's temptation, the philosopher's anxiety, to find some magical intermediary between rules and actions. As David Pears wrote:

> The point is not just that there is often a need to interpret rules by defining their terms, but also that the process of defining a term and then defining the terms in the definition cannot possibly close all gaps, because sooner or later there will have to be a leap, not guaranteed by any definition, from language to the world.[17]

There is a sense in which even Pears's discussion concedes too much to Wittgenstein's opponents: to write of 'gaps' and 'a leap

[13] S. Blackburn, 'The Individual Strikes Back', 58 *Synthese* 281, 285, 288 (1984).
[14] See Kripke, *Wittgenstein on Rules and Private Language*, 61–9.
[15] C. Wright, critical notice, 98 *Mind* 289, 303 (1989).
[16] Wittgenstein, *Philosophical Investigations*, sec. 201.
[17] D. Pears, *The False Prison*, 2 vols. (Oxford: Clarendon Press, 1987–8), ii. 432.

. . . from language to the world' implies that language can be understood separate from its applications to and in the world, a position Wittgenstein would not have endorsed. (Elsewhere, Pears himself wrote: 'No rule can be completely laid down in words and the complete expression of any rule must include its actual applications.')[18]

In easy cases at least, we all apply the rule in the same way. For example, we would all continue the series 'add 2': '1,000, 1,002, 1,004, . . .'[19] The 'we' of the previous two sentences would include all those who share the same form of life, who have been trained in the same rules in the same way. (I will discuss Wittgenstein's concept of a form of life later in the next section.) In these easy cases, it is not fuel for scepticism that nothing more can be offered in justification for how the rule is applied. The sceptic's complaint is unwarranted because there is nothing more that *could* be offered as justification and there is nothing more that is needed as a justification.[20] To the sceptic who keeps asking why, a different form of response is eventually necessary. 'If I have exhausted the justifications I have reached bedrock, and my spade is turned. Then I am inclined to say: "This is simply what I do." '[21] One might also reply to Kripke's sceptic: 'that is just *what we call* "adding 2" (or "the colour red", and so on).'[22] There is no room in the language game for further justification or for further doubt. 'If after full training and all the recommended checks I still "doubt" whether I am using a word correctly, my "doubt" goes beyond the particular language-game and is automatically transformed into a request for an answer to the conceptual question "What counts as following a rule?" '[23]

The 'correct response' is identical with the way we are inclined to go on, but the *fact* that we all go on the same way is not what makes it correct (though, as I will discuss later, it is what makes our practices sensible). The distinction in Wittgenstein's work is

[18] Pears, *The False Prison*, ii, 468.

[19] See Wittgenstein, *Philosophical Investigations*, secs. 185–7.

[20] See Wittgenstein, *Tractatus Logico-Philosophicus*, sec. 6.51 (London: Routledge & Kegan Paul, 1961). Unlike most aspects of his early thought, Wittgenstein never changed his position on or his approach to the question of scepticism. See Hacker, *Insight and Illusion*, 79.

[21] Wittgenstein, *Philosophical Investigations*, sec. 217.

[22] Baker and Hacker, *Scepticism, Rules and Language*, 78, 85.

[23] Pears, *The False Prison*, ii. 442.

sometimes subtle, between the background fact of agreement and the internal relation between a rule and the acts that accord with it. Without the background agreements in judgement, we would not follow the rules in the same way that we do now, but it is not those agreements we look to when we adjudge another person's applications as correct or incorrect. When we are explaining what makes a judgement or application 'correct', we need to see what criteria are used; or, to put the matter differently, we need to see how the concept of 'correctness' is used.[24] We do not determine whether a flower is red by first asking everyone around what they think the flower's colour is.[25]

Like H. L. A. Hart, Wittgenstein sought a middle position on rules. Wittgenstein 'attempt[ed] to point to an alternative account of normativity to the "rules-as-rails" imagery of Platonism, to explain how there can be a standable middle ground between the hypostatization of rules and the denial of their existence'.[26] On the one hand, Wittgenstein did not want to ascribe the application of rules to the rules themselves *qua* metaphysical entities. On the other hand, he did not wish to deny that (it makes sense to say that) a rule determines its correct application or interpretation.[27]

DISAGREEMENT AND 'FORMS OF LIFE'

Wittgenstein's discussions on rule-following in *Philosophical Investigations* focused on easy cases, like the mathematical series 'add 2'.[28] In section 240, he wrote:

> Disputes do not break out (among mathematicians, say) over the question whether a rule has been obeyed or not. People don't come to blows over it, for example. That is part of the framework on which the working of our language is based (for example, in giving descriptions).

Wittgenstein focused on 'easy cases' because he was interested in dispelling certain misunderstandings and mythologies regarding

[24] See Baker and Hacker, *Wittgenstein: Rules, Grammar and Necessity*, 171–2.

[25] See Wittgenstein, *Zettel*, sec. 431 (Berkeley, Calif.: University of California Press, 1970); see also his *Remarks on the Foundations of Mathematics* rev. edn., 336–7 (Cambridge, Mass.: MIT Press 1978).

[26] Wright, critical notice, 297.

[27] See Baker and Hacker, *Wittgenstein: Rules, Grammar and Necessity*, 81–106.

[28] Wittgenstein, *Philosophical Investigations*, secs. 185–7.

what makes these instances of applying a word or continuing a series easy. There cannot be a fact which determines how to go on: no mental state, inner voice, or disposition, and no Platonic rule-entity that we somehow grasp. For Wittgenstein, there is no mediating entity which can justify or explain why we all go on the same way when continuing the series 'add 2' or applying the colour-word 'red'. It simply is the case that people who share the same form of life and are trained in the same way go on in the same way in following rules. As John McDowell described Wittgenstein's position: 'nothing . . . keeps our practices in line except the reactions and responses we learn in learning them.'[29]

The analysis is complicated somewhat by the recognition that for Wittgenstein concepts like 'the same' and 'agreement' cannot be understood a priori or otherwise independently of the problem of rule-following:

> The word 'agreement' and the word 'rule' are *related* to one another, they are cousins. If I teach anyone the use of the one word, he learns the use of the other with it.
>
> The use of the word 'rule' and the use of the word 'same' are interwoven. (As are the use of 'proposition' and 'true'.)[30]

The following may help to explain Wittgenstein's point about the relation between rules and 'the same': if we say that two people are 'going on in the same way' (for example, that they are playing the same game, applying the same concept, or creating the same mathematical series), any attempt to justify that conclusion is likely to end up with the assertion that they are following the identical rule or set of rules.[31]

For Wittgenstein, the clarity of clear cases derives from certain background facts regarding agreement in judgements, agreement in social context, and stability of the world. In *Philosophical Investigations*, section 242, he stated:

> If language is to be a means of communication there must be agreement not only in definitions but also (queer as this may sound) in judgments . . . It is one thing to describe methods of measurement, and another to

[29] J. McDowell, 'Non-Cognitivism and Rule-Following', in *Wittgenstein: To Follow a Rule*, 149 (S. Holtzman and C. Leich, eds., London: Routledge & Kegan Paul, 1981).

[30] Wittgenstein, *Philosophical Investigations*, secs. 224–5; see id., *Remarks on the Foundations of Mathematics*, 344.

[31] See Wittgenstein, *Remarks on the Foundations of Mathematics*, 392–3.

obtain and state results of measurement. But what we call 'measuring' is partly determined by a certain constancy in results of measurement.

Briefly, 'judgements' here includes all the connections we make (through our actions) between language and the world: between a rule and its application, between how we have used a term in the past and whether we apply it to a particular new instance, between how we have been trained to understand a practice (for example, adding or measuring) and how we perform it ourselves, and so on.[32]

It is a matter of fact that we all go on the same way in the series 'add 2' after we have been trained in mathematics; we do not tend to diverge in our answers upon reaching 1,000. After learning how to use a ruler, all of our measurements of the same object will be the same. Similarly, after being taught the colour words by ostensive definitions, we will all agree that this particular tomato is red and that patch of grass is green.[33] If differences in individual judgements created divergences in the way people continued the series 'add 2' or if instabilities in the world caused us to get different results every time we measured the same object, then the concepts within those practices—and the practices themselves—would cease to have meaning.[34] At one point, Wittgenstein wrote: ' "If humans were not in general agreed about the colours of things, if undetermined cases were not exceptional, then our concept of colour could not exist." No—our concept *would* not exist.'[35] One could say that the fact that we all go on the same way in our practices and in our uses of words after rudimentary training is just a happy coincidence, though a coincidence without which communication would be impossible.[36] David Pears wrote: 'We could say that this is fortunate, except that this would be like saying that it is fortunate that life on earth tolerates the earth's natural atmosphere. What we ought to say is that there is as much

[32] See C. McGinn, *Wittgenstein on Meaning*, 57 (Oxford: Basil Blackwell, 1984), equating 'judgement' with 'unreflective and "blind" application of a sign'.

[33] See Wittgenstein, *Remarks on the Foundations of Mathematics*, 342.

[34] See e.g. Wittgenstein, *Philosophical Investigations*, sec. 142; see also id., *Remarks on the Foundations of Mathematics*, 38, 382.

[35] Wittgenstein, *Zettel*, sec. 351. For a more detailed discussion of how agreement in judgements and stability in nature work as presuppositions in our concepts, see Baker and Hacker, *Wittgenstein: Rules, Grammar and Necessity*, 229–51.

[36] See Wittgenstein, *Philosophical Investigations*, sec. 242, quoted above.

stability as there is.'[37] In section 241 of the *Investigations*, Wittgenstein wrote: ' "So you are saying that human agreement decides what is true and what is false?"—It is what human beings *say* that is true and false; and they agree in the *language* they use. That is not agreement in opinions but in form of life.' The following is from one of Wittgenstein's unpublished manuscripts:[38]

> How is the application of a rule fixed? Do you mean 'logically' fixed? Either by means of further rules, or not at all!—Or do you mean: how is it that we agree in applying it thus and not otherwise? Through training, drill and the forms of our life.
>
> This is a matter not of a consensus but of forms of life.

'Form(s) of life' in part sums up, and in part hints at an explanation for, the fact of our general agreement.[39] Rudolf Haller has shown that Wittgenstein used this phrase in at least two different ways: (1) (in the singular, *Lebensform*) to summarize 'the common human way of acting', that which is distinctly and universally human; and (2) (in the plural, *Lebensformen*) to emphasize diversity between societies and even between different communities within a single society.[40]

The role the concept 'form of life' might play in explaining disagreement will be discussed in a later part of this section. For now, one can get an overview of Wittgenstein's analysis of agreement: we go on the same way because of commonalities in our training and in our nature. It is far from inevitable that all people will always react in the same way in all matters; where we do not go on the same way there will usually be no stable practice.[41]

[37] D. Pears, *Ludwig Wittgenstein*, 179 (Cambridge, Mass.: Harvard University Press, 1986).

[38] It is quoted in Baker and Hacker, *Wittgenstein: Rules, Grammar and Necessity*, 258, and labelled 'MS 160, 51'.

[39] For an overview of how Wittgenstein used the concept of 'form(s) of life', see R. Haller, *Questions on Wittgenstein*, 129–36 (Bristol: Routledge, 1988).

[40] Haller, *Questions on Wittgenstein*, 130–6. One example of the second usage appeared in Wittgenstein, *Lectures and Conversations on Aesthetics, Psychology and Religious Belief*, 58 (C. Barrett, ed., Oxford: Basil Blackwell, 1978): 'Why shouldn't one form of life culminate in an utterance of belief in a Last Judgment?'

[41] It is difficult to judge to what extent areas like art, politics, and morality are counter-examples to this claim. I discuss these type of discourses, where there is significant disagreement and, at best, only mixed evidence of any underlying agreement about paradigms or criteria, later in this chapter. I think that it would be open to argument either (1) whether these types of discourse are in fact counter-examples, or even (2) whether they are in fact practices rather than a chaos of opinions and attitudes that sometimes take the appearance of coherent practices.

In contrasting Wittgenstein with certain Critical Legal Studies theorists, I do not mean to imply that there is any basis in his thought for denying the Critical Legal Studies theorists' point that some 'clear cases' are clear because of political or ideological consensus rather than because of some more peremptory claim about the correct or incorrect use of words. That a certain practice is or is not a violation of 'equal protection' may seem clear and obvious to us; but the clearness of the question may disappear if we go either forward or backward one generation in time. Finally, I am not sure that there is a bright line between those 'clear cases' that fit under the rubric of Wittgenstein's rule-following considerations and those that do not. That is, I am not sure that a theorist can usually (if ever) be confident in determining which interpretative questions are completely beyond the pale of legitimate debate ('outside the language game').

OVER-READINGS OF WITTGENSTEIN I: LANGILLE

'Philosophy is in fact the synopsis of trivialities.'[42]

If there is a danger—exemplified by Kripke and others—of reading Wittgenstein's rule-following considerations as scepticism which undermines meaning and certainty, there is also an opposite danger of over-reading Wittgenstein's message of assurance. Wittgenstein wanted to assure us that despite (because of) the absence of some 'internal' or Platonic facts of the matter, we can speak of 'correct' and 'incorrect' in our most basic normative behaviour. The over-reading danger occurs when Wittgenstein's message is read as guaranteeing ascriptions of correctness or the achievement of consensus in more controversial matters. For example, while Brian Langille argued correctly that legal theorists could not use Wittgenstein to ground positions of radical indeterminacy,[43] he went too far in implying that a correct

[42] Wittgenstein, *Wittgenstein's Lectures: Cambridge 1930–1932*, 26 (D. Lee, ed., Chicago: University of Chicago Press, 1980). The preceding sentence reads: 'But the proper synopsis of these trivialities is enormously difficult, and has immense importance.'

[43] B. Langille, 'Revolution Without Foundation: The Grammar of Scepticism and Law', 33 *McGill Law Journal* 451 (1988); see also A. Hutchinson, 'That's Just the Way it Is: Langille on Law', 34 *McGill Law Journal* 145 (1989).

appreciation of Wittgenstein could be used to rebut all sceptical analyses of law.

In his article, Langille focused on 'strong claims about the indeterminacy of language and the impact of this alleged indeterminacy upon our ideas about the nature of constitutional discourse'.[44] His particular targets were those theorists who claimed that Wittgenstein's writings were the basis of their arguments. For the reasons given earlier, I agree with Langille that Wittgenstein did not believe that language was radically indeterminate, and that Wittgenstein's writings could not be used to support the conclusions of the indeterminacy theorists.[45] However, I dissent from Langille's attempt to take his reading of Wittgenstein one step further, writing of 'the explication of the grammar of law, and . . . the grammar of constitutional jurisprudence'.[46] My objection is simple: Wittgenstein used the term 'grammar' when talking about words and concepts, and, as I will argue below, it is at best misleading to move that analytical tool to a different set of topics: here, social practices.

Wittgenstein used 'grammar' in a way somewhat broader than, but clearly connected to, the ordinary usage of that term.[47] 'In [Wittgenstein's] sense the grammar of a term includes a wide variety of practices connected with its use and the criteria and background conditions that govern its normal application.'[48] A phrase's grammar is constituted in part by the rules which determine how that phrase can be used, such that if those rules are violated the resulting sentence will have no sense. For example, it is part of the grammar of numbers that colours cannot be ascribed to them and part of the grammar of pain that one cannot claim to be in doubt about one's being in pain.[49]

Wittgenstein argued that many philosophical problems resulted

[44] Langille, 'Revolution Without Foundation', 452.

[45] See ibid. 452–75, 486–95.

[46] Ibid. 498. See also B. Langille, 'The Jurisprudence of Despair, Again', 23 *University of British Columbia Law Review* 549, 558–62 (1989).

[47] See generally Hacker, *Insight and Illusion*, 181–5; Baker and Hacker, *Wittgenstein: Rules, Grammar and Necessity*, 34–64. For Wittgenstein's claim that his use was *not* different from the ordinary use, see Wittgenstein, *Wittgenstein's Lectures: Cambridge 1930–1932*, 97–8.

[48] E. Wolgast, *The Grammar of Justice*, p. x (London: Cornell University Press 1987).

[49] See Wittgenstein, *Philosophical Investigations*, sec. 246 and p. 221.

from violating grammatical rules (for example, by mistakenly applying the grammar of material-object statements to first-person psychological statements).[50] If we would only follow a term's grammar strictly and stay within the language game we are considering, he argued, we would avoid metaphysical muddles and temptations to scepticism.[51]

When Langille used Wittgenstein's arguments about the relevance of human nature and human practices to the meaning of simple terms to ground his own statements about 'the grammar of law' and law 'being grounded in a bedrock of practice',[52] he was not following Wittgenstein's ideas, he was flouting them. He was doing just what Wittgenstein warned against, taking terms—in this case, Wittgenstein's concepts of 'grammar', 'practice' and 'bedrock'—outside their usual context, outside their language game. These concepts belong to Wittgenstein's analysis of 'clear cases' and unreflective applications.

The jump from the grammar of language to 'the grammar of law' implies that, analogous to Wittgenstein's discussions of meanings and mathematical series, the definitions of legal terms and the moves within the legal discourse cannot sensibly be challenged and are not in need of further justification. I am not arguing that Wittgenstein's approach, or even his analysis in terms of 'grammar', could never be helpful in the analysis of social institutions or social theory.[53] However, Langille makes the significant move to 'the grammar of law' without either arguing for the transition or even noting that argument might be needed.

The idea of 'grammar' (and the related idea of 'criteria') is central to Wittgenstein's work, but it is also controversial. It is an idea that is used to turn aside challenges to (apparent) knowledge-claims (for example, 'how do you *know* that the next number in the series should be "12"?') and the viability of the idea is thus crucial to Wittgenstein's response to scepticism. Much of what makes the idea controversial is doubt as to whether Wittgenstein has done enough to show that certain connections are 'merely grammatical'.

[50] See Wittgenstein, *Zettel*, sec. 434; see also id., *Philosophical Investigations*, sec. 290.

[51] See e.g. Wittgenstein, *Philosophical Investigations*, secs. 90, 520.

[52] Langille, 'Revolution Without Foundation', 497–8.

[53] Cf. Wolgast, *The Grammar of Justice*.

This is why I am hostile to a casual borrowing of Wittgenstein's idea of 'grammar'. Even if we accept that this form of analysis is warranted where Wittgenstein used it, there is no reason to believe that it will be warranted in a completely different context (and a number of reasons to believe that it would *not* be warranted). The burden is always on the theorist who proposes a simple answer to scepticism; large portions of Wittgensteins work are devoted to trying to show that he had rebutted scepticism—whether he succeeded or not is beyond the scope of my current project. Langille has not offered any comparable arguments for using the anti-sceptical arguments in a different context. To use Wittgenstein's analysis casually and out of context is to invoke his authority falsely, to fail to recognize what was difficult in the original materials, and to make no attempt to take on the burden of showing why the analysis should be extended.

Langille's comments here were brief and cryptic, but they hint at an argument that cannot be sustained. Along with his reference to 'the grammar of law' and 'the grammar of constitutional jurisprudence', Langille described Owen Fiss as having created 'the "structural conditions" for a Wittgensteinian view of law—the existence of a set of constraining rules utilized by judges as a social group',[54] and stated that 'Hart's idea of judges utilizing social rules from the internal point of view is the bringing of Wittgenstein's fundamental point about rule following to the judicial rule'.[55] Within their context, these comments seem to imply that for Langille the practice of law is like the series 'add 2' and the application of the colour-term 'red' in needing no further justification (and that any present consensus in law can be explained in much the same way as Wittgenstein explained our all going on the same way in the series 'add 2').

If Langille in fact held this position—and perhaps he did not—then I must disagree with him. The analogy does not hold. Unlike the matters with which Wittgenstein was concerned, law is a reflective activity: the participants consider, discuss, and argue over how they should go on. Contrary to Wittgenstein's descriptions of mathematicians and mathematical series,[56] disputes do break out in law over the question of whether a rule has been

[54] Langille, 'Revolution Without Foundation', 498.
[55] Ibid. 499.
[56] Wittgenstein, *Philosophical Investigations*, sec. 240, quoted above.

obeyed or not. Legal practice, locally and generally, *is* subject to criticism and *is* in need of further justification.

(Though I believe that Wittgenstein's analysis is most useful in 'clear cases', where there is a consensus as to the appropriate response and choices are made automatically and unreflectively, I do not mean to foreclose the argument that a Wittgensteinian approach might have a role within a proper analysis of 'hard cases', where our judgements and choices diverge. For example, one might argue that we disagree about the meaning of terms like 'democracy' because we disagree about which criteria should be used as necessary and sufficient conditions for the term's application, but that at the level of the criteria themselves, whether a criterion is met or not is a question we would decide unreflectively and about which there would be an agreement in judgements.)[57]

An initial and basic point in understanding the limitations of applying Wittgenstein's rule-following considerations to legal theory (at least the limitations of any *direct* application) is seeing how those considerations were meant to leave language and life just the way they are. Though Wittgenstein (and some commentators on Wittgenstein) may at first or on a superficial level seem to have been proposing a sceptical position on meaning, the only role scepticism plays in his rule-following considerations is as the absurd consequence of mistaken premisses he sought to correct: '*if* this conception of the facts were the right one, *then* we wouldn't know such and such, but we do, so we need this other conception of the facts.'[58] Words *do* have meaning, and there *are* unique correct answers to simple mathematical questions. These are the starting-points both for us in our daily use of language and for Wittgenstein in his rule-following considerations. Wittgenstein's aim is 'to alter our conception of the facts we take ourselves to know';[59] but whether he succeeds or fails in persuading us, we have no reason to create or apply rules differently from the way we do now. Most, if not all, of the problems in law and legal theory occur at a different level of abstraction (or in a different area of philosophy altogether).[60]

57 This argument is based on a suggestion made to me by Joseph Raz.
58 S. Blackburn, *Spreading the Word*, 99, n. 17 (Oxford: Clarendon Press, 1984).
59 Ibid.
60 See Schauer, *Playing by the Rules*, 64–8.

OVER-READINGS OF WITTGENSTEIN II: PATTERSON

Dennis Patterson used discussions of legal theory to offer a possible solution to problems raised in Wittgenstein's rule-following considerations. He then, in turn, used his reading of Wittgenstein as the basis for a particular view of law.[61] His emphasis was on constructing a new approach to law and to legal interpretation. Going somewhat against the focus of his article, I will discuss it primarily in terms of how well it works as a discussion of and application of Wittgenstein's ideas. Though Patterson's approach is more sophisticated than Langille's, I fear that it is vulnerable to many of the same criticisms.

Within Wittgenstein's discussions of rule-following, it remained a difficult question what it was that made one application (extension) of a rule rather than another correct. Patterson considered two responses within the secondary literature on Wittgenstein: those who believe that it is the rule itself which somehow determines 'how to go on' and those who believe that only a community consensus about how to go on makes one approach rather than another correct.[62] In thinking about the problem of rule-following within law, Patterson offered an approach half-way between those two. According to this third approach, the extension of a rule is not determined by the rule alone or merely by a consensus within the relevant community about the right answer. There is a reference to the community, but it is to determine the rule's point or purpose, and it is by reference to this point or purpose that the extension of the rule can be determined.[63]

Once we are talking about interpreting law according to the purpose of particular statutes (or the purpose of the area of law in general or the purpose of law itself), a collective, ongoing debate to 'construct' the purpose, and 'law as narrative', the similarities between Patterson's approach and that of Ronald Dworkin (or Lon Fuller) become obvious.[64] I do not want to focus here on the

[61] D. Patterson, 'Law's Pragmatism: Law as Practice and Narrative', 76 *Virginia Law Review* 937 (1990). [62] See ibid. 942–52. [63] Ibid. 953–7.

[64] See ibid. 959–65, 980–9. While Patterson did not discuss the affinities between his approach and Dworkin's, he did point out the similarities between his approach and Fuller's: ibid. 960–3.

end-product, on the merits of Patterson's (or Dworkin's) approach to law, but rather to focus on the way he claimed that his approach was grounded in Wittgenstein's ideas. The first thing worth noting is the strangeness of applying Wittgenstein's rule-following considerations to law at all. Though the name is the same, 'rules' within Wittgenstein's discussions are quite different from 'rules' in legal theory and practice.

The published article pulled back somewhat from the exegetical claims that had been made in an earlier, unpublished version of the same paper. In one footnote in the published article, Patterson wrote in passing: '[t]he present Article is an explicit attempt to move beyond Wittgenstein', and in another footnote he added, '[f]or the sake of accuracy, I should reaffirm that my primary interest in discussing Wittgenstein's thoughts on rule-following is *not* in rendering an authoritative interpretation of Wittgenstein'.[65]

Nevertheless, much of the article was devoted to a detailed discussion of Wittgenstein's works and the relevant secondary literature, so I believe a focus on Patterson's ideas as a reading of Wittgenstein is proper (though more detailed exegetical questions will not be raised). For example, I do not think one can invoke Wittgenstein's discussions of rule-following, and then reply to the criticism that one is using a completely different idea of 'rules' from the one Wittgenstein used by stating merely that correct exegesis is not one's primary objective. If one is deviating in substantial ways from the original project, then it is misleading at best to invoke that project (without further substantial justificatory work) in support.

Wittgenstein was concerned with the way we follow the 'rules' in the use of descriptive language and in simple mathematics, the unreflective way in which we (for example) apply colour terms to objects and continue simple mathematical series (for example, '2, 4, 6, 8, 10, . . .'). Wittgenstein's purpose in his discussions was not to teach us how to continue series or apply terms in more complicated cases, or to assert in the easier cases that we were not in fact following a rule. His purpose was to deny some philosophers' views about what goes on when we follow a rule and to begin work towards creating an alternative view. (The extent to which his discussions include a full alternative view rather than

[65] Ibid. 940, n. 11, 971, n. 124.

simply some suggestions and questions regarding an alternative view remains controversial in the secondary literature, but it is not important for our purposes.)

In Wittgenstein's terms, one is confusing language games if one tries to use the concepts and analyses of the unreflective application of colour terms to understand the application of rules which attempt to guide and co-ordinate human behaviour. While the application of legal rules in some situations may seem as easy and as obvious as the easiest cases of applying colour terms, this will not be the case with the 'hard cases' with which Patterson was primarily concerned. To see the difficulty, consider one of Patterson's conclusions: hard cases in the application of legal rules are decided by the construction of plausible narratives of the point of the practice (whether that is the point of the practice of law in general or the point of a practice within law, like making wills).[66] Whatever value this analysis might have for difficult legal cases, it is out of place in the areas Wittgenstein used to discuss rule-following: the application of colour terms, simple mathematical series, reading, and so on. Wittgenstein might have found some sense in the notion that the practice of mathematics has a point (perhaps some connection with the way we operate in commercial life), but reference to that purpose would not help us to solve a difficult mathematical problem (or to create a consensus for a solution where none had been before).

Wittgenstein did urge us to look at language from the perspective of the role the words play in our lives. For Wittgenstein, emphasizing use within a process of ascertaining meaning is a way to avoid imputing inappropriate metaphysical overtones to the concepts we have. As the problem of metaphysicizing concepts is as problematic in law as anywhere,[67] I certainly would not deny that Wittgenstein's approach could be usefully applied to law. In fact, I think it would be fair to describe the approach Hart used in two of his early articles in analyzing legal concepts as Wittgensteinian in his emphasis on how concepts are actually used.[68]

[66] D. Patterson, 'Law's Pragmatism: Law as Practice and Narrative', 983–95.

[67] A good discussion of this problem is given in F. Cohen, 'Transcendental Nonsense and the Functional Response', 35 *Columbia Law Review* 809 (1935).

[68] H. L. A. Hart, *Definition and Theory in Jurisprudence* (Oxford: Clarendon Press, 1953); 'Theory and Definition in Jurisprudence', *Proceedings of the Aristotelian Society*, suppl. vol. 29, 239 (1955).

Patterson's approach may have great merit on its own terms; however, as an explication of or a derivation from Wittgenstein's rule-following considerations I believe it falls short.

HARD CASES AND 'CONTESTED CONCEPTS'

Wittgenstein's discussions of rule-following centred on what explanations can and cannot be given in understanding the consensus that pervades most of our uses of language (and mathematics). My interest in this paper has been in whether those remarks, though aimed specifically at 'clear cases'—in particular, at explaining (causally and conceptually) our agreement in such cases—can also help us understand what explanations can and cannot be given for our failure to reach consensus in other ('hard') cases. There are ample reasons to believe that we cannot directly apply Wittgenstein's ideas, meant for clear cases, to hard cases. As Simon Blackburn has pointed out, it is the 'automatic and compelling nature of rule-following' in clear cases that made them interesting to Wittgenstein.[69] The way we think about clear cases—and about 'correct' and 'incorrect' in clear cases—differs sharply from our thinking in hard cases. As Blackburn wrote, 'we [may] have some title to regard ourselves as thinking the truth when (as when we accept a proof) we can form no conception of what it would be to think differently. But it would not follow at all that we have the same title when we are all too aware of the possibility of thinking differently.'[70]

John McDowell offered some suggestions on how Wittgenstein's ideas about clear cases might be extended to hard cases (though he admitted that these thoughts might be *extensions* of Wittgenstein's ideas).[71] First, in cases where there is no consensus on whether to apply some word or concept (particularly common with evaluative concepts), it might still be the case that, to one person, how to go on seems obvious. Though that person knows that other people disagree, he may not be able to understand how they could. His reaction to them might be: 'But surely you can see . . . ?'[72] That

[69] S. Blackburn, 'Rule-Following and Moral Realism', in *Wittgenstein: To Follow a Rule*, 170.

[70] Ibid. 170–1.

[71] McDowell, 'Non-Cognitivism and Rule-Following', 160, n. 14.

[72] Wittgenstein, *Philosophical Investigations*, sec. 231; McDowell, 'Non-Cognitivism and Rule-Following', 151–2.

quote from *Philosophical Investigations* continued: 'That is just the characteristic expression of someone who is under the compulsion of a rule.'[73] In other words, McDowell is suggesting that in many hard cases, some people have the same feelings that they have in clear cases, in cases of consensus.[74] In an analysis that parallels the work of Stanley Fish, he hinted that the difference between clear cases and hard cases might reflect the difference between people who share the same 'whirl of organism'[75] and those who have (belong to) different ones. Thus, there could be seen to be a variety of intermediate situations between the clearest of clear cases and the hardest of hard cases. There are two parameters: the extent of agreement amongst people and how many believe that their chosen result is obvious (they could not imagine a contrary conclusion). For example, there could be consensus about the result without any participant having the same (type of or level of) certainty he or she would have in (for example) continuing the series 'add 2'.[76]

McDowell's second suggestion was that in the background of hard cases there might be an underlying agreement about what arguments are reasonable or acceptable.[77] This reflects a viewpoint that seems to have strong intuitive appeal within the legal community.[78] Lawyers and legal theorists often argue that though there may be little agreement about results, legal practice is kept relatively stable and orderly by some rough consensus regarding what kind of arguments lawyers and judges can use. I will not consider the validity or power of that position at this point.

If we cautiously move forward from Wittgenstein's comments—knowing that generally what we say cannot be ascribed to him, but

[73] Wittgenstein, *Philosophical Investigations*, sec. 231.

[74] See Wittgenstein, *Remarks on the Foundations of Mathematics*, sec. 115.

[75] McDowell, 'Non-Cognitivism and Rule-Following', 151–3; Fish's analogous concept is 'interpretive communities', Wittgenstein's is 'forms of life'. For an elaboration of Fish's analysis, see S. Fish, *Is There a Text in This Class?*, 1–17, 167–73, 303–71 (Cambridge, Mass.: Harvard University Press, 1980); id., *Doing What Comes Naturally*, 82–4, 141–60, 302–5, 580, n. 3 (Oxford: Clarendon Press, 1989).

[76] cf. Wittgenstein, *Remarks on the Foundations of Mathematics*, sec. 1: '. . . people . . . who react to [the order "add 3"] with perfect certainty, but each one in a different way.'

[77] McDowell, 'Non-Cognitivism and Rule-Following', 160, n. 14.

[78] See e.g. J. Bell, 'The Acceptability of Legal Arguments', in *The Legal Mind*, 45–65 (N. MacCormick and P. Birks, eds., Oxford: Clarendon Press, 1986); O. Fiss, 'Objectivity and Interpretation', 34 *Stanford Law Review* 739 (1982).

at best can only be said to follow from his ideas or to be in the same spirit as his writings—there are a number of ways in which we might begin to analyse or explain the disagreement in hard cases. In such cases, everyone involved does not react the same way; there is no broad 'agreement in judgements'. We can follow McDowell and Fish—and even have some warrant in ascribing the position to Wittgenstein—and say that in some cases people react differently because they have (or 'participate in') different forms of life. The social contexts, cultures, practices, and training are different. Within the subgroups of people who share the same form of life, there would (by definition) be no divergence in reaction, and these same cases would seem to be 'clear cases'. (Stanley Fish, in his analysis of 'interpretive communities', was particularly good in describing scenarios in which issues seem obvious within a subgroup but highly controversial across subgroups.)[79]

There would also be hard cases where the divergent reactions could not be ascribed to the fact that the people had (come from) divergent forms of life. In some cases, different individuals might simply tend to go on differently even when given the same initial training. Along this line (and moving away from analyses based on Wittgenstein's work), W. B. Gallie suggested that the controversy over the use of terms like 'democracy' and 'work of art' might be explained by the fact that different people interpret differently (in Wittgenstein's terminology, 'go on in different ways from') paradigm examples to which all agree that the terms should apply (analogous to the initial ostensive definition).[80] Such concepts, which allow for substantive disagreement about the concept and not just differences about which concept to apply, Gallie termed 'essentially contested concepts'. S. L. Hurley gave the following, more technical summary of Gallie's position: 'essentially contested concepts [are] appraisive and applicable to objects of an internally complex character that may be described in various ways by altering one's view of the significance of descriptions of their component features.'[81] (It is interesting to note that according to

[79] See e.g. Fish, *Is There a Text in This Class?*, 272–92 and *Doing What Comes Naturally*, 298–305.

[80] W. B. Gallie, 'Essentially Contested Concepts', 56 *Proceedings of the Aristotelian Society* 167 (1955–6).

[81] S. L. Hurley, *Natural Reasons*, 46 (Oxford: Oxford University Press, 1989).

Hurley, concepts of what ought to be done, what the law requires, distributive justice, and contract are all essentially contested concepts.)[82]

To see whether Gallie's discussion has added anything to our understanding of substantive disagreement, his analysis must be considered more closely. What would it mean for two people to disagree about the application of a concept but to agree that the touchstone for understanding the concept is a particular example? There seem to be two possibilities, which I will describe as a strong paradigm and an absolute paradigm.

In a strong paradigm case, a person would say, for example, 'if anything is law, a traffic statute is law',[83] or 'if any place ever had a democratic form of government, ancient Athens did'. Here the paradigm coincides well with one's pre-reflective intuition about the concept ('law' or 'democracy'), but it is not used to set the terms of the concept. It is possible, if unlikely, that one may someday conclude that this particular example does not, in fact, instantiate the concept.[84] For example, upon deeper reflection, one might conclude that ancient Athens excluded too many of its residents from the *polis* to be considered a democracy, or one might learn that new archaeological discoveries rebut the picture of ancient Athens one had accepted. In the strong paradigm case, it is the criteria we derive from (or associate with) the paradigm rather than the paradigm itself which are important.

In the absolute paradigm case, the paradigm *defines* the concept, such that the paradigm could never be understood as *not* exemplifying the concept and any change in belief about the paradigm would result in a change in belief about the concept. An instance of this approach appears in religious thinking: for example, some people believe that living a good life consists in living as much as possible like Jesus.[85] If such people were to be convinced that their beliefs about how Jesus had acted or what he had commanded were wrong, they would make analogous modifications in their beliefs about what ought to be done. This approach is always sensitive to some version of Socrates' challenge: is something holy because it is dear to the gods or is something

[82] S. L. Hurley, *Natural Reasons*, 46–7.
[83] See Dworkin, *Law's Empire*, 87–91.
[84] See ibid. 87–90.
[85] cf. Gallie, 'Essentially Contested Concepts', 168, 180–1.

dear to the gods because it is holy?[86] If the good can be separated from what God commanded (or from how a divine figure had lived), then, at least in principle, the concept of good could be defined and delimited independent of the paradigm and the paradigm might even be found to have diverged from goodness at some point. In other words, there is always the risk that an absolute paradigm case will evolve into a strong paradigm case. Only if the respondent would be willing to answer Socrates that something is good because and only because God ordered it are we still in an absolute paradigm case.

The absolute paradigm case itself is nothing more than an elaborate form of guidance by ostensive definition—'do as I do' or 'follow me'—with all of the confusions and uncertainties that come with that process.[87] Gallie's analysis seems to offer nothing new in understanding the source or the nature of disagreement in such cases. If essentially contested concepts usually reduce to a set of criteria, as they appear to, then disagreement about concepts is nothing more and nothing less than disagreement about which criteria are sufficient and necessary for that concept to apply. Gallie's analysis described a convergence—the reference to a particular example as a paradigm—that may be due merely to custom or practice.[88] The problem of disagreement is at best pushed back one step: for whatever reason, we may agree on a paradigm, but derive different criteria from the paradigm; why we do so is not explained.

Perhaps I have given too flat a reading of Gallie's idea. S. L. Hurley attempted a richer characterization of essentially contested concepts. She wrote that the 'component features' or criteria to which the concepts are responsible 'characteristically compete with one another to influence' the concept's application.[89] She used her reading of Gallie to explain how moral, political, and legal disagreements are 'substantive disagreements' rather than 'mere conceptual disagreements'. Meaningful disagreement is possible only if there is a foundation (or, to change the metaphor,

[86] Plato, 'Euthyphro', 10c–11b, in *The Dialogues of Plato*, i. 319–20 (B. Jowett, trans., Oxford: Clarendon Press, 1953).
[87] See e.g. Hart, *The Concept of Law*, 122–3.
[88] See Dworkin, *Law's Empire*, 65–6, 87–91.
[89] Hurley, *Natural Reasons*, 46–7.

a background) of agreement.[90] Substantive disagreement must be contrasted with merely apparent (or 'conceptual') disagreement, where the parties are actually talking about different things, as when we say different things about 'banks' because you are talking about financial institutions while I was talking about the slopes at the sides of rivers. According to Hurley, we judge whether our disagreement with another person is substantive rather than conceptual by determining whether there is a baseline of agreement regarding paradigm cases, the relevant criteria, the rules for constructing theories about the criteria (how to determine whether the concept applies when the criteria conflict), and paradigm examples of such theorizing.[91]

However, it may be that Hurley's analysis, like Gallie's analysis, displaces and postpones the problem of explaining divergence without solving it. Even if we sense that someone else agrees with us regarding the component features of an essentially contested concept and regarding the general process of creating a theory about that concept which is some function of those features, we may still wonder about the situation when the other person disagrees with us about which theory is the best.[92] How should we understand the disagreement at the level of theory?

Perhaps that disagreement is conceptual rather than substantive. Hurley's response had been that both at the level of the specific practices the theories are about and at the level of theorizing, 'the distinction between conceptual and substantive difference is drawn by reference to practices'.[93] At both levels, 'the conceptual *locus* of disagreement is participation in world-embedded practices and customs and the criterion of conceptual divergence is inability to participate in those practices'.[94] Here, Hurley was appealing indirectly to a Wittgensteinian idea that meaning does not come from self-interpreting entities, but that it derives in part from the

[90] See Davidson, 'On the Very Idea of a Conceptual Scheme', 196–7.

[91] Hurley, *Natural Reasons*, 47–8.

[92] For Hurley, essentially contested concepts are 'non-centralist' in that the identification of discrete specific values or criteria is the starting-point for analyzing more general concepts, and a theory must be constructed to give an account of the relationships of interdependence between the particular values or criteria and the general concept. The best theory is the one 'that gives the best account of the relationships among the specific values [or criteria] that apply to the alternatives in question'. Ibid. 11.

[93] Ibid. 48.

[94] Ibid. 49.

practices, customs, and institutions in which the speaker participates (and which collectively constitute a 'form of life').[95]

Hurley's recharacterization of Gallie's work may make it sufficiently subtle and sophisticated for use in other philosophical discussions, but in the context of my project it only brings us back to where we began: sharing a 'form of life' may explain how we come to talk about the same things or to understand them in the same way, but we still lack an explanation (at least an explanation more nuanced than 'differences in "form of life" ') as to why we sometimes seem to understand the same things differently.

CONCEPTS AND CONCEPTIONS

Hurley's elaboration of Gallie's work might not have resulted in a better explanation of why we disagree, but that was not her intention. Hurley was not trying to salvage the idea of 'essentially contested concepts' as an explanation, but as a description: a description of theoretical disagreement as substantive disagreement, which allows that there is conceptual common ground for the disputants.[96] When there is significant disagreement about the definition or application of some term, and there seems to be no hope that further discussion will bring the various sides closer to consensus, there is always the suspicion that the disputants are not actually talking about the same thing.[97] This issue is relevant to my inquiry indirectly. The fact that a disagreement is a substantive disagreement rather than just two people talking past one another does not answer the question why we diverge in our understanding or application of a concept. However, it is a prerequisite for asking the question.

At the level of concepts—as contrasted with words which refer to particular material objects—some theorists wonder if it is even *possible* for people who ascribe different meanings to concepts to be talking about the same concept. For example, Colin McGinn wrote:

> we have not, in the case of concepts, the idea of a single meaning-bearing item (word) about which we can press the question what establishes constancy in its meaning; there isn't the gap between a concept and its

[95] See ibid. 33–8. [96] See ibid. 30–3. [97] See e.g. ibid. 175–6.

content that there is between a word and its meaning—a concept *is* (so to speak) its content. . . . we cannot . . . make sense of employing a concept with a different content from that originally intended—it would just be a *different concept*.[98]

Perhaps in part to get around this argument, Ronald Dworkin wrote of having 'different conceptions of [the same] concept'.[99] He is not always clear, however, about what it is that makes these different 'conceptions' different conceptions of the *same concept* rather than simply being different concepts. To the extent that we could show that the former is the case, we would be justified in thinking of our disagreements as substantial.

In *Law's Empire*, Dworkin explained the difference between concept and conception (for the purpose of that book) as being 'a contrast between levels of abstraction at which the interpretation of the practice can be studied'.[100] In that discussion, the concepts are concepts *of a practice*; what ties different conceptions together is that (echoing Gallie's work) they purport to describe the same practice.[101] In Dworkin's discussion of creative interpretation of social practices, the disputants are by definition talking about the same thing: a particular practice (defined tentatively at a 'pre-interpretive' stage)[102] in a particular community. The interpretations are kept convergent by a requirement of substantial fit with the pre-interpretative content and by a shared world-view.[103] (However, since Dworkin's interpretative approach is meant to act on the level of *prescription for* the practice as well as on the level of *description of* the practice,[104] the extent to which the practice limits the scope of possible interpretations is different in kind from (and probably less restrictive than) the way (for example) Gallie's paradigms would limit different understandings of those paradigms.)

I note in passing that Dworkin may have too quickly dismissed the possibility that lawyers and legal theorists talking about law could be talking about different things. At most, Dworkin's discussion[105] showed that 'the law' has a relatively stable single

98 C. McGinn, *Wittgenstein on Meaning*, 146, 147.
99 Dworkin, *Taking Rights Seriously*, 128.
100 Dworkin, *Law's Empire*, 71.
101 Ibid. 43–9, 68–76.
102 Ibid. 65–6.
103 Ibid. 87–9.
104 See e.g. J. Finnis, 'On Reason and Authority in *Law's Empire*', 357–63.
105 Dworkin, *Law's Empire*, 44.

reference in that a number of interrelated institutional processes go on every day under that name. However, the fact that lawyers (and social scientists) are not talking past each other about 'the law'—the rules and procedures that operate within a particular community at a particular time—does not show conclusively that they are not talking past one another when they talk about 'Law'—a particular form of social institution common to many communities.

Dworkin's fleeting discussions of concepts and conceptions may conflate two different types of analytical moves. When he wrote of different conceptions of the same concept, John Rawls's earlier use of that distinction was implicitly invoked. Rawls wrote about people having a shared concept of justice in the sense that 'they understand the need for, and they are prepared to affirm, a characteristic set of principles for assigning basic rights and duties and for determining what they take to be a proper distribution of the benefits and burdens of social cooperation'.[106] For Rawls, there is an agreed concept (of which there are varying conceptions) because 'justice' is used merely as the name of a particular subsection of moral thought. To the extent that the shared concept has substantial content, it is only whatever (if anything) is presupposed ('a priori' or 'grammatically') by a moral approach to social ordering. (It would be left open, I believe, for other theorists to argue that there is no necessary or a priori content (or structure) to theories of justice.)

On the other hand, when Dworkin wrote in *Law's Empire* about different conceptions of the same concept of courtesy, he was closer to Gallie's analysis of 'essentially contested concepts', discussed above. For Gallie, divergent theories are sometimes related by being different interpretations of the same practice. The Rawls approach is not suited for interpretation of practices, and the Gallie approach is not suited for purely abstract concepts, and imprecise analysis might result if the two approaches are confused.

CONCLUSION

Both proponents and opponents of radical indeterminacy in legal questions have tried to use Wittgenstein's discussions on rule-following to ground their positions. In my opinion, both sides find

[106] J. Rawls, *A Theory of Justice*, 5 (Oxford: Clarendon Press, 1972).

more in Wittgenstein than is actually there. The rule-following considerations do, however, have some limited use in understanding the problem of clear cases and hard cases.

Some clear cases are clear—in large part—because of the (short-term) determinacy of descriptive terms. Our consensus in applying such terms is due to some combination of our common human nature, our common training, and our common way of life. Wittgenstein did not discuss extensively the situation when consensus was absent, though some potential explanations for hard cases can be derived from his writing: for example, that the people involved may have different forms of life.

3
Clear Cases

I conclude that there is no such thing as a language . . .[1]

THE IDEA OF EASY CASES

I have been using the problem of legal determinacy as a context for considering the role of language within law. The usual focus within this area is the question whether there are unique correct answers even for the most difficult and controversial legal problems (sometimes given the shorthand name 'hard cases'). Before exploring that issue further, I want to see what can be learned from situations at the other extreme: legal questions that seem so obvious that there is no question as to what their proper resolution should be (these go under various names in the literature: for example, 'clear cases', 'plain cases', 'easy cases').

Hart had stated: 'Particular fact situations do not await us already marked off from each other, and labelled as instances of the general rule, the application of which is in question; nor can the rule itself step forward to claim its instances.'[2] Yet in clear cases, judges do speak of having a sense of being confined, of the answer being (pre)determined. It may be only a coincidence that everyone believes that a certain case should come out a particular way. It may be that the consensus is made up of people who would give different answers if asked why the case should come out that way or how difficult they thought the case was. However, the convergence of opinion may well be more than coincidence; the consensus may be due to a shared belief regarding the meaning of words or the scope of legal concepts. Most of the writing about

[1] D. Davidson, 'A Nice Derangement of Epitaphs', in *Truth and Interpretation*, 446 (E. LePore, ed., Oxford: Basil Blackwell, 1986); the sentence continued '. . . not if language is anything like what many philosophers and linguists have supposed'.

[2] Hart, *The Concept of Law*, 123.

'clear cases' is not about the sociology of chance convergences; it is about this language-based determinacy. Of course, there may be other reasons behind the convergence of opinion—for example, a consensus about moral or political matters—but those situations are not directly relevant to the present project.

Problems about the nature and basis of agreement arise in J. W. Harris's discussion of clear cases. He tried to avoid one set of difficulties by excluding the 'deviant' or 'non-serious' interpreter in determining whether a consensus about a legal interpretation existed.[3] The fact that some person or small group of people disagreed could be discounted, Harris argued, if the dissenters were clearly wrong. However, this only brings us back to the beginning: by what standard are we judging the dissenters as clearly wrong and their opinions not relevant to determining whether a case is a clear case, if it is only by reference to consensus that we feel comfortable in characterizing the case as easy in the first place? Robert Alexy expressed a similar point as follows:

> Whoever claims that a decision is uncontroversial is to be understood as asserting that there are no arguments which might give rise to serious doubts. Such arguments are, however, always conceivable. The assertion that every such counter-argument is bad or legally irrelevant does not follow conclusively from the set of presupposed norms. In view of this one might wish to assert that the categorization of a case as 'clear' constitutes a 'negative value-judgment' with respect to all potential counter-arguments.[4]

We must ask: at what point are the number of dissenters sufficiently large or sufficiently high in proportion that we are no longer allowed to dismiss their interpretations even though we find them untenable? Is the majority or established interpretation immune by definition from *ever* being labelled as 'untenable' or 'off-the-wall'?

In law, we want to be able to say that some interpretations are 'objectively right'; at the least, we want to be able to say that some are 'objectively wrong'. However, as Gerald Frug argued in the context of 'bureaucratic theory', there is no separating the objective from the subjective, at least when considering human

[3] Harris, *Law and Legal Science*, 6.

[4] R. Alexy, *A Theory of Legal Argumentation*, 8 (Oxford: Clarendon Press, 1989). See also A. D'Amato, 'Aspects of Deconstruction: The "Easy Case" of the Under-Aged President', 84 *Northwestern University Law Review* 250, 251 (1989).

practices and institutions.[5] Objectivity, in the sense of a 'correct' interpretation of a written text or spoken words, refers to getting the meaning right. The problem is that the correctness of a meaning is usually seen to be determined directly or indirectly by consensus: either agreement as to the correct interpretation, agreement as to which authority to defer to, or agreement about which decision-procedure to use. The 'objective' (neutral, independent) is thus, in a sense, only a sum (or a particular function of) the 'subjective' (individual, perspectival).

In language—and to a lesser extent in law—there is a continual tension between consensus/dissent and authority, between whether whatever everyone does is right and the imposition of a standard of correctness (and the branding of 'error') from without. If some persons started using 'cow' to mean horse, the writers of dictionaries and other guardians of proper usage would label that usage as 'incorrect'. However, if enough people took up that usage, with time it would become acceptable, and perhaps standard (moving from idiolect to dialect to accepted usage). Similarly, at a certain level of legal analysis, there is no practical difference, except perhaps one of time, between an evaluation (of whether officials' statements about what the law is were correct) and a description (of what the officials' statements were); for certain limited purposes, whatever is, is right.[6]

Various theorists have commented on clear cases, though sometimes these comments shed more light on the theorists' own general approaches to law than they did on the specific issues regarding consensus in law. The analyses by Dworkin and Schauer I will discuss focused on rule-application; by contrast, Harris's analysis focused on language and intent.

Dworkin argued that the clarity of a clear case is a conclusion we reach after considering the interpretative question (that is, the correct interpretation of past legal and political actions), not a matter which is present ahead of time.[7] He based this argument in part on our willingness to read exceptions into apparently unambiguous language (for example, inheritance according to a will's clear language . . . except for murderers; no vehicles in the

[5] G. Frug, 'The Ideology of Bureaucracy in American Law', 97 *Harvard Law Review* 1276, 1286–92 (1984).

[6] See e.g. Hart, *The Concept of Law*, 144–50 (uncertainty in the rule of recognition).

[7] Dworkin, *Law's Empire*, 350–4.

park . . . except for statues; and so on). For Dworkin, clear cases are cases where only one theory of the law adequately fits the historical materials in the light of our ideas of justice and fairness. The latter clause is important; it is not merely a question of fit. For it is our feelings about justice and fairness which may compel us to read an exception into an apparently clear rule. Thus, 'someone whose convictions about justice and fairness were very different from ours' would disagree about which cases were 'easy cases'.[8] I do not disagree with the conclusion, though it seems driven less by a study of clear cases than by the need to maintain a certain kind of uniformity in the application of an interpretative approach to law.

Frederick Schauer offered an argument similar to Dworkin's, though in the context of a theory about rule-application rather than a grand theory about law. Schauer argued that the conclusion that a directly applicable legal rule could be mechanically applied to resolve a particular legal problem was only the first step in the analysis.[9] Almost all legal systems contain a variety of 'rule-avoiding norms', and may also authorize judges to create new ones. (Schauer noted that in theory it would be possible for there to be legal systems 'in which no rule-avoiding norms exist at all'.[10] Such systems, however, would be wholly static, incapable of adapting to new situations.) These 'escape routes' allow judges 'to ameliorate the rigidity of rules' 'to avoid the arguably unjust consequences of mechanical application of the most directly applicable rule'.[11] Such rule-avoiding norms might include general references to justice or equity as well as 'less locally applicable general principle[s] [such as] no person should profit from his own wrong'.[12] Until one considers such escape routes, Dworkin's favourite case, *Riggs* v. *Palmer*[13]—in which a general wills statute was held to implicitly prohibit a murderer from inheriting from the grandfather he murdered—would be a clear case coming out the other way.[14] Our understanding of clear cases must thus factor in not only the clarity or non-clarity of language in general and the language of a particular text, but also the availability of rule-avoiding norms and the conditions under which judges feel

[8] Ibid. 354.
[9] Schauer, 'Formalism', 515–20.
[10] Ibid. 520.
[11] Ibid. 519.
[12] Ibid. 518, n. 31.
[13] 115 N.Y. 506, 22 N.E. 188 (1889).
[14] Schauer, 'Formalism', 518, n. 31.

compelled (or, to put the same point from the opposite perspective, under which judges feel free) to use them.

The clarity of the language in a legal rule, that it is straightforward relative to the facts to which the rule will be applied, is not sufficient (and perhaps may not be necessary) for the application of that rule to be a clear case. Even if we disregard situations where other rules may apply and indicate a contrary result, we must still consider the 'outlet' or 'safety valve' moves a legal system may authorize (or order) a judge to make in extreme circumstances: either rejecting the literal reading of a rule in this case in favour of one consistent with the rule's purpose, or refusing to follow the plain meaning of the rule in this case because it would lead to an absurd or unjust result (these two analyses overlapping to some extent).

J. W. Harris ascribed the clarity of clear cases not to the clarity of the words used, but to the clarity of intention.[15] He gave the example of the rule, 'no child under the age of ten years may be convicted of any criminal offence', and then considered whether a judge might none the less conclude that this exclusion should not be granted to a particular seven-year-old boy (justified on some ground—for example, that he was from an allegedly inferior ethnic group). Harris concluded that if such an interpretation were proffered, 'legality would manifestly have been breached'.[16] He argued that the interpretation is not excluded logically but on the basis of the author's intent—more specifically, our understanding of the author's intent: 'it would be clear to everyone that that was not the purpose of the rule.'[17] He relied on intention, but he offered no source for his conclusion regarding intention other than the words of the rule themselves; 'intent' is inferred more than determined. We could conclude that his interpretation of what a speaker meant did not in fact depend on intention; to the contrary, what 'intention' Harris would have us *ascribe* to an author must depend on how we had already interpreted the author's words.

Harris's ideas about meaning and intention could be seen as reflecting the English courts' approach to statutory interpretation. Before the 1992 decisions of the House of Lords in *Pepper* v. *Hart*,[18] neither advocates nor judges in English courts were

[15] Harris, *Law and Legal Science*, 3–7.
[16] Ibid. 4.
[17] Ibid. 5.
[18] *Pepper* v. *Hart* [1992] 3 W.L.R. 103.

allowed to refer to records of legislative debates to support conclusions about what the legislators meant by a particular phrase. When the English courts referred to 'the intention of Parliament', they meant nothing more and nothing less than what certain words or phrases mean (given their context).[19] Lord Scarman stated:

> If Parliament . . . says one thing but means another, it is not, under the historic principles of the common law, for the courts to correct it . . . We are to be governed not by Parliament's intentions but by Parliament's enactments.[20]

Harris's discussion of intention in 'clear cases' follows the English courts' 'literal rule' of statutory interpretation: 'Where the application of the law is clear . . . no evidence of the Legislature's, or anyone else's, individual purpose is required.'[21] As a policy matter, this may be a wise approach to statutory interpretation, but its reference to 'intention' can be misleading.[22]

To avoid the problem of the 'deviant interpreter', Harris later clarified that 'everyone' need mean only all persons who would be 'accepted as serious participants in such a debate'.[23] As I noted earlier, this attempt to brush aside the problem of deviant interpreters hints at circularity. Whether someone would be accepted as a serious participant in a debate may turn on whether we find that person's proffered argument tenable or off-the-wall. Consensus is thus maintained only by excluding from consideration anyone who disagrees. (There is one set of circumstances in which Harris's response to the problem of the deviant interpreter would not be circular. If someone had an established reputation in the community, built on many competent (and some excellent) interpretations, we would probably accept him or her as a serious participant in a debate on a new issue, even if for once the

[19] See R. Cross, J. Bell, and G. Engle, *Statutory Interpretation*, 2nd edn., 21–30 (London: Butterworths, 1987).

[20] 418 House of Lords Debates, col. 65 (9 Mar. 1981), quoted in Cross, Bell, and Engle, *Statutory Interpretation*, 22; see also *Saloman* v. *Saloman & Co. Ltd.* [1897] A.C. 22, at 38 (Lord Watson); *Stock* v. *Frank Jones (Tipton) Ltd.* [1978] ICR 347, at 354.

[22] In discussing judges' use of the phrase in cases of statutory interpretation, one commentator described 'intentions of Parliament' as 'not so much a description as a linguistic convenience': Cross, Bell, and Engle, *Statutory Interpretation*, 26. I return to the topic of Parliamentary intent in Ch. 6.

[23] Harris, *Law and Legal Science*, 6.

interpretation this person offered struck us as untenable. Because of the person's good reputation, we might give the apparently 'untenable' interpretation more serious consideration than we otherwise would.)

Wittgenstein's approach to psychological statements may help us to understand (and evaluate) Harris's approach. According to Wittgenstein, there is a first person/third person asymmetry for psychological concepts like 'intend', 'hope', and 'plan'.[24] When I say 'I plan to go to London tomorrow' or 'I intend by "bank" to refer to the financial institution, not the side of a river', I am not describing something, at least not in the sense that one describes a room or a painting. The grammar is different; the grammar of a description is that the descriptive proposition could be wrong (false), according to whether it does or does not correspond to the object described. By contrast, when I *express* my plans or intentions, I am not describing some inner state. If such expressions were like descriptions, it would make sense to be wrong about the matter, and to say later 'I thought I was planning to go to London, but I was wrong' or 'I was mistaken in believing I intended "bank" to refer to the financial institution'. However, such comments are without sense.[25]

By contrast, third-person psychological statements do follow the model of descriptive statements: one can speak of knowing another person's plans or intentions, and one's claims about such matters can be wrong. It is not that one cannot speak of 'knowing' what another person intended by a statement when one has only the statement itself to go by; it is only that this knowledge is defeasible. When one tries to determine what meaning another person intended by a particular utterance, the utterance itself is the primary (and usually the only) evidence. However, there may be other evidence as well: other past utterances, the gestures made while speaking, answers to the follow-up question 'what did you mean by that?', and so on. When the only information we have for determining what someone intended is the utterance itself, our guess of the speaker's intent could be rebutted (or at least made uncertain), for example, by the speaker's later declaration that he had meant something different. Rephrasing Harris's position in

[24] See Wittgenstein, *Philosophical Investigations*, secs. 288–303, 574, 585–6; pp. 221–5; see generally Hacker, *Insight and Illusion*, 276–306.

[25] See Wittgenstein, *Philosophical Investigations*, secs. 246, 408.

the terms used by some Wittgensteinians, we can be 'certain' what a speaker meant when she used a particular phrase, but it is a certainty which allows that we should change our opinion if further, contrary evidence comes to light.

For Harris, the clarity of clear cases comes from a consensus or convention about what the drafter's intention must have been in using particular words ('no child under age ten . . .'). There is a tension in his position, in that he has constructed a judgment purportedly independent of individual views (the clear case for interpretation, the interpretation with which no serious participant could disagree) from a series of individual views (what the legislators intended). This relates to the connection, and tension, mentioned earlier between consensus and authority.

In the terms of the above analysis, Harris has not allowed for the defeasibility of claims that derive intention directly from the primary text. There is no reason why a legislator could not, on one occasion, intend an age restriction to be read flexibly rather than absolutely. If that occurred, Harris's standard would disaggregate, and the judge would need to choose between convention and legislative intent. In the terms of the distinction discussed earlier, Harris has tried to equate what the speaker meant with what the words mean, despite the fact that these two do diverge from time to time. (There are, however, limits to the divergence, limits probably derived from the nature of thought and the nature of language. It simply is quite difficult to say (or write) 'it is cold here' while meaning 'it is warm here', or to say 'the sky is clouding over' while meaning 'there is no odd perfect number'.)[26]

The limited importance of subjective intention (as contrasted with interpretations based solely on the primary text) probably reflects an aspect of the nature of legal systems. It is characteristic of certain types of social systems, including legal systems, to favour words' meaning over speakers' meaning. The effectiveness of legal rules in guiding and co-ordinating behaviour depends on citizens generally being able to figure out without great effort how the rules will be applied.[27] If judges often preferred the rule-

[26] M. Dummett, 'A Nice Derangement of Epitaphs: Some Comments on Davidson and Hacking', in *Truth and Interpretation*, 471; see Wittgenstein, *Philosophical Investigations*, sec. 510.

[27] See e.g. L. Fuller, *The Morality of Law*, rev. edn., 33–94 (New Haven, Conn.: Yale University Press, 1969).

makers' (actual or subjective) intention over the semantic meaning *and* if those intentions often diverged significantly from that meaning, then the ability of citizens to act according to the rules (that is, to predict how they would be later interpreted by the judges) would be undermined.

One can approach the question of language and clear cases in an entirely different way, a way which allows one to accept Harris's conclusions without incurring the disaggregation problem (discussed earlier) that comes with relying on legislative intention. The argument would be that there are conventions within language not only regarding the meanings of words and phrases, but also regarding the amount of leeway in interpretation (and application) delegated to the listener. For example, our conventions seem to hold that general descriptive terms (for instance, 'a mature person') delegate a great deal of discretion, while numerical descriptions (for instance, 'a person at least thirty-five years old') greatly curtail that discretion. 'Buy me an inexpensive chess book' leaves a greater role to my listener's judgement than 'buy me a chess book that costs less than ten pounds'. Such conventions are understood by all competent users of the language, and knowledge of such conventions is a criterion of that competence. Assuming such a convention is present in the case of numerical limitations, we need no recourse to purpose. It would be no more necessary in that case to ponder whether legislators wanted us to use our discretion when they used a numerical limitation than it would be to ponder whether they meant 'horse' when they wrote 'cow' (though in both types of cases, one can still imagine a speaker intending to use words contrary to the language's conventional rules).

LANGUAGE AND DISCOURSE

Sometimes a proposition that would seem clear in meaning and application in a descriptive context seems to become uncertain, fuzzy at the edges, when used in a normative context; in such situations, one might say that the meaning of a term changes when we move from descriptive to normative discourse. One (Fregean) approach would be to claim that there is and could be no such change. According to that approach, sentences can be analyzed into content and force, and a change of force should not be confused with a change in content.[28] For example, under this approach there is only a change of force between 'there are no vehicles in the park' ('no vehicles in the park' plus declarative force) and 'no vehicles in the park!' ('no vehicles in the park' plus imperative force).

Under a different (arguably Wittgensteinian) approach, the fact that words occur within a rule changes their meaning.[29] In particular, absolutes—'no', 'all', 'every', and so on—seem to have different meanings in rules compared to what they have in descriptions. One should note how differently—perhaps, how much more clearly—one thinks about the 'open texture' (in Hart's sense) of 'vehicle' in a descriptive sentence. If someone says 'there are no vehicles in the park' despite the existence of a skateboard, it might either be that the person did not see the skateboard or that the person did not consider skateboards to be 'vehicles'. However, if an emergency vehicle were present, we would surely correct the speaker if he continued to insist that no vehicles were present. It is only when we move from the descriptive to the normative that we are tempted to say that 'vehicle' might not include emergency vehicles, and that, I suggest, is because we are being led by our judgement to consider that applying the (otherwise reasonable) rule in a way that excluded emergency vehicles would be 'absurd' or 'wrong'. The description 'there are no vehicles in the park' means that there are zero vehicles in the park. However, the rule 'no vehicles in the park' is taken by many commentators to mean something slightly different: that there shall be zero vehicles in the park, *except under special circumstances*.[30]

The point may be more general. In different 'language games', the extent to which terms are understood literally rather than metaphorically, 'rigidly' rather than 'flexibly', varies along a

[28] See e.g. M. Dummett, 'Can Analytic Philosophy be Systematic, and Ought it to be?', in *Truth and Other Enigmas*, 449–50 (London: Duckworth 1978); 'Frege's Distinction between Sense and Reference', ibid. 117–18.

[29] For opposing evaluations of how well the Fregean sense/force distinction survives a Wittgensteinian critique, see J. Katz, *The Metaphysics of Meaning*, 86–101 (Cambridge, Mass.: MIT Press, 1990), and Baker and Hacker, *Language, Sense and Nonsense*, 47–120 (Oxford: Basil Blackwell, 1984).

[30] See Harris, *Law and Legal Science*, 5–6; A. M. Honoré, *Making Law Bind*, 80–1 (Oxford: Clarendon Press, 1987): 'the prima-facie universal character of rules'.

spectrum. In exaggerations, '*no one* in class is ever prepared!' probably means that very few students are; in moral discourse, '*always* do what you promise' is understood to mean that one should do so unless one has a very good reason not to; and so on. Universals in rules may be just another example of a language game in which such terms are used 'flexibly'.

Of course, it remains possible to maintain the Fregean line even if one accepts the 'prima facie' approach to absolutes in rules. Frederick Schauer would argue that the second (non-Fregean) approach confuses a theory about language (what sentences mean) with a theory about how rules should be applied. For Schauer, if we decide that 'no vehicles in the park' does not justify excluding emergency vehicles, this is not because we think 'no' or 'vehicle' have a slightly different meaning in the normative context. We decide this way because we believe that rules should not be strictly applied if to do so in a particular instance would lead either to an 'absurd' result or to a result contrary to the rule's underlying purpose.[31] According to Schauer, it remains open to us to have a strict approach to rule application, one that would never diverge from the meaning of the words in the rule formulation, one that would warrant excluding the emergency vehicle in that case. However, Schauer did not give any examples where that approach to rule application actually prevails.[32] In the end, the data seem to be indeterminate in choosing between a Fregean and a non-Fregean approach to analyzing (the meaning of absolutes in) normative discourse. (Given that judicial decisions involve both semantic analysis and policies regarding rule-application, it is not clear that anything of importance turns on the choice between the two characterizations of the same phenomenon.)

LANGUAGE AND DIALECT

The non-Fregean approach is based in part on an analogy with other specialized or deviant forms of normal speech: dialect and jargon. The literal meaning of a word is the meaning that participants from the relevant community would unreflectively assign to it, and the same word or phrase might have different

[31] See Schauer, *Playing by the Rules*, 53–62; 'Formalism', 524–5.
[32] Schauer, 'Formalism', 520.

literal meanings in different contexts. The notion of literal meaning (or, in the terms of American judicial rhetoric, 'plain meaning') can be understood in terms used in Chapter 2, when discussing Wittgenstein's rule-following considerations: we apply a term we know in an unreflective way; on such occasions, we are not 'interpreting' the term (that is, interpreting the rule for the term's application), we simply grasp its meaning.[33] It is instructive to notice the contrast here between Wittgenstein's approach to understanding and that of Donald Davidson: in contrast to Wittgenstein's idea of simply grasping meaning, Davidson believed that in understanding even simple sentences (correctly used and in our native language), we are interpreting, applying a theory of meaning.[34]

A word can be described as having a 'literal' or 'plain' meaning only relative to competent speakers of a particular language or dialect. When I am listening to someone describing an ice-hockey match, the 'plain meaning' of 'check' is different for me than it would be if I were listening to a description of a chess game: slightly different contexts (the jargon of the two different games), different meanings for the same word, yet the same immediate, unreflective grasp of meaning. The ability of words to carry different 'plain meanings' even for the same interpreter when the context is altered is exemplified by some situations in (American) contract law. Consider the following exchange between Richard Posner and Stanley Fish.

Richard Posner discussed the example of a contract which had clauses stating that the written text was the final and complete expression of the parties' agreement and that the price agreed would be $100 per pound. He argued that the parol evidence rule would foreclose a party from claiming that the parties had in fact agreed that the price would be $120 per pound after the first ten pounds, adding emphatically: 'The document is not ambiguous . . . [I]t is silly to think that every document is unclear.'[35] Stanley

[33] See Wittgenstein, *Philosophical Investigations*, secs. 201 ('there is a way of grasping a rule which is *not* an *interpretation*'), 228–32.

[34] See Dummett, 'A Nice Derangement of Epitaphs: Some Comments on Davidson and Hacking', 464–8; S. Mulhall, 'Davidson on Interpretation and Understanding', 37 *Philosophical Quarterly* 319 (1987), and *On Being in the World*, 91–106 (London: Routledge, 1990).

[35] R. Posner, 'Law and Literature: A Relation Reargued', 72 *Virginia Law Review* 1351, 1371 (1986).

Fish criticized Posner's ascription of ambiguity or clarity to the contract itself: 'The document is neither ambiguous nor unambiguous in and of itself. The document is not *anything* in and of itself, but acquires a shape and significance only within the assumed background of circumstances of its possible use.'[36] If the context of Posner's contract had been an industry where it was the usual practice and the general understanding that a set price is only for the first ten pounds, and thereafter a 20 per cent escalation applies, Fish argued, Posner's contract 'would have, and have obviously and without dispute, the meaning Posner scoffs at'.[37]

Contrary to the misleading characterizations used by both Posner and Fish, the problems of interpreting the contract come not from the strange quasi-metaphysical task of trying to locate meaning either 'in' the physical document or 'outside' it. The choice of interpretations here turns instead on which language the contract is read against. The 'plain meaning' of a particular phrase might be quite different in a particular industry sub-community than it is in normal everyday speech. If both parties to a contract are part of a particular sub-community, it is not clear why the 'plain meaning' doctrine should not be applied in terms of that sub-community's understandings.

It is important to see why this example is different from Balkin's example discussed earlier, where two contracting partners chose to mean horse by the word 'cow'. In the Balkin example, the speakers are imposing a meaning on a word that does not otherwise carry that meaning. In the business contract example, the speakers are merely following the meaning they unreflectively associate with the term, the meaning that the sub-community has collectively given to the term. That is, it is the difference, not a trivial one, between the idiolect of one or two people, and the dialect of sub-community.

Continuing with examples from contract law, prior to the development of the Uniform Commercial Code in America, normal business practices could not be introduced to contradict the apparent meaning (or clarify the true meaning) of the written terms of an agreement, unless it could be shown that the parties had intended those practices to have that priority. However, that

[36] S. Fish, 'Don't Know Much about the Middle Ages: Posner on Law and Literature', 97 *Yale Law Journal* 777, 784 (1988).

[37] Ibid.

business practices were *not* intended as the starting-point or the reference point for interpreting the written terms was assumed rather than argued for by the courts at that time.[38] That approach was fatally circular. When speakers treat a dialect as normal or natural, they see no need to tell one another or anyone else that they have chosen to use this dialect rather than 'conventional language'. Also, one cannot simply argue that since the contractual language did not explicitly mention background practices, no reference to such practices is necessary in interpreting the contractual language. The judges in the cases prior to the Uniform Commercial Code saw themselves as privileging the linguistic meaning over the authors' intentions, when in fact what they were doing was privileging everyday speech over the dialects spoken in particular business sub-communities.

CONCLUSION

Many theorists discuss 'clear cases' as though the nature and basis of such cases were themselves clear and obvious. However, a close analysis discloses a variety of issues and factors. Among the things that can make an apparently clear case unclear, or an apparently hard case easy, are issues of speakers' intention, dialects and idiolects, context, community practices and assumptions, views about justice, and ideas about rule-application, as well as the issues of vagueness and 'open texture' that were raised in earlier chapters.[39]

[38] See D. Patterson, 'Good Faith, Lender Liability, and Discretionary Acceleration: Of Llewellyn, Wittgenstein, and the Uniform Commercial Code', 68 *Texas Law Review* 169, 186–99 (1989).

[39] I return briefly to the question of 'clear cases' in Chap. 6.

4
Ronald Dworkin's Right Answer Thesis

> I myself am often accused of thinking that there is almost always a right answer to a legal question; the accusation suggests that if I were to confess to that opinion anything else I said about legal reasoning could be safely ignored.[1]

INTRODUCTION

Unlike the earlier chapters on Hart's concept of 'open texture' and on the application of Wittgenstein's rule-following considerations to legal theory, the focus of this chapter and the following one will be broader: an entire legal theory (for this chapter, the legal theory of Ronald Dworkin, for the next, that of Michael Moore). I want to discuss a viewpoint rather than a question, a whole way of looking at law rather than a single debate. However, the advantage of a broader scope brings corresponding disadvantages; trying to discuss so much material in so limited a space means that the resulting exegesis and critique may be only an outline, and that my discussions may be in risk of becoming either conclusory or superficial. I will do my best to treat the ideas with the seriousness and the respect they deserve despite the limited space within which I work.

The opening sections of this chapter will be about ideas from Dworkin's earlier writings regarding whether there are unique right answers to legal questions. Part of my discussion will go beyond the range of the main debate in the literature to consider questions of the possible scope of a right answer theory and the problem of incommensurability. The remaining sections in the chapter will deal with Dworkin's later work on an interpretative approach to law. After briefly summarizing his approach, I will consider a series of challenges to it, moving from more surface objections to objections that go to the heart of Dworkin's ideas.

[1] Dworkin, 'No Right Answer?', 58.

THE CONCEPT OF 'RIGHT ANSWERS'

Much of the English-language literature on legal determinacy has focused on the work of Ronald Dworkin. He has consistently advocated the position that there is a unique right answer for the vast majority of legal cases. However, the nature of his 'right answer thesis', as well as the arguments put forward in its support, has changed substantially over the years. At first, Dworkin's 'right answer thesis' was a direct response to Hart's arguments about 'open texture' and judicial discretion; aspects of that debate were discussed earlier in Chapter 1. Dworkin did not view the limitations and complexities of language as a serious obstacle to his 'right answer thesis'. As I discussed earlier, he initially argued that ambiguities and uncertainties could be overcome by burdens of proof, presumptions, and the like. As was noted, there are problems with that response, for while it concedes the difficulty of drawing borderlines in one part of the analysis or definition, it assumes just that ability for some other part of the analysis or definition.

Dworkin's more recent work has had a different focus and direction. Few of the arguments deal directly with the determinacy of language or of rules; he seemed to abandon his earlier approach to the problem of ambiguity, and replace it with a different method of circumventing that problem. If legal concepts or statutory language are ambiguous, open-textured, or otherwise unclear in their application, this uncertainty simply supports the belief that more than one statement of what the law is, is initially tenable. The uncertainty does not trouble Dworkinian judges because they have a set process for how to choose between alternative readings of what the law is. That the meaning of the relevant legal language favours one reading over another—or that it is indeterminate between the two—is only one aspect of evaluating the two readings (part of the evaluation of a reading's 'fit' with the relevant legal materials). The final decision can always be made in part on the basis of political morality. A judge may not be able to decide whether, as a matter of linguistic meaning or legislative intent, 'vehicle' includes skateboards, but the judge may be able to include or exclude skateboards on the basis of which interpretation creates a better social order or which interpretation better serves the value of 'integrity'.

There is one issue I want to put aside. Dworkin's claim that there are unique right answers to almost all legal questions could be separated into two sub-claims: that there are unique correct answers, and that these answers are determined by legal considerations—no extra-legal considerations are necessary. One might accept that there was a unique right answer to a case without thinking that it was what the law required. There is a spectrum along which such matters might lie. At one extreme, material that all theorists would consider 'legal' determines a unique right answer. At the other extreme, there are right answers to many disputes because there are unique right answers to moral questions, so that though the law in some hypothetical system gives no guidance at all to judges, there would be a unique correct way to resolve the (legal) dispute. In between, there would be situations where the law ordered (or authorized) judges to apply whatever moral standards were relevant (without specifying them in advance), and situations where there were specific legal standards to apply, but these standards included broad moral language (for example, requiring 'fair treatment' or 'reasonable behaviour'). As discussed in Chapter 1, Dworkin tends to be a maximalist on when to describe considerations as 'legal' considerations, but even he would probably stop short of the extreme case where judges were acting without any instructions. Raz tends to be a minimalist in these matters, and probably would not include even the case of moral standards embedded in specific statutes, if those standards had not been narrowed or clarified by earlier decisions. Though some theorists find the argument about this 'sub-claim' important and interesting, I will largely leave it aside (except for the comments I made in the earlier chapter), and focus primarily on the first 'sub-claim', that there are unique right answers.

Other aspects of Dworkin's later work will not be considered until later in this chapter. I first want to consider more closely the idea of a right answer thesis, both in the abstract and as it was elaborated in Dworkin's earlier work.

What does it mean to say that there is a right answer to a legal question? Does it even make sense to talk of 'right answers' before a court has spoken on an issue? A critique of Dworkin's ideas about right answers offered by A. D. Woozley is a good place to begin considering these questions, though I will argue that it is the weaknesses rather than the strengths of his argument which are instructive. Woozley offered an extreme answer to the question of what it means to say that there is always a 'right answer' to legal problems. His answer seemed to comport with a basic legal intuition, but in the end the answer proves to be quite unhelpful. Woozley argued that because 'law is what the courts say', a legal problem as a right answer only if the courts have given their answer to that problem.[2] In other words, the 'right answer' to a question within a particular legal system is whatever answer that system gives to the question. Until the point when an official answer is proffered, we can try to predict what the courts will say and we can argue about which judicial response would be the most reasonable (given precedent, public policy, and so on), but 'we are not [thereby] saying anything about truth.'[3]

Woozley wanted to distinguish a judge coming up with the best answer given the circumstances from the judge stating what the law *already was* before the decision was rendered:

> The judge's answer may have been more reasonable than the contrary answer would have been; and in that case it *was* the right answer for him to have given . . . but its having been the right answer for him to have given is not the *same* as its having been the right answer to the question of law.[4]

Woozley did not deny that one could speak of a court's ruling as having been 'reasonable' or 'unreasonable' (or even of its having been 'right' or 'wrong').[5] Therefore, even if we accept his analysis, it may succeed only in pushing our inquiry about right answers back one step. The question now becomes, as Dworkin pointed out, whether in difficult cases 'one answer might be the most reasonable of all, even though competent lawyers disagree about which answer is the most reasonable'.[6] Though I believe that Dworkin's response might be seen to end the debate, I think it worthwhile to continue on, to consider Woozley's argument on its own terms.

Woozley seemed to assert that one cannot speak of the 'truth' of a legal statement until a judge has rendered a decision in a particular case.[7] It is important to note that there is no reason why

[2] A. D. Woozley, 'No Right Answer', in *Ronald Dworkin and Contemporary Jurisprudence*, 180 (M. Cohen, ed., London: Duckworth, 1984).

[3] Ibid. 179. [4] Ibid. [5] Ibid. 179–81.

[6] Dworkin, 'A Reply by Ronald Dworkin', 278.

[7] Woozley, 'No Right Answer', 176–80.

Woozley's analysis, if accepted, would not extend to 'clear cases' as well as the more controversial cases. Woozley seemed to pull back a bit from that conclusion, though the position he then took is probably not consistent with the remainder of his argument. Throughout the article he distinguished between the 'truth' about legal, literary, and historical matters on one hand, and speculation (what should happen or what would have happened) based on coherence with the known facts on the other. At one point Woozley seemed to allow the possibility that a counter-factual statement could have a truth value if the coherence of the statement (or its opposite) with known facts was 'overwhelming'.[8] He went on to state, without further elaboration, that there are 'legal analogue[s]' to these counter-factual statements.[9] So it seems that Woozley might allow ascriptions of truth value to legal propositions in the clearest of clear cases even before the courts have spoken on the matter (and such clear cases, presumably, would include legal propositions derived solely from statutes as well as those based wholly or partly on judge-made standards). As I noted earlier, I do not think that this position can be made consistent with what he was arguing elsewhere in the article.

We could also extend this analysis in a different direction, and say that statements about the law have no truth value until the *highest* court has spoken on the subject, for the lower court's judgment could always be overturned. (And even with the highest court's judgment, the 'truth' would be tentative, for that court could always overrule its initial decision.)

With each level of analysis, the idea of legal 'truth' implicit in Woozley's discussion becomes more and more intricate. Woozley had made matters easier for himself by assuming a strange conception of 'settled law':

> The judge has to try for whatever in his system counts as narrative fit, but if he is thought by higher or later courts to have failed, they will write a different ending. Eventually some ending gets accepted into the legal system, and the statement of that becomes the right answer; it was the answer which sooner or later was given and endured.[10]

It is easier to equate legally true propositions with judicial promulgation if there is a great deal of finality and stability within the system. Woozley seemed to assume that a proposed answer to

[8] Ibid. 177. [9] Ibid. 180. [10] Ibid. 179.

a legal question eventually 'becomes' a legally true proposition after (say) a sufficient number of sufficiently important courts approve of it. The problem is that the 'settledness' of a legal proposition in most systems is always relative to a point in time. For example, though the 'separate but equal' reading of the American constitutional requirement of equality was accepted by all courts for decades, it was eventually questioned and then rejected.[11] If it is always possible for the highest court to rethink an issue and to overturn what was until then settled law, then the language of Woozley's approach must change. Instead of being able to say '*as of now*, this proposition is (finally) legally true', we can only say '*for now*, this proposition is legally true'.

Along with the problem of time-frame, there is also a problem of specificity. Woozley's argument tended towards the claim that only the most specific legal propositions (more specific than the rules in the rule-books, and case-law only as confined strictly to the facts of each case) can have a truth-value. The implication is that the next case, no matter how clearly it seems to be subsumed under the general rule or how similar its facts seem to be to the facts of the prior case, could be decided either way. However, there is a countervailing tension: legal opinions are given (and characterized) in words and concepts which are by nature general; any attempt to describe the result in a particular case will use or imply a legal proposition at a higher level of generality than the specific case from which it derived. In common-law systems, a judge does not merely say, 'given the facts of the case as I have found them (A, B, C, . . . , X), judgment for plaintiff'. If that were the case, then rulings might be able to be limited tightly to the facts of the original case. Since the next case did not involve exactly the same date, time, characters, and so on, the prior case would not then seem to require any result in *any* subsequent case, no matter how close the facts. As it is, judges must give reasons for their rulings, and those reasons will necessarily be couched in terms which will make them at least in principle applicable to other cases. Similarly, a judge must give a reason for distinguishing a prior case. The judge cannot simply say, 'in that case, the events occurred on a Tuesday in March, and in this case the events

[11] See e.g. L. Tribe, *American Constitutional Law*, 2nd edn., 1474–80 (Mineola, New York: Foundation Press, 1988).

occurred on a Thursday in April: therefore, even though plaintiff won in the earlier case, in this case, defendant wins'. The judge must give a reason for why that difference is significant to the case, and that reasoning will have some applicability to actual or hypothetical future cases.

Someone might wish to argue against my characterization of Woozley. The alternative reading would go: what he was arguing was that a proposition is only legally true if it has been promulgated by a court; however, many judicial promulgations are quite general. I make a mistake by confusing the specific decision the court made (for example, under this fact situation, plaintiff wins) with the legal conclusions the court promulgated in deciding the case. A court might conclude, for example, that a particular implied warranty should apply generally to all sales, even though the case before the court involved only a sale of hardware.

However, if we accept this alternative reading, Woozley is led into all the difficulties that occur in the theory of precedent in England and America.[12] Most basically, later court decisions (and legal commentators) will often read an earlier decision more narrowly (or differently) than that decision had been characterized in the original opinion, without that new reading being seen either by its authors or by commentators as (necessarily) a new piece of judicial rule-making. (In more technical language, even if the original opinion says that X, Y, and Z are the *ratio decidendi* of a case, later courts and commentators may disagree; the original declaration will not be conclusive on the issue.) The only thing that is constant among the changing readings of a past case is consistency with the facts of the case and the conclusion as to which side won. If Woozley equated 'legally true' with whatever a judge has said, then Woozley's approach would be inconsistent with legal practice in England and America at a basic level, in that a judge's characterization of the case is often (implicitly) rejected as a correct reading of what the case 'meant'. That is why I prefer to read Woozley as equating 'legally true' with the minimal holding of a case: under these facts, the court has held that this party should prevail.

[12] See e.g. M. Moore, 'Precedent, Induction, and Ethical Generalization', in *Precedent in Law*, 184–90 (L. Goldstein, ed., Oxford: Clarendon Press, 1987).

Woozley's position could be viewed as a kind of extreme legal realism. An alternative might be to read Woozley as simply equating the term 'truth' in the legal context (or the phrase 'legally true') with the description 'promulgated in a judicial decision' (or 'promulgated by a decision of the highest court'); that is the reason why we cannot speak of legally true statements until an official has granted judgment. However, this reading would make Woozley's position both irrefutable and meaningless. It does not make sense to treat a legal realist ('law is a prediction of what the courts will do and nothing else') as merely offering either a stipulative definition or a linguistic analysis. These theorists were trying to make an analytical or conceptual point about the nature of a social institution and the way its participants act.

Under a legal realist or positivist approach, one must distinguish true statements from 'legally true statements'. The following illustrates the difference between true and 'legally true': while it may be true that we have a (moral) duty to care for our elderly parents, it is not *legally* true (within our legal system) that we have a (legal) duty to care for our elderly parents. For the type of extreme legal realism I am discussing, a statement is legally true if and only if it has been promulgated by a proper authority (say, a judge).

Woozley tied the set of 'legally true' propositions very tightly to the set of official promulgations. It appears that for him every judicial decision adds to the set of legally true propositions. Though the proposition 'no one can park on a double yellow line' might be legally true (as the text of a valid statute), for him the proposition 'Robert Smith cannot park on a double yellow line' is not legally true until it is stated by a judge as part of a judicial decision (since it is not explicitly stated in the statute).[13]

The problem with tying the set of legally true propositions to actual court pronouncements is that it seems to discount the role of reason within law. There are standards of correct inference within a legal system (most reflecting general notions of correct inference, though some may be peculiar to legal systems) which

[13] One can find roughly similar claims, that even straightforward applications of rules create new norms, in the work of other legal theorists. See e.g. H. Kelsen, *General Theory of Law and State*, 132–6 (New York: Russell & Russell, 1945); J. B. White, *Justice as Translation*, 246 (Chicago: University of Chicago Press, 1990).

participants of a legal system use to argue for particular outcomes in particular cases, to predict how a court will resolve particular cases, and to praise or criticize past court decisions. Within the discourse of most legal systems, it is not nonsensical (though it may often be unjustified) to claim that a particular court decision was wrong. The idea of legal mistake means that there is conceptual space between what a court actually said and what the court should have said.[14]

Ignoring the concept (and the problem) of legal mistake has created difficulties for various legal theories. For example, John Austin ignored the problem of legal mistake in one of his arguments against natural law theory. He posited that if he violated an unjust statute—one which would not be valid according to a natural law theory—which carried the death sentence, the natural law argument would not get him very far: 'if I object to the sentence, that it is contrary to the law of God . . . the court of justice will demonstrate the inconclusiveness of my reasoning by hanging me up, in pursuance of the law of which I have impugned the validity.'[15]

The story was meant to be about the difference between legal validity and morality: that a statute could be valid without being moral. In fact, at most the story is about the difference between legal validity and political power, or about legal mistake. To see this, we need only modify the story slightly. If the narrator was to be hanged for violating a particular statute, it might be equally futile to argue that the statute was not a valid law under the governing rule of recognition (for example, that it was somehow procedurally deficient), *even if that argument was correct.* Judges can make mistakes (and even act deliberately contrary to the law)—though here, of course, the 'can' denotes physical possibility, not authorization.

Because of the possibility of legal mistake, Austin was wrong to

[14] The going is tricky here, and I am trying to be careful in my wording. To have written (instead of what I did write) that there is conceptual space between what a court actually said and what *the law was* (at least before the court's decision was handed down) would have been implicitly to have taken a position about where to draw the line between 'legal' and 'extra-legal'. I discussed some of the difficulties and subtleties of that debate in Chap. 1.

[15] J. Austin, *The Province of Jurisprudence Determined*, 185 (London: Weidenfeld and Nicolson, 1955), quoted in Hart, 'Positivism and the Separation of Law and Morals', 616.

conflate the fact that an official acted *as if* a statute was valid law with the statute *actually* being valid law. The connection Austin drew between enforcement and validity is shown by two sentences which occurred slightly before the section quoted above:

> Now, to say that human laws which conflict with the Divine Law are not binding, that is to say, are not laws, is to talk stark nonsense. The most pernicious laws, and therefore those which are most opposed to the will of God, have been and are continually enforced by judicial tribunals.[16]

I am not, of course, arguing that a workable legal theory could ever make legal validity completely independent of enforcement. Arguably, and this simplifies the matter somewhat, some legal positivists do equate *over the long term* what officials enforce as law and what the law is.[17] However, only a caricatured form of legal realism would equate *in the short term* what the law is with whatever officials characterize (or enforce) as law.

Woozley equated the set of all true statements within a legal system with some set of propositions declared or decided by judges. To admit the concept of legal mistake is to say directly that it may be that not all judicial conclusions are true statements within a legal system and to say indirectly that there may be some such statements that have never been part of a judicial declaration. The debate then is over what additional elements can be used to justify a claim that a certain proposition is true within a particular legal system (and not just that it *should be made true* within that system) even though no statute or precedent states it explicitly.[18]

In loosening the connection between the set of legally true propositions and official promulgations, I want to assert both (1) that some judicial statements and decisions do not add to the list of legally true propositions, that is, that there are legal mistakes; and (2) that some propositions are legally true even though never promulgated by the relevant authority. The second assertion is illustrated by Joseph Raz's definition of 'legal justification':

> The statement 'It is the law that P' legally justifies the statement 'It is the law that R' just in case 'It is the law that P' is true and there is a set of true statements (legal *or non-legal*) <Q>, such that <Q> and it is the law that

[16] Austin, *The Province of Jurisprudence Determined*, 185.

[17] Consider, for example, H. L. A. Hart's discussion of the 'rule of recognition', Hart, *The Concept of Law*, 97–107.

[18] See J. Raz, 'Legal Rights', 4 *Oxford Journal of Legal Studies* 1, 9–12 (1984).

P state a complete reason to believe that R (and <Q> by itself does not state such a reason).[19]

Here it may be the case that 'it is the law that P' is a judicial pronouncement (that is not challenged as mistaken) or a statute, but the derived 'it is the law that R' is not. Most legal practitioners and legal theorists would accept derivations of this kind, but Woozley appeared not to.

As for the first assertion, that not all judicial conclusions about the law add to the set of legally true propositions, consider the situation if two judges within the same jurisdiction promulgated norms with contradictory contents, for example, one saying that bookshops in the jurisdiction could not be open for business on Sundays and the other saying that those same shops *could* be open for business on Sundays. In this situation, one would believe that even the extreme legal realist would have to admit the occurrence of 'legal mistake', that one of the judges, even though formally acting within his or her authority, had not added to the set of legally true propositions. The extreme legal realist has a difficulty here. On one hand, he cannot claim that both promulgations are legally true without severing all connections between law and norms: it is part of the 'grammar' of normative discourse that it makes no sense to say both that one has permission to do X and that one is also prohibited from doing X. On the other hand, if the extreme legal realist refers to some principle to justify dismissing one of the two promulgations as mistaken, that admits that the institutional source of a proposition is not the only criterion and not a conclusive criterion for describing the proposition as legally true. The extreme legal realist is forced to concede that at least some of the time judicial conclusions about the law do not add to the set of legally true propositions.

A slightly less extreme form of legal realism is still possible: someone might argue that among different properly promulgated norms, a legal interpreter may occasionally have to treat some of the promulgations as invalidated, limited, or modified by other promulgations in order to maintain minimal consistency in the legal system's orders. By minimal consistency, I mean only avoiding actual or potential contradictory contents in the norms[20]

[19] Ibid. 7–8 (emphasis added).
[20] See Harris, *Law and Legal Science*, 70–83.

(I do not mean any broader consistency of values and purposes among the various legal norms, as in Dworkin's value of 'Integrity').[21] These principles are merely the principles of non-contradiction and derogation traditionally used in legal analysis.[22] This concession, the somewhat extreme positivist would argue, does not entail the further concession that some propositions are legally true despite never having been promulgated by a relevant authority.

One can see, from this brief critique of Woozley's approach to right answers in the law, how the issue of legal determinacy is connected with many other issues in legal theory. The discussion has also confirmed the less surprising conclusion that notions of 'right answers' and 'legally true' depend on contingent procedures and institutions, and therefore that those concepts may vary from one legal system to another.

THE SCOPE OF A RIGHT ANSWER THESIS

I want to consider briefly a matter rarely mentioned in the literature, the scope of 'right answer' theories: that is, to what types of legal questions such theories extend. Dworkin has generally limited his discussions to the question of whether the plaintiff or the defendant in a civil law suit has a right to win. In his earlier works, he specifically allowed that judges have discretion in the strong sense for some of their other decisions: for example, the setting of a prison sentence or the framing of equitable relief.[23] It is not clear why a 'right answer' theory should exempt even these areas. Assuming that a particular approach to judicial reasoning (for Dworkin, the balance of 'fit' and 'best light' and the value of integrity) does yield a right answer as to who should win the lawsuit, it might also do so for other judicial decisions: evidentiary motions, procedural motions, the setting of jury instructions, sentencing, and so on.

Dworkin's discussions on the application of his 'right answer' thesis to matters other than civil verdicts were mixed and seem to have changed somewhat over time. In an early work, he argued

[21] cf. Dworkin, *Law's Empire*, 225–58.
[22] See Harris, *Law and Legal Science*, 70–83.
[23] See Dworkin, *Taking Rights Seriously*, 71.

that the proposition that judges have discretion in the strong sense 'must be established affirmatively, on the balance of argument', and that in the case of sentencing and equitable relief judges have reached that decision.[24] I am sceptical that the discretion in these areas was claimed only after it had been 'established affirmatively, on the balance of argument' (nor is it entirely clear why the decision should be made by judges rather than, say, legislators). Also, I do not see why this conclusion of discretion would be immune from the same arguments Dworkin used against legal positivist claims for judicial discretion.

Later discussions did seem to assume a wider scope for Dworkin's right answer theory, though he never discussed the question of scope directly. In *Law's Empire*, he implicitly extended the theory to include determining the appropriate remedy in civil law suits (at least for those cases with particularly wide social consequences).[25] In another discussion, he argued that it followed from the right of the innocent not to be convicted of a crime and the right of certain parties to win their civil suits that citizens have the right to have a particular level of accuracy in their trial procedures. He wrote that citizens have a right that the state, in its selection of trial procedures, give the appropriate weight to potential 'moral harm' (the injustice to those directly affected by incorrect verdicts) as against the interest in efficiency.[26]

If theorists do not feel inclined to extend 'right answer' theories to judicial decisions other than the judgments in civil suits, it may be because in those other decisions they are confident that though some answers can be labelled as wrong, there is more than one right answer. However, the notion of a 'right answer' in sentencing decisions is not so strange that it has no takers. Michael Moore seemed at least somewhat inclined towards such a position. His attempt to give a metaphysically realist analysis of the legal concept of 'malice' turns on a judge being able to determine the exact punishment that a particular criminal deserves.[27] In a sense,

[24] Ibid.

[25] Dworkin, *Law's Empire*, 389–91 (discussing the appropriate remedy in the desegregation case of *Brown* v. *Board of Education*, 349 U.S. 294 (1955)).

[26] R. Dworkin, *A Matter of Principle*, 72–103 (Cambridge, Mass.: Harvard University Press, 1985).

[27] M. Moore, 'The Interpretive Turn in Modern Theory: A Turn for the Worse?', 41 *Stanford Law Review* 871, 886 (1989).

whoever believes in either a pure retributivist or a pure utilitarian approach to punishment might believe that there is (in principle) a single correct sentence for each offender—after calculating, however this is done, either the level of moral turpitude of the act or the best way to maximize utility. Of course, it may be the case that due to problems with the theories themselves, utilitarianism or retributive theory cannot reach unique right answers for the relevant moral-legal questions.[28] However, such disputes are beyond the scope of my project.

One reason right answer theories may be thought of as only applying to judgments is that it is there that the rhetoric of general practice seems best to match a right answer theory. The argument is that we speak of a litigant having a right to win his or her suit in a way that we do not speak of the litigant having a right to a particular level of damages or a particular rule of evidence. However, in areas other than civil judgments, even if we do not often speak of a person *having a right*, we do (at least sometimes) speak of there being *a right thing to do*: for example, that it is wrong to have rules excluding certain kinds of evidence (for example, hypnotically enhanced testimony)[29] or that the sentence the defendant received was neither too severe nor too lenient. There are subtle and interesting differences between the rhetoric of rights and the rhetoric of 'the right thing to do', but the concepts are certainly related,[30] and both types of rhetoric would support or encourage a right answer theory.

We should note that in many decisions other than the final judgment, judges' decisions are bound to some degree. By stating that a judge's decision is bound I mean (at a minimum) that if the decision transgressed certain boundaries, it would be reversed by a reviewing court. For some of these decisions, the judges could be said to have 'discretion', though it is not (or is not treated by the reviewing courts as being) as limited as Dworkin's 'weak sense' of discretion or as broad as his 'strong sense' of discretion.[31] Dworkin

[28] See e.g. J. Raz, *The Morality of Freedom*, 267–366 (Oxford: Clarendon Press, 1986), arguing against consequentialism; H. L. A. Hart, *Punishment and Responsibility*, 161–3 (Oxford: Clarendon Press, 1968), discussing the difficulties of retributive theories of punishment.

[29] See *Rock* v. *Arkansas*, 483 U.S. 44 (1987).

[30] For a discussion of the connections and differences, see J. Finnis, *Natural Law and Natural Rights*, 205–10 (Oxford: Clarendon Press, 1980).

[31] See Dworkin, *Taking Rights Seriously*, 31–3.

noted that what he called the 'strong sense' of discretion is 'not tantamount to licence', in that decisions made under such discretion, like all decisions, are still held to 'standards of sense and fairness'.[32] This, however, is not sufficient to capture the bindingness judges feel in many of their 'discretionary' decisions. Dworkin also referred in passing to 'that jurisprudential favourite, "limited discretion" ', but dismissed it as merely being where the judge has discretion in the weak sense for part of the decision and discretion in the strong sense for another part.[33] This again fails to capture the way judges and reviewing courts experience and view such decisions.

The fact is that the rhetoric (not meant here as a pejorative term) judges use in decisions on procedural or sentencing matters—decisions which Dworkin tends to characterize as involving strong discretion—often matches that of judgments in implying that there are a limited range of right answers or a unique right answer. This observation is not meant as conclusive on any issue, only as a caution against accepting (or rejecting) judges' rhetoric as evidence supporting or opposing a right answer theory (given that the rhetoric might be similar in types of case we wish to treat differently regarding the question of right answers, or different in types of cases we think should be treated the same).

An alternative model with some suggestive power is to see some 'discretionary' judicial decisions as analogous to the American rules as to when a judge can direct a jury's verdict. 'The trial judge allows a case to go to the jury only if the evidence suffices to support a verdict either way.'[34] Within a certain range, *any* decision would be 'right' or 'acceptable'. This model is reproduced in many discussions of the judicial review of actions by administrators or lower-court judges. When the standard of review is 'deferential'—for example, the 'clearly erroneous' standard and the 'abuse of discretion' standard in American law—the reviewing court often speaks of not 'substituting its opinion for the opinion of the trial court', or that even if the reviewing court 'might have decided the issue differently', it will still uphold the lower court's

[32] Ibid. 33.

[33] Ibid. 32, n. 1.

[34] C. Nesson, 'The Evidence or the Event? On Judicial Proof and the Acceptability of Verdicts', 98 *Harvard Law Review* 1357, 1370 (1985).

decision. An American federal appellate court described a relevant standard of judicial review as follows:

We cannot simply substitute our judgment for that of the district court to reverse under the [abuse of discretion] standard, but must be left with the definite and firm conviction that the court committed a clear error of judgment in reaching its conclusion after weighing the relevant factors.[35]

A cynical reading of deferential judicial review would view this language as saying to the initial decision-maker: 'you can be wrong, as long as you are not *far* wrong ("clearly erroneous")'. A more sympathetic reading would echo the analysis of directed verdicts: within a range of decisions, no decision will be considered wrong.

Similar models—there being incorrect answers, but also a range of correct answers—may be found in various legal theories. For example, for John Finnis the translation of the principles of practical reasoning into concrete legal rules often requires an act of implementation (*determinatio*) that goes beyond simple deduction. Though the legislator's choice is strongly guided, it does involve ('arbitrary' or 'judgement') choices among equally correct alternatives.[36] Hans Kelsen similarly implied a certain discretionary range within which a judge acts when the judge 'individualizes' or 'concretizes' a general norm to apply it to a particular case.[37] For the most part, these 'ranges of right answers' do not refer to the extreme situations discussed above, where either a guilty verdict or an innocent verdict might be equally acceptable, but to less dramatic situations, as in the different ways of applying a vague statute or extending a common law rule to a new factual situation.

(We seem uncomfortable with the idea that two alternatives could be equally justified if the choice between them could have significant consequences for individuals, as would be the case for verdicts in some civil suits. However, there will also be many significant consequences in the choice between two equally good co-ordination schemes (for example, two different anti-pollution plans)—for example, businesses ruined, other businesses bene-

[35] *Frank Brisco Co.* v. *Clark County*, 857 F.2d 606, 613 (9th Cir. 1988).

[36] Finnis, *Natural Law and Natural Rights*, 282–9; 'On "The Critical Legal Studies Movement"', 30 *American Journal of Jurisprudence* 21, 23–6, 37–8 (1985).

[37] See Kelsen, *General Theory of Law and State*, 134–6; *The Pure Theory of Law*, 230–6 (Berkeley, Calif.: University of California Press 1967); J. W. Harris, *Legal Philosophies*, 68 (London: Butterworths, 1980).

fited, and people forced to move—but here we seem less bothered by the idea that the alternatives may both be 'right answers'.)

Regarding whether standards of review are helpful in considering the problem of right answers, much may turn on how one views the difference between the judgment having been 'erroneous' and its having been 'clearly erroneous' (assuming one finds the distinction sensible at all). The United States Supreme Court once defined the 'clearly erroneous' standard as having been met if 'the reviewing court on the entire evidence is left with the definite and firm conviction that a mistake has been committed'.[38] What comes to mind are the situations where we recognize that there are good arguments (whether moral arguments, policy considerations, or factual evidence) for more than one possible resolution of a problem or dispute, and while we may choose one conclusion (and thus tentatively conclude that it is 'right' and the alternatives 'wrong') we understand how other people could arrive at different conclusions. Our lack of certainty can be contrasted with the 'definite and firm conviction'[39] that the Supreme Court equated with the 'clearly erroneous' standard.

It is then not clear if the considerations of the difference between judgements of 'erroneous' and 'clearly erroneous' gets us any further towards finding or justifying an alternative to the 'one right answer' position. Both responses assume that there are right and wrong answers—the distinction between the two judgements seems to turn either on the certainty of the reviewing court or on the tenability of the original response—and the distinction neither advances nor hinders the suggestion that there may be more than one correct answer. The distinction is only helpful if we equate the judgement that a decision was '[merely or not-clearly erroneous' with the decision having been correct. Let me explain: from the perspective of the original decision-maker, what is important (among other things) is that the decision not be reversed upon appeal. Both decisions that the reviewing court considers correct and those it considers '[merely] erroneous' will be upheld—and if the decision is upheld, it will be a valid legal norm. From the perspective of the law (the reviewing court considering the original

[38] *United States* v. *United States Gypsum Co.*, 333 U.S. 364, 395 (1948).

[39] cf. Wittgenstein, *Philosophical Investigations*, sec. 231: ' "But surely you can see . . . ?" That is just the characteristic expression of someone who is under the compulsion of a rule.'

decision, just like the trial judge considering the (possible) verdicts of the jury), both answers would be 'right'.

Consider a different standard of review: the standard of 'substantial evidence' is used in America in reviewing findings of fact by both juries and administrative agencies.[40] If there is adequate support for a factual finding—the support need not be indubitable or conclusive—the reviewing court will uphold it. What is significant is what is not said, but is a background truth of the practice: both in normal trials and in administrative procedures, regarding the most hotly disputed factual questions, there usually is (what would be considered) 'substantial evidence' for contrary factual findings. Again, in such situations, if correctness is equated with what will be upheld by the reviewing court, there will be more than one right answer. (This conclusion is slightly paradoxical because here the underlying subject can be the discovery of historical truth—the facts about what happened—and we assume that there should only be one right answer for such questions.)

One final example: American courts review with some deference administrative agencies' decisions regarding what rules to promulgate, and whether to promulgate any rules at all.[41] The example, not coincidentally, looks similar to Finnis's discussion of *determinatio*: analogous to legislative choices within the limits of natural justice are the agency's choices within the limits of its statutory instructions. Judicial deference here is partly a recognition that the agencies have greater expertise in administrative decisions and partly a recognition that the legislative grant of power implied a certain amount of discretion.[42] For both of these reasons, administrative rule-making is one legal area where it seems most justified (and least paradoxical) to talk about there being a range of correct decisions (while there are also decisions which are legally wrong—both in the sense of being *ultra vires* and in the sense that they will/should be invalidated by a reviewing court).

The discussions in this section were meant to be suggestive, not conclusive, on issues relating to the 'right answer' theory. Among the suggestions are that a theory regarding the limits of judicial

[40] See e.g. K. C. Davis, *Administrative Law Treatise*, 2nd edn., v. 351 (San Diego: K. C. Davis Publishing Co., 1984).

[41] See e.g. ibid. 332–63.

[42] See e.g. ibid. 343–4.

discretion need not begin and end with the topic of final judgments, and that one can speak—that at least in the American legal system, practitioners and theorists often *do* speak—of there being situations where judges' discretion is substantially bounded *and* there is more than one correct result. I leave the development of these theories to another time or another person.

A few words about the status of the claims I have been making (directly and indirectly) in this section: my examples are all drawn from the American legal system, and I do not presume that they exemplify any (necessary or essential) aspect of all legal systems. I see no reason to believe that either the structural elements I have described (division of functions between judge and jury, review of lower court decisions by appellate courts, and delegation of some legislative and judicial functions to administrative agencies combined with judicial review of administrative actions) or the dynamics within the structure (the criteria of evaluation used within the system that sometimes allow one to speak of there being more than one correct—or 'acceptable'—answer to a legal question) are present in all other, or even most other, legal systems. However, that such elements are present even in one legal system is a matter worth noting.

It is my impression that if one were to make a global claim about legal *indeterminacy*, it would have to be made at the level of language or at the level of rules and rule-application, claiming that because of the nature of one or the other, there would always be cases where there is more than one right answer (and claims of that kind were considered in Chapter 2). There would be obvious difficulties in making a global claim about legal *determinacy*, that it is part of the nature of law that there are always unique right answers to legal questions, in that it always seems open to a society to create rules or review-processes which incorporate strong discretion for the decision-makers.

It is conceivable that someone could put forward an argument that systems which condone strong discretion by their decision-makers, or that are structured in such a way that there are *not* always unique correct answers to legal problems, are not 'really' *legal* systems (or not legal systems 'in the fullest sense of the term'). However, as I cannot now imagine how that position might be justified, I will not now concern myself with it.

INCOMMENSURABILITY

The final topic in this short survey on right answer theories is the problem of incommensurability. It is a difficult issue, still somewhat undeveloped in the philosophical literature, but it is very important for any consideration of legal determinacy. The idea of incommensurability is that some things—whether values, options, books, or people—cannot be compared in terms of 'better/worse' and 'best'.

The problem incommensurability poses for Dworkin's right answer thesis was first raised by John Mackie; he argued that the strength of considerations in favour of two sides of a legal problem 'may be imperfectly commensurable, so that neither of the opposing cases is stronger than the other, and yet they are not finely balanced'.[43] When we consider the two sides of a legal question which are in rough equipoise, if we then discover minor support for one side in an obscure precedent or statute, that small piece of evidence should in theory make us choose the favoured side. The fact that the evidence often does not have that effect could indicate an incommensurability of factors.[44] Dworkin did not offer a substantive reply to this initial formulation of the problem (his response to Mackie focused on questions of the proper characterization of 'fit' and of the role of 'fit' within a theory of judicial reasoning). On the subject of incommensurability, Dworkin stated merely that his theory 'presupposes a conception of morality other than some conception according to which different moral theories are frequently incommensurable'.[45]

The challenge was picked up, and elaborated, by John Finnis. He wrote: 'a claim to have found the right answer [in hard legal cases] is senseless, in much the same way as it is senseless to claim to have identified the English novel which meets the two criteria "shortest and most romantic" (or "funniest and best", or "most English and most profound").'[46] According to Dworkin's approach (in both his earlier and later writings), there are two separate criteria for evaluating theories of what the law requires,

[43] J. Mackie, 'The Third Theory of Law', in *Ronald Dworkin and Contemporary Jurisprudence*, 165.

[44] Dworkin, 'A Reply by Ronald Dworkin', 272.

[45] Ibid.

[46] Finnis, 'On Reason and Authority in *Law's Empire*', 372.

and 'in the absence of any metric which could commensurate the different criteria (the dimensions of fit and inherent moral merit), the instruction to "balance" (or, earlier, to "weigh") can legitimately mean no more than bear in mind, conscientiously, all the relevant factors, and *choose*'.[47] Finnis wrote of there being no single metric to combine the two criteria[48] and 'no principle by reference to which [one] could criticize as unreasonable or immoral' those who combine the criteria in a different way or with a different result.[49]

In other words, Finnis's claim is that the fact of incommensurability scuttles the right answer thesis. If judicial reasoning involves at least two values, and these are not commensurable, then on many occasions it would be incorrect to say (before a decision is made) that one decision is the unique right way to resolve the dispute, that one decision is better than all the potential alternatives.

Dworkin's reply to Finnis[50] was that the incommensurability argument remained unproven. Finnis had assumed, but had not shown, that the judgments of 'fit' and political-moral soundness were incommensurable. Given that we are all the time making 'all things considered' judgements in all sorts of situations which involve disparate criteria, the burden should be on those claiming incommensurability to put forward some argument to support their position.[51] Such an argument would refer to the objectives of the practice or the ideas underlying various criteria to explain why the criteria cannot be made commensurable.

In response to an argument on incommensurability by Raz,[52] Dworkin argued[53] that the fact that a judge considering a hard case (or a person making a difficult career choice) did not now see a

[47] Ibid. Finnis pointed out that in *Law's Empire* Dworkin had retreated from his earlier position that 'fit' was merely a 'threshold' criterion: ibid. 372–4. In any event, '[t]his solution was empty, for he identified no criteria . . . for locating the threshold beyond which the criterion of soundness would prevail': ibid. 373.

[48] Ibid. 374.

[49] Finnis, *Natural Law and Natural Rights*, 116.

[50] Given in lectures at Oxford University, 18 and 25 Jan. and 1 Feb. 1989; 20, 21, and 27 Feb. 1990; see R. Dworkin, 'On Gaps in the Law', in *Controversies about Law's Ontology*, 88–90 (P. Amselek and N. MacCormick, eds., Edinburgh: Edinburgh University Press, 1991).

[51] See K. Kress, 'Legal Indeterminacy', 77 *California Law Review* 283, 335–6 and n. 215 (1989).

[52] J. Raz, *The Morality of Freedom*, 321–66.

[53] Given in lectures at Oxford University, 20 and 27 Feb. 1990.

reason for preferring one claim (or one decision) over another (and might not be able even to imagine ever finding such a reason) is different from and does not entail that the alternatives (or the underlying evaluative criteria) are incommensurate. That second step, he argued, requires a further, substantive argument.[54]

Dworkin argued that the best evidence we have that 'all things considered' judgements can be made—whether combining various aspects of 'best novel', various aspects of 'friendship', or the elements of 'fit' and 'moral worth'—is that we do make such judgements all the time. The argument strategy is similar to one Dworkin used in support of his right answer theory: that the arguments offered for a right answer in particular disputes are the best evidence (if not the only evidence) that can be offered to show that there are right answers to (almost) all legal questions.[55] The underlying argument is that neither his position—right answers and commensurability—nor his opponents' position can be proved on a global scale. Each decision or choice must be considered separately, to see whether the relevant criteria can be made commensurate or (a related matter) whether there is a unique right answer to a particular problem.

This response is not entirely satisfactory. The fact that we make numerous choices involving allegedly incommensurable values *may* prove that those values were not in fact incommensurable, or it may only prove that a larger percentage of our choices than we might have thought are 'open' or 'arbitrary' (in the sense that we cannot claim that the choice we made was better than all the choices we rejected). To those who are not worried about commensurability, the second option seems unlikely; to those who are worried about commensurability, the first option appears to be unlikely. The argument seems stalemated.

As the argument regarding incommensurability has developed in the legal philosophy literature, the structure of arguing about the burden of proof remains, but it now occurs one step further on. In a recent article, Dworkin argued that there are two kinds of

[54] See Dworkin, 'On Gaps in the Law', 89–90.

[55] See e.g. Dworkin, 'A Reply by Ronald Dworkin', 280; see also R. Dworkin, 'My Reply to Stanly Fish (and Walter Benn Michaels): Please don't Talk about Objectivity Any More', in *The Politics of Interpretation*, 298–301 (W. J. T. Mitchell, ed., London: University of Chicago Press, 1983), offering a similar argument strategy against scepticism about interpretation.

incommensurability. In the first, 'conceptual incommensurability', as an aspect of understanding two concepts, one can see that they cannot intelligibly be compared (as an example, he wrote: 'Which is the more clear, an argument by Descartes or the Greek sky?').[56] In the second kind of incommensurability, the comparability of two matters cannot be discovered a priori, but is a matter of substantive argument. For example, it is a matter of aesthetic theory whether one can intelligibly ask whether Shakespeare was a greater playwright than Molière. Similarly, Dworkin argued, it is a matter of political morality whether one can ask whether one interpretation of a statute is superior to another[57] (and, for Dworkin, when that question is asked, the answer will also—in part—be a matter of political morality). Thus, for Dworkin, someone who claimed the incommensurability of 'fit' and moral value in judicial reasoning must present an argument why this is true.

Both John Finnis and Joseph Raz have recently given arguments allowing for comparisons of mixed-value goods, but only after one has established a structure within which comparisons can be made intelligible. Finnis pointed out that once one *chooses* a structure for comparing values, either through arbitrary assumptions or through a personal commitment (say) to a particular life-plan, then one can claim that one mixed-value good is superior to another.[58] For example, though one cannot normally say that spending the afternoon reading legal philosophy is better or worse than spending the afternoon walking in the park, the situation is different if one adds the fact that the subject wants to become a solicitor, the jurisprudence exam is in two weeks, and the results of the exams are crucial to that person's ability to be hired.

Raz (in an article that was directed primarily at questions of moral, not legal, philosophy) argued that the comparison of goods of mixed values is often justifiable, but this occurs within the context of a new inherent standard. For example, the value of a novel is not merely an aggregate of individual constituent values, but is an independent good of its own 'which is constituted by the constituent goods being present in the right way and in the right

[56] Dworkin, 'On Gaps in the Law', 89. [57] Ibid.

[58] J. Finnis, 'Concluding Reflections', 38 *Cleveland State Law Review* 231, 238–41 (1990).

proportions'.[59] Further, the 'right' mixture of values would be different even for slightly different variations of the social form: for example, what makes for a good detective novel is quite different from what makes for a good satire. The particular social form offers the structure within which comparisons can intelligibly be made. However, across forms, the absence of a common metric remains a problem (for example, whether a particular detective story is better or worse than a particular satire).

Dworkin argued that commensurability is a matter of substantive argument within a practice, but what argument does he offer for the commensurability of 'fit' and moral value in considering alternative theories about a legal issue? One suspects that he would point to the fact that such judgements are made all the time, the fact that in particular cases judges argue (for example) that in this particular area consistency with past decisions is (or is not) very important, and therefore the theory which is better in matters of 'fit' is superior (or inferior) to the theory which is better in matters of moral value. However, this would not be a substantive argument about commensurability, but only a substantive argument that (apparently) assumes commensurability. To be frank, I am not sure what a substantive argument in this area *about* commensurability would look like.

On the other hand, there are also problems for Raz's approach. He had allowed that there are certain types of mixed-value goods (usually supported by social practices) that have their own standards, which allow for comparisons. First, what would stop someone from arguing that legal reasoning is one of the social practices which justifies comparisons between different interpretations of the law? Secondly, one could argue that Raz's analysis does not help us much in understanding why choices between mixed-value goods are sometimes commensurable. If we start by assuming that social practices support the mixed-value good, 'the thriller novel', with an optimum mix of three parts plot and one part character, how does Raz's structure help us understand the comparison between two sub-optimal examples from the genre? If one novel had slightly too much plot and too little character, and the second had too little plot and too much

[59] J. Raz, 'Mixing Values', *Proceedings of the Aristotelian Society*, supp. vol. 65, 83, 88 (1991) (emphasis omitted).

character, it seems like we would be back to the normal incommensurability problem.[60]

Another challenge for those who believe that most values are incommensurable is to explain or respond to our intuition that though one cannot usually choose between two options, one can if there is a great deal of one good and very little of the other.[61] For example, though we might be reluctant to say that Picasso was a better or worse painter than Rembrandt, we might feel less uncomfortable saying that Picasso was a better painter than the pet-portrait artist at the local market. Similarly, while we might not be able to say that a walk in the woods is better or worse than an afternoon reading Aristotle, we might feel more likely to reach a conclusion if the competition for Aristotle was a trip to Paris.

James Griffin explained our different attitude in extreme comparisons by claiming that the underlying values are commensurable, but can become incomparable in close cases for epistemic reasons.[62] Even if we accept this model rather than a stronger claim about incommensurability, it may not be enough to salvage Dworkin's right answer thesis. For in the difficult cases in which we are most concerned, the choice is likely to be between an answer with slightly better fit and one with slightly better moral value; it is not likely to involve (for example) choosing between an answer with vastly better fit and one with a trivially better moral value. In other words, assuming that there is incomparability in close cases, there would remain no right answer in hard cases.

The problem of choice in the face of apparently incommensurable values comes up regularly in the literature on moral decision-making. An interesting example for our purposes is S. L. Hurley's book *Natural Reasons*, which put forward a theory of moral choice which is structurally similar to Dworkin's approach to law, and which was based in part upon and claimed applications to legal theory. Dworkin had argued that judges should decide cases by building a theory of what the law is in the area in question, a theory which would incorporate different values, including fit and

[60] J. Griffin, 'Mixing Values', in *Proceedings of the Aristotelian Society*, suppl. vol. 65, 101, 104–5 (1991).

[61] See e.g. ibid. 108–9, 111. Finnis explicitly denies that values become commensurable in such situations: Finnis, 'Concluding Reflections', 238–40.

[62] Griffin, 'Mixing Values', 108–9, 111.

moral worth. Hurley argued similarly that an all-things-considered judgement of what ought to be done should be based on the theory that does the best job of displaying coherence among the various values that apply.[63]

Hurley did not claim that the various values that her theory must take into account are commensurable. That judgement, she argued, could only be made *after* we found the best theory about the relationship between the values. That theory *might* turn out to be monistic (like the simpler forms of utilitarianism), in which case the values would be commensurable, or the theory might turn out to be pluralist, in which case the values would not be commensurable.[64] Here, Hurley was distinguishing between 'commensurability in the weak sense of merely formal unity' and 'commensurability in some more substantial sense':[65] the weak sense occurs when decisions are made despite the existence of different values; the strong sense occurs when all the different values are reduced to a single value or a function of a particular unit of measure. Values are (always) commensurable in the weak sense for Hurley because the product of our theorizing will be a ranking of alternative actions which does take into account the various values. However, this theorizing does not make the values commensurate in the strong sense, in that it does not offer a common metric.

At one point in her text, Hurley described the role coherence could play in reaching a legal judgment. The hypothetical case involved resolving a conflict in Contract Law between the doctrines (and underlying values) of consideration and estoppel in a situation where the promisor had made a gratuitous promise which induced detrimental reliance in the promisee and which the promisor would reasonably have expected to induce the promisee's reliance. The issue for judgment was, was the promisor under a legal obligation to the promisee?[66] She analysed the arguments for and against liability, determined how the conflicting arguments had been resolved in various contexts in past cases, and then constructed a theory consistent with past decisions to show under which circumstances a particular argument would prevail. The

[63] See Hurley, *Natural Reasons*, 193–6. Hurley explicitly noted the parallels between her work and Dworkin's. See e.g. ibid. 201, 212.

[64] Ibid. 260–70.

[65] Ibid. 270.

[66] Ibid. 205–06.

hypothetical case was then resolved according the theory (concluding that liability does exist).[67]

There are two things to note here. First, Hurley's coherence approach to legal decisions made the different practical reasons commensurate only in the weaker sense, in that a choice was made which took the various reasons into consideration. Secondly, what made the ultimate decision the correct one for Hurley was that it fitted better with past decisions (and the decisions we would reach in hypothetical decisions) than the alternatives.[68] In the example, the problem of commensurability seems to drop out: we bring together and order various values for this choice according to the way we have done so before. However we made the values commensurate (here, in the weak sense) before, we shall do so again; it is a kind of 'bootstrap argument'. The later decisions are 'right' if they are consistent with the collection of past decisions (and choices one would currently make in hypothetical cases). (There may yet be some difficulties in filling out the notion of 'consistency' here, but I leave that issue aside.)[69] The question then is, what made those initial decisions—which ground all later decisions—right. One might answer, 'nothing made the initial decisions "right"; we just chose (choosing for a reason, but allowing that reason would have allowed other decisions),[70] and now we are acting consistently with those past choices because there is a value to acting consistently and a value to acting in accord with who one is (and with how one has been affected by one's past choices)'. Leaving aside evaluating the merits of that position, I want only to note that this approach does not so much solve as circumvent the core problem of incommensurability. There is no claim in the abstract that right answers can be given when different values are involved; the approach directs us only to combine the values in a way consistent with the way we have done

[67] Ibid. 203–19.

[68] I am simplifying Hurley's position somewhat. For Hurley, 'to say a certain alternative ought to be done, all things considered, is to say that the theory that does the best job of displaying coherence favours that alternative': ibid. 193. I have passed over a step—the construction/selection of the best theory, which is then used to determine the correct ultimate decision—that she would consider important, but which I do not believe relevant for my purposes.

[69] cf. M. Moore, 'Metaphysics, Epistemology and Legal Theory' (book review), 60 *California Law Review* 453, 480–1 (1987), discussing Dworkin's concept of 'fit'.

[70] cf. Raz, *The Morality of Freedom*, 339–40 (choosing between incommensurable options).

in the past. There is a 'right' or 'best' answer only in a derivative or secondary sense of those terms.

The issue of incommensurability is quite difficult, and the arguments in the philosophical literature in the area are still undeveloped (though as the field is growing, there is promise of greater sophistication). I am not able in this short section to give the complexities of the area due consideration. I can only offer my initial reaction to the application of the arguments in this area of legal theory.[71] However, I thought it important to raise the question of incommensurability and to outline some of the problems in that debate, since it is clearly central to any attempt to defend a right answer theory. If the evaluative criteria of Dworkin's theory are incommensurable, then the claim that there are unique right answers to most legal problems must fail. Whether that challenge can be overcome I must leave to others to determine.

There is one more matter I should consider before I go on to other topics. This section and the previous one have suggested that there may be more than one right (or 'acceptable') answer to some legal questions, either because the alternative answers are incommensurable, because the legal system is indifferent to how a particular question is resolved, or because different responses would be (by the relevant criteria) of equal merit. If this is the case, the question then is, how should the judge (or other decision-maker) decide between the alternative answers? Would flipping a coin be legitimate? (Contrarily, would any procedure other than a random one, like flipping a coin, be legitimate?)

One line of response is that while the duties and principles within past legal actions may not yield a unique answer to particular legal questions, other sets of values or principles could—or perhaps should—be applied to make the decision. For example, H. L. A. Hart wrote that there may be 'characteristic judicial virtues' which judges can and should use in cases where

[71] I offer the following sample of some of the interesting work on incommensurability: J. Raz, 'Mixing Values'; J. Griffin, 'Mixing Values'; B. Williams, 'Conflicts of Values', in *Moral Luck*, 71–82 (Cambridge: Cambridge University Press, 1981); T. Nagel 'The Fragmentation of Value', in *Mortal Questions*, 128–41 (Cambridge: Cambridge University Press, 1979); J. Griffin, 'Are there Incommensurable Values?', 7 *Philosophy and Public Affairs* 39 (1977).

there is discretion. (Hart listed 'impartiality and neutrality in surveying the alternatives; consideration for the interest of all who will be affected; and a concern to deploy some acceptable general principle as a reasoned basis for decision'.)[72] One could just as easily say, the judge should decide the case as he or she thinks best, all things considered. Under this line of response, the underlying idea is that there is more than one right answer in some legal cases only because the law requires or offers only a limited set of sources, principles, and duties; with the addition of other moral principles, policy considerations, or perhaps aesthetic considerations, there might yet be unique right answers.

A second line of response would be more appropriate for alternatives of equal merit and for incommensurable alternatives. In such cases, decisions should be made (and, arguably, are being made in actual practice) much the same way that people generally decide between incommensurable alternatives: after long consideration of the options, and the reasons for each, the decision-maker slowly begins to identify with one alternative rather than the others.[73] This option thereafter seems right to the decision-maker *because* it was chosen, even though it remains the case that its superiority to the alternatives cannot be demonstrated (because it is apparent rather than real). Judicial opinions in (arguably) incommensurable cases look much like personal justifications in the analogous situations: 'conceding that the option(s) not chosen had the advantages of reasons *a*, *b*, and *c*; however, because of reasons *x*, *y*, and *z*, we (must) conclude for the option we have chosen.' Judicial opinions written with that structure are fairly common, and if incommensurable alternatives are involved, it is clear why such opinions persuade only those who are already persuaded. (Such opinions are largely honest, in that they express all that could be expressed about why a particular decision was reached in an incommensurable case. They deceive, to the extent they do deceive, only by sometimes implying that the reasons offered *required* the choice made. I leave to others the question of how useful and how common judicial deception and self-deception are.)[74]

72 Hart, *The Concept of Law*, 200.

73 See J. Raz, 'Facing Up: A Reply', 62 *Southern California Law Review* 1153, 1222 (1989).

74 See e.g. S. Altman, 'Beyond Candor', 89 *Michigan Law Review* 296 (1990).

As an afterword, it is interesting to consider why we recoil at the idea of cases (where the right decision is not clear) being decided by a coin-flip. There is in fact at least one documented instance of an American judge deciding the guilt or innocence of traffic violators by the flip of a coin when he could not decide the case on the basis of the testimony.[75] Not surprisingly, this practice was the basis of an action against the judge before the state commission on judicial fitness.

I cannot go into this interesting question in any detail, but I will briefly offer two possible explanations. One explanation is that we do not want important decisions made in a random or irrational way: we might be able to accept judges acting on policy grounds as quasi-legislators or as moral legislators, but to flip a coin is to offer no *reasons* for the choice offered. The second explanation would explain the opposition to coin-flipping in line with the resistance to believing that judges legislate in difficult cases rather than discovering what the law already is. This explanation is based on the idea that we ask and expect judges to determine matters of blame and excuse, a delegation one would only make if one were confident that those judgments were based on decisions of what actually happened, as a matter of fact. The idea of the past being indeterminate sits very uncomfortably with us.

INTERPRETATION AND DISAGREEMENT

In his later works, Dworkin offered what he called 'an interpretive approach' to law.[76] In *Law's Empire*, he argued 'that legal claims are interpretive judgments and therefore combine backward- and forward-looking elements; they interpret contemporary legal practice as an unfolding political narrative'.[77] According to Dworkin, every time a judge is confronted with a legal problem, he or she should construct a theory of what the law is. That theory must adequately fit the relevant past governmental actions (legislative enactments and judicial decisions),[78] while making the law the best it can be.[79] 'Judges who accept the interpretive ideal

[75] *International Herald Tribune*, 30 Sept. 1991, p. 6.

[76] Dworkin, *Law's Empire*, 46–8.

[77] Ibid. 225.

[78] Ibid. 227–8, 245–58.

[79] Ibid. 52, 143.

of integrity decide hard cases by trying to find, in some coherent set of principles about people's rights and duties, the best constructive interpretation of the political structure and legal doctrine of their community.'[80]

The argument for the right answer thesis in the later Dworkin is largely implicit. (Perhaps it is significant that at the end of *Law's Empire*, he referred not to there being a 'right answer' to a hard case, but a 'right way . . . to decide a hard case'.)[81] However, his discussion of 'law as integrity' in *Law's Empire* incorporated by reference the arguments in *Taking Rights Seriously* that one party to a suit has a pre-existing right to win and that only judicial actions consistent with the right answer theory would be properly based on principle rather than policy.[82] Other arguments offered in the later works for there being unique right answers were more indirect: it is consistent with the rhetoric we (judges, lawyers, and legal theorists) use in legal discourse,[83] global scepticism about the possibility of right answers is not tenable,[84] and most modern legal systems have sufficient legal sources for subtle judgements to be made about the superiority of one theory of what the law is over all alternatives.[85]

Dworkin admitted that though he believed that there is a right answer to most hard cases, that answer will not be *demonstrably* right—that is, its superiority over other answers will not always be demonstrable to the satisfaction of all (or even most) competent lawyers.[86] It is certainly correct that it does not follow from the fact that the right answer to some problem cannot be demonstrated, or from the fact that the problem is a matter of great controversy, that there is no right answer.[87] However, the presence or absence of demonstrability will have important practical consequences. An approach to legal problems that

[80] Ibid. 255.

[81] Ibid. 412.

[82] Ibid. 244, 439, n. 7.

[83] See e.g. Dworkin, *A Matter of Principle*, 144–5.

[84] See e.g. ibid. 167–77.

[85] See e.g. ibid. 143–4.

[86] See e.g. Dworkin, *Taking Rights Seriously*, 335–8; *A Matter of Principle*, 137–42, 153, 162, 171–2.

[87] cf. Moore, 'Metaphysics, Epistemology and Legal Theory', 480–3 (arguing that, to be consistent, Dworkin must adopt at least a weak demonstrability thesis: that the right answer would be demonstrable to fully rational persons with full information).

espouses a procedure for finding right answers but offers neither a promise of consensus nor a process for approaching consensus may create divergent pronouncements of what the law is.

Two aspects of Dworkin's theory make it probable that different judges applying it to the same legal question would reach different results. First, given the divergence of moral and political values among people, how the criterion of moral soundness ('best light') is filled out will vary from one judge to another.[88] This divergence of moral soundness criteria might only result in an occasional divergence in judicial decisions if the criterion of moral soundness played only a small and clearly circumscribed role within the judicial process; in such a situation, only rarely would the judges need to have recourse to the criterion of moral soundness, for the decision would almost always be determined by the other criterion ('fit' with the relevant legal materials). However, a second aspect of Dworkin's theory makes that situation unlikely. Dworkin does not pre-set what level of 'fit' a theory about what the law requires must have or what weight the criterion of 'fit' should have as against moral soundness in judging between two alternative theories.[89] He also does not offer any process or algorithm for ensuring that different judges will treat 'fit' similarly in similar cases. If judges give 'fit' a small role to play, then differences in moral and political beliefs will more often result in divergent decisions. And if judges have markedly different ideas about the relative importance of 'fit' and moral soundness in a particular area of law, a large divergence of results is likely even if the judges otherwise had quite similar political and moral beliefs.

In Dworkin's interpretative approach, where propositions of law are part descriptive and part evaluative,[90] there will be as many different 'descriptions' of a given legal system as there are persons thinking seriously about that system. In the final analysis,

[88] See Mackie, 'The Third Theory of Law', 165–6; cf. K. Kress, 'The Interpretive Turn', 97 *Ethics* 834, 847 (1987), arguing that if a Dworkinian judge used some version of conventional morality rather than the judge's own (critical) morality, law would be 'more knowable and therefore better at promoting efficient coordination of citizens' lives . . . [and it would also be] more coherent'.

[89] See Dworkin, *Law's Empire*, 240–66; Finnis, 'On Reason and Authority in *Law's Empire*', 370–6.

[90] Dworkin, *A Matter of Principle*, 147 ('propositions of law . . . are interpretive of legal history, which combines elements of both description and evaluation but is different from both').

Dworkin's scheme results in there being *for each judge that considers a case* one right answer. What the right answer is, is 'subjective', in the sense that the judge's view of the answer will vary predictably—if not inevitably—from one judge to another.[91]

(There is a different sense in which the right answer is 'objective', at least if one believes (as Dworkin appeared to) that there is a right or best answer regarding what standard of morality to apply and what level of fit to demand in all cases. However, if as an epistemic matter few judges are likely to discover these truths, and if those few are either unable to demonstrate the truths or unable to persuade their colleagues to adopt those standards, the right answer will be continually shouted down by the various and conflicting wrong answers that occur within (and partly constitute) legal practice.)

Dworkin affirmed the likelihood that different judges following his approach would reach different decisions,[92] but did not seem to find it troubling. By contrast, John Finnis pin-pointed exactly what is troubling about a prescription for judicial interpretation that makes it likely that the outcome will vary depending on which judge is presiding: litigants would suffer from 'the excruciating sense that if their case had been tried *on the same day* by the judge next door it probably would have been determined differently'.[93] Dworkin might argue that in principle there should be no divergence. After all, that was the whole idea of the right answer theory, that there is a unique correct answer to the vast majority of legal issues. If there is a divergence in actual results, it would have to be, under his approach, because many judges were getting it wrong (perhaps because they were applying an incorrect moral-political theory or an incorrect balancing of that theory with the value of 'fit'). If every judge would go through the process 'correctly', the argument would go, the problem of divergence would not come up. What this response would miss is the concrete problems of theories that have practical consequences.

If one puts forward a theory about the correct way to interpret ancient (secular) texts, and the theory is such that even if

[91] See Posner, *Law and Literature*, 227–8; Mackie, 'The Third Theory of Law', 165; see also B. Bix, 'Dancing in the Dark: The Philosophical Moves of Ronald Dworkin' (book review), 23 *Harvard Journal on Legislation* 307, 315–20 (1986).

[92] See e.g. Dworkin, *A Matter of Principle*, 17, 162.

[93] Finnis, 'On Reason and Authority in *Law's Empire*', 379, n. 35.

interpreters try to follow it many are likely to come to erroneous conclusions, then the real-world loss is minimal. If only a few persons are interpreting the texts correctly, and most others are coming up with different (and erroneous) interpretations, the result is unfortunate, but the consequences beyond the world of this discipline would be small. The area of judicial reasoning is different. It is of course of value for judges to come up with *the right answers*, but there is also a separate and independent value in judges coming up with *the same answers*. In the next section, I will consider a critique of Dworkin that is based largely on this consideration.

Dworkin's response might be that it is far from clear that law would be less predictable or less settled if judges acted as his theory claimed they should rather than in the way claimed by the positivists' theories—which, after all, hold that discretion or 'judicial legislation' is required in hard cases. The difference here might not be in the result—different judges offering different responses to the same legal problem—but in the characterization of the result. The legal positivist judge, unlike the Dworkinian judge, would not claim to be discovering the (predetermined) right answer.

Dworkin might also remind us that his theory is meant to be a theory *of our practice*, an interpretation of the American legal system, and it is a commonplace among practitioners and observers that the outcome of cases in this system *does* depend on (vary with) which judge(s) happen to be presiding. Dworkin's theory can be seen as putting this unfortunate phenomenon in its best possible light: it is not that judges are often biased (for example, pro-business or anti-government), but that they often hold sincere but mistaken beliefs about the correct political-moral theory or the correct weight to be given to 'fit'.

Though Dworkin characterized his approach as an interpretation of our practice, he cannot divert criticisms by saying that his theory is 'merely a description'. Interpretation for Dworkin is a matter of choosing among the theories that adequately fit the relevant data the one that is morally best. The argument might be that even if we accept Dworkin's interpretative approach to legal theory, he has chosen the wrong theory of law (or the wrong theory of the American or English legal systems), in that a theory which not only condones but accentuates the problem of divergent judicial decisions cannot be the morally best among the possible theories.

Dworkin's holistic[94] approach leaves us suspended (as he himself asserted)[95] between description and prescription. No text or past judicial utterance is itself law; such things are *nearly* law; to be law they must be seen in their best light.[96] No real judge actually gets the interpretation right; it would take a superhuman judge (Dworkin's fictional 'Hercules') to discover what the law *actually* is. It may be that Dworkin's right answer thesis cannot be effectively rebutted directly, but only indirectly. In considering the merits of the conclusion of a right answer thesis, one's focus must be on the premise which supports that conclusion while leaving aside for the moment the unusual view of law just described: the premise is that we should take an interpretative and holistic approach to what the law is/what the law requires. That focus will be taken up in the final sections of this chapter.

INTERPRETATION AND CONSENSUS

Robert Cover argued that there is an incongruity—a lack of 'fit', if you will—between a theory like Dworkin's, that would lead to the law having a different content for different individual judges, and the manner in which many legal systems (in particular, the American system) actually operate. Cover wrote: 'there is no set of secondary rules and principles more fundamental than those which make it impossible for any single judge, however Herculean her understanding of the law, ever to have the last word on legal meaning as it affects real cases'.[97] In appellate courts, a decision must have the support of a majority of the panel hearing the case, and even if the initial decision is made by a single trial judge, that decision is usually subject to an appeal to another judge or panel of judges. The law may speak with a single voice, Cover argued, but this is not a voice derived from 'a single coherent and consistent' interpretation of the legal materials, but from a

[94] I discuss the nature of this 'holism' later in this chapter.

[95] See above, n. 90.

[96] cf. Dworkin, *Taking Rights Seriously*, 214 ('A citizen's allegiance is to the law, not to any particular person's view of what the law is').

[97] Cover, 'Violence and the Word', 1625.

consensus—or majority view—often born of compromise among various views of the law.[98] Hence, a theory of judicial interpretation that would condone, and perhaps encourage, diverging individual views of what the law is would fall short, both descriptively and prescriptively.

Dworkin claimed that legal theory is primarily, if not exclusively, the interpretation of *a particular legal system*. His view was that an analysis that applied equally well to all of the many diverse (actual or possible) legal systems would have to be of such generality as to be of little value.[99] A judge (or legal theorist or layman) who followed Dworkin's interpretative approach in determining what the law was on some issue in his or her society would construct a theory that was grounded strongly in the legal structures and political system of that society.[100] Therefore, according to Dworkin himself, part of the evaluation of his approach to law should be how good an interpretation it gives (or it is) of our own society's practices. Cover was arguing that Dworkin's approach failed at least in its interpretation of and application to the American legal system. Dworkin's approach did not offer a good interpretation of the American legal system because it did not fit the actual practice (decision by agreement of many rather than the vision of one) and it discounted the values that lay behind the decisions (which were made in a variety of forums and at many different periods in American history) to establish that structure at all levels of the American legal system.

Cover's argument supported an approach to judicial reasoning in which different judges' descriptions (interpretations) of what the law is would be more likely to converge.[101] He argued that a right answer theory should conform not only with our ideas about the nature of language and rules and the nature of law and authority, but also with the specific institutional structures of the

[98] Cover, 'Violence and the Word'; see also Kornhauser and Sager, 'Unpacking the Court'.

[99] Lecture by Ronald Dworkin at Oxford University, 16 Jan. 1990; see R. Dworkin, 'Legal Theory and the Problem of Sense', in *Issues in Contemporary Legal Philosophy*, 16 (R. Gavison, ed., Oxford: Clarendon Press, 1987); *Law's Empire*, 102–3.

[100] See Dworkin, 'Legal Theory and the Problem of Sense', 14–15; cf. *Law's Empire*, 72–3 (the role of paradigms in interpreting social practices).

[101] For one elaboration and defence of that approach, see J. W. Harris, 'Unger's Critique of Formalism in Legal Reasoning: Hero, Hercules, and Humdrum', 52 *Modern Law Review* 42 (1989).

particular legal system concerned: for example, the structure and hierarchy of the court system and the relationship between the judiciary and the legislature.

Cover's criticism did not attack Dworkin at the highest—most general—level in Dworkin's hierarchy of interpretations. Cover might have agreed with Dworkin that law is an interpretative concept and that legal theories are attempts to make particular legal systems the best they can be; his argument worked one level lower: that Dworkin's theory did not in fact offer the best possible interpretation of the American legal system. (I will discuss some criticisms that challenge Dworkin's approach at higher levels of generality later in this chapter.)

I once heard Cover's approach described as 'a complacent-seeming acceptance of judicial horse-trading'. This accusation may have some force, but it misses the complexity and subtlety of the position at hand. There is a paradox in the attitude of an American judge which is similar to the paradox of the voter that political theorists discuss.[102] A voter who participates in and accepts a majority-rule system will hope that programme A is adopted or candidate A elected because that voter believes that programme A or candidate A is the best choice among the alternatives; at the same time, the voter also hopes that an alternative (programme B or candidate B) will be adopted if that alternative gets the majority of the votes cast.

It is important to note that even though the voter believes that policy decisions should be based on majority rule, he does not determine what position he will advocate (questions of tactics and strategy aside for the moment) based on an evaluation of which position seems most likely to gain a majority. The voter advocates a position because he believes it to be the right position (or the best position among the alternatives available), but he accepts whatever decision gets a majority of the votes because he recognizes the value of majority rule. The situation for an American judge is analogous. The judge wants the case in question to be decided a certain way, because he or she believes that this decision would reflect correct conclusions about the law and the

[102] See R. Wollheim, 'A Paradox in the Theory of Democracy', in *Philosophy, Politics and Society*, 2nd ser., 71–87 (P. Laslett and W. G. Runciman, eds., Oxford: Basil Blackwell, 1972).

facts. However, the judge also wants the case to be decided according to the majority vote of the panel on which he or she is sitting (or, if it gets that far, the majority vote of the appellate panel), even if that vote reflects a view of the law or the facts contrary to the judge's own, because the judge sees a value to that form of decision-making.

Thus, in one sense, the overall structure of the judicial hierarchy is irrelevant to the individual judge's decision-making: the judge should still try to determine what the right answer is, even if that answer will eventually be rejected in favour of another that has greater support. The process of requiring interchange among judges on a panel, review of lower-court decisions by higher courts, and panel decisions by majority rule, may affect decision-making in the sense that it makes it more likely that mainstream, conventional views will prevail—though this need not prevent individual judges (or lawyers) from forcefully advocating more unconventional views. However, the process does weigh against a lawyer or judge claiming that his or her unconventional view describes *what the law is* even though (1) that view has never been embodied in a judicial opinion, (2) if it were to be put forward by a judge, one would predict that it would be reversed by a reviewing court, and (3) given the current rough consensus among judges and academic commentators, that view is unlikely to be accepted as the correct characterization of the law at any time in the foreseeable future.

In some ways, language may work better than voting as an analogy. Consider a person whose task it is to revise an old dictionary or to write a new one. The starting-point for the task is the way words are actually used by the relevant population. The dictionary-writer could (and should) dismiss certain usages as wrong, but it is in the nature of language that if a term is used in a certain way by enough people for a long enough time, it becomes part of that term's meaning. It just does not make sense to say (for example) that the way the vast majority of people have used a term for the past hundred years is wrong. As I noted in Chapter 3, in law as in language there is a tension between authority and consensus: what is right is to some extent determined by experts, but there are also occasions when expertise must defer to practice.

From the discussion of Cover and the earlier discussion of Woozley, it can be seen that I am arguing for a middle position. I criticized Woozley for equating too strongly the set of judicial pronouncements and the set of legally true propositions. In my support of Cover's position against Dworkin, I am accusing Dworkin of not making a strong enough equation between the two.

One problem for Cover's argument is that while it criticizes Dworkin's interpretation of the American legal system, it only gives a partial answer regarding what should be offered as an alternative. To say that consensus is important, without more, makes law (and judging) into an exotic co-ordination game. It is similar to the weakness of the extreme legal realist's analysis that law is merely a prediction of what the courts will do. While such an analysis may be useful enough for a lawyer advising a client, or even for a lower-court judge deciding a routine case, the analysis is useless for the highest court deciding a novel question. There are situations when trying to predict what other people would do cannot help. The same thing happens with a consensus analysis: at least for the highest court and for novel cases, something more must be added to the analysis. Also, a focus on agreement and consensus, without more, makes it difficult to understand what people who disagree about the nature of legal rights and duties are disagreeing *about*; in fact, the whole notion of substantive disagreement in law under such an approach becomes almost meaningless.[103] Cover did not suggest in his article what the additional, non-consensus element in the theory of law should be.

The trick is not just to reach agreement, but also to have an idea of what we are agreeing *about*. It could be that Cover's critique could fit within a modified Dworkinian view. Under such an approach, judges would still focus on trying to view law as if it expressed a coherent, principled perspective, but the mechanics of deciding individual cases would be altered slightly from Dworkin's prescriptions. Though the same structure of balancing 'fit' and moral value could remain in place, either 'fit' would have to be transformed to include fit with the current (and likely future) views of other judges or 'moral value' would have to be transformed to reflect society's conventional morality rather than the judge's own critical morality. This would make it more likely, though still far from certain, that particular judges' assessments of

[103] cf. Dworkin, *Law's Empire*, 37–44 (offering a similar criticism of 'semantic theories' of law).

moral value would converge. (I do not endorse this approach; I am only trying to show that a modified version of Dworkin's approach could incorporate Cover's critique.)

This discussion hints at a second problem with Cover's critique. Dworkin could concede its force while still maintaining his basic approach to law and to legal theory. Dworkin's response to Cover could be: if you believe that predictability is one of the primary purposes of the American legal system and that consensus is an important value within the system, then a judge working within the system could—and should—incorporate an appropriately high emphasis on those values when interpreting the law. The interpretative approach to law and to legal theory is unaffected by claims that particular interpretations do not 'fit' the legal system or do not show the system in its best light. The question is whether an effective criticism of Dworkin's approach can be made against a more basic level of his theory. That will be the focus of the final sections of this chapter.

As a postscript to the discussion in this section, I want briefly to consider ways in which Dworkin's interpretation may work better or worse for the English legal system than it does for the American legal system. As I noted earlier, Dworkin sees legal theory as properly the interpretation of a particular legal system; however, perhaps because he teaches in both England and America and his work is read in both countries, he often presents his interpretation as equally applicable to both countries' legal systems.

While the two legal systems are very close both in structure and in content, there are a number of significant differences. Relevant to Cover's critique, it is far more common for English judges sitting on panels to render individual judgments *seriatim* rather than simply joining in an opinion written by one judge for all (or a majority) of the court (though cases in which the other judges on the panel simply concur with the judgment given by one of their colleagues are far from rare). The attitude of English jurists towards individual opinions might be exemplified by two comments: the first is by Lord Reid discussing the Judicial Committee of the Privy Council, the one English court in which there is only one opinion given for the majority and one for the dissent, if there is one. He wrote that he thought that this 'single opinion rule' made the opinions of the Privy Council inferior to the speeches in the House of Lords, and the reason he gave was a reason central to the analysis offered above regarding American law: 'a single judgment must get the agreement of at least all in the majority so it tends to be no more than the highest common factor of all the views.'[104]

The second comment was made by Lord Justice Roskill in a Court of Appeal decision. He wrote that he wanted merely to concur in another judgment given by his colleague, but he considered it disrespectful:

> to do so [not to deliver a separate judgment] would perhaps be less than courteous to the two careful arguments which we have had from Counsel, and I shall therefore endeavour to express my own views in my own way very briefly, while echoing what [Lord Justice Megaw] said.[105]

This shows a marked difference from American courts, where judges believe they must justify writing a 'separate opinion' (that is, an opinion other than the opinion for the court or for the majority); even with dissenting opinions, judges often feel the need to explain writing a second dissenting opinion if one of their colleagues is filing one.

Whether we think it better or worse to have opinions written for the majority rather than each judge writing separately, the fact remains that the situation is significantly different. The advantages that might be gained by 'uncompromised', higher-quality opinions may be balanced out by the confusion that comes when the judges that make up the majority offer varying justifications for the results or varying standards to apply, so that it is difficult for citizens, lawyers, or lower-court judges to determine from the decision what the law is or how they should act. (Extreme examples of such cases include the House of Lords decisions in *R.* v. *Inland Revenue Comrs. ex. p. National Fed. of Self-Employed and Small Businesses Ltd.*[106] and *Esso* v. *Commissioners of Customs and Excise*.)[107] The point, however, is that Dworkin's interpretation of a legal system, in which individual judges are instructed to construct their own view of what the law requires, without much consideration of how other people—even their

[104] Lord Reid, 'The Judge as Law Maker', 12 JSPTL 22, 29 (1972), quoted in S. H. Bailey and M. J. Gunn, *Smith and Bailey on the Modern English Legal System*, 2nd edn., 96 (London: Sweet & Maxwell, 1991).

[105] *Mallozzi* v. *Carapelli*, [1976] 1 Lloyd's Law Reports 407, at 413.

[106] [1982] A.C. 617, [1981] 2 All E.R. 93.

[107] [1976] 1 W.L.R. 1, [1976] 1 All E.R. 117.

colleagues on a judicial panel—view the law, fits the English legal system far better than it fits the American legal system. (By contrast, some commentators have maintained that Dworkin's description/prescription of the judiciary as the forum of principle, in contrast to the role of policy in legislation, fits the American legal system far better than the English system.)[108]

DIFFERENT PERSPECTIVES IN LAW

Perhaps Dworkin's approach to legal theory could usefully be re-characterized as guidance to judges as to how they should act in particular circumstances.[109] His theory did not simply advise a (potential or hypothetical) judge what the law is; rather, the theory advised the judge how to make the all-things-considered judgement about how to act when deciding the case: given that legal officials in the past have acted in certain ways, the judge's implied acceptance of the legal system by taking a role in it, the high value of predictability and consistency in legal matters, and the sometimes contrary force of other values, and so on, *this* is how you should decide *this case*. (The alternative approach would include the traditional distinction between what the law requires and how particular cases should be decided. This distinction creates conceptual room not only for notions of judicial discretion and judicial legislation, but also for the assertion that judges should sometimes decide cases contrary to what the law requires.)[110] Dworkin's discussions, not coincidentally, sometimes resembled discussions of whether there are unique right answers to moral questions. The question he considered is what should I (as judge) do, all things considered—an only slightly modified version of a straightforward question of practical reasoning. It is therefore not surprising that Dworkin's most heated arguments in this area have concerned problems that trouble similar positions in moral theory: global scepticism and incommensurability.

[108] S. Lee, 'Law's British Empire' (book review), 8 *Oxford Journal of Legal Studies* 278, 281–2 (1988).

[109] See J. Raz, 'The Problem about the Nature of Law', 210–11.

[110] See Raz, 'Dworkin: A New Link in the Chain' (book review), 74 *Southern California Law Review*, 1115–18. I should note that Dworkin also wrote about occasions where he thought judges should act contrary to what the law requires. See Dworkin, 'A Reply by Ronald Dworkin', 258–60.

That Dworkin's approach is limited in this way may be indicated by the difficulties that result from trying to argue that his approach should be adopted by normal citizens as well as by judges. When each citizen is trying to determine 'what the law is' through an analysis that includes their own (various) moral theories as well as past official actions, it is difficult to understand either what the purpose of this exercise is or what the purpose of law is thought to be on this conception.

The purpose of the exercise cannot be to determine what the citizen, all things considered, ought to do, for Dworkin's approach gives far too much weight to past official actions for it to be a likely description of how we do make difficult moral choices, or prescription for how we should.[111] (For example, we may have good reasons for ignoring the pronouncements of a wicked legal system, even if those pronouncements are seen in their best light.) If, on the other hand, we take Dworkin's characterization at face value, and the purpose of the citizen's analysis is to determine 'what the law is', then we must ask what vision of law and the law's function Dworkin's approach assumed. As I discussed earlier, Dworkin's approach carries a high risk that different persons using it will regularly come to substantially different conclusions regarding what the law requires. This is troubling in an obvious way if the interpreters are judges; it is troubling in a different way if the interpreters are citizens. If citizens' beliefs about what the law requires vary greatly, then the law will fail in the two functions often ascribed to it by modern legal theorists: guiding behaviour and co-ordinating social action. For these functions to work, it is better for citizens to predict how the courts will interpret the legal rules[112] rather than acting on the basis of their own readings of those rules (to the extent that the two diverge).

None of this is to say that there is not a role (and value) for citizens to advocate alternative readings of legal rules, especially those legal rules whose application requires judgements about general moral concepts like 'equality' or 'due process'.[113] The

[111] cf. Raz, *The Morality of Freedom*, 70–105 (offering one analysis of when a citizen has an obligation to obey the law).

[112] See O. W. Holmes, 'The Path of the Law', 10 *Harvard Law Review* 457, 457–61 (1897).

[113] See generally R. Cover, '*Nomos* and Narrative', 97 *Harvard Law Review* 4 (1983).

point is only that it does not make sense—descriptively or prescriptively—to see challenges to the usual understanding of legal rules as normal and usual rather than as special and exceptional.

The above arguments depend on two assumptions. First, law's co-ordination function requires that all concerned understand the instructions in roughly the same way. I assume that citizens (some advised by lawyers) predicting how officials will interpret a rule will come closer to consensus or will reach consensus more often than these same citizens would if each were interpreting the law for himself or herself using Dworkin's 'protestant' approach. Secondly, law's guidance function requires that the rule-maker's intentions not be greatly distorted by the rule-appliers (or by the citizens' prediction of how the rule-appliers will act). I assume that (to use the American example) either the judges will remain largely faithful to the legislature's intentions or the legislature will step in to clarify its prior intentions if and when the judges' reading of those intentions is badly wrong. (If these assumptions are incorrect, it will primarily affect the possibility that law can ever act to guide and co-ordinate action, and only incidentally affect the evaluation of Dworkin's approach. A fuller investigation into the warrant of these assumptions and the consequences if they are unwarranted is beyond the scope of this book.)

THE ROLE OF 'PURPOSE'

The most effective way to evaluate Dworkin's current approach to legal theory is probably to get to the core of the matter: to consider his interpretative attitude to law, which is basic to all his pronouncements in this area.

According to Dworkin, an interpretative attitude towards a practice is warranted if two facts are present: (1) the practice has a purpose 'that can be stated independently of just describing the rules that make up the practice'; and (2) the rules or requirements of the practice are sensitive to its purpose, 'so that the strict rules must be understood or applied or extended or modified or qualified or limited by that point'.[114] Dworkin justified his

[114] Dworkin, *Law's Empire*, 47.

application of an interpretative approach to law by the fact that it succeeds where other approaches fail in explaining the significant amount of substantive disagreement that seems to occur within law (that is, frequent and detailed disagreement about 'what the law requires in this case').[115]

One initial difficulty to consider: the possibility that Dworkin's key requirement for an interpretative attitude, as described, is not sufficiently strong to distinguish that approach from a descriptive approach to law. Most legal positivists would not disagree with the idea (or at least would not think it inconsistent with non-interpretative positivism) that a legal rule should be 'extended . . . or qualified or limited' according to some view of the purposes of that particular rule, that doctrinal area, or law in general. This is a weak claim, which could be seen to follow from beliefs that judges legislate on the penumbra, that words must be read in their context, and that legislation is best understood (for the purpose of application) if the problems to which it is responding are kept in mind. None of these claims, individually or jointly, entail an interpretative attitude. I do not think Dworkin believed that this weaker claim was sufficient for an interpretative attitude, though it is a reading his text allowed.

At other times, Dworkin made it clear that he had in mind a stronger claim, that substantial portions of a practice are vulnerable to be changed if that would make the practice more consistent with its purpose, and that there may be no aspect of the practice which is immune. For example, Dworkin described the paradigm of the practice as being 'concrete examples any plausible interpretation must fit',[116] implying that other aspects of the practice could be rejected for the sake of consistency with the purpose. Further, even a paradigm could be rejected one day if it was found to be inconsistent with the claimed purpose.[117]

It is crucial to ask: what does it mean to say that a practice has a purpose? Courtesy, the example of a practice Dworkin often used, is constituted by a large collection of detailed rules. A legal system is far more complex: it includes not only rules which impose duties

[115] See ibid. 3–6, 38–44, 87–90.

[116] Dworkin, *Law's Empire*, 72.

[117] Ibid. 72–3. cf. H. Putnam, 'Is Water Necessarily H_2O?', in *Realism with a Human Face*, 60 (London: Harvard University Press, 1990): the defeasibility of paradigms in the analysis of substance–identity.

on citizens, but also norms which empower citizens or officials to create new rules, higher-level norms which indicate how rules should be interpreted and applied, and an institutional structure through which the whole process operates. Along with this structural complexity, most legal systems also have a very broad scope, covering almost every area of human behaviour. Though it may be possible to discuss the purpose of practices like courtesy with their relatively simple internal structure and relatively limited scope, it is far more difficult to speak of *the* purpose of a legal system. (Though in Dworkin's examples he always refers to 'the' purpose of courtesy or of law, and only mentions one such purpose, perhaps his analytical structure could contain a view that a particular social practice has a number of identifiable defining purposes. I will briefly consider such possibilities later.)

Also, with any complex entity about which we might want to talk about purposes and uses, whether this entity is a social practice, a social institution, a human product, or an animal, one must be careful to distinguish attributes which are present *because* they serve a particular purpose, and attributes, unavoidably there, for which a purpose has been found.

Consider the example of the spandrels of San Marco, an example that has been used by evolutionary theorists to discuss the subtleties of 'purpose' in their field. The spandrels in St Mark's Cathedral in Venice work well as a location for mosaics, but they are there not by choice, but as the necessary by-product of mounting a dome on rounded arches on a rectangular base. Attributes may be present because they are the structural correlates of other things desired; this occurs not only in architecture, but also in other areas, including genetics, where an attribute may be 'favoured' because it is genetically closely linked with a highly advantageous trait. Also, attributes may be present even though they do not now serve a purpose, if they once did, and if though they are not now similarly useful they have not become so detrimental that the attribute is selected against.[118] The natural reference is again to evolutionary theory, but consider the analogy to archaic laws that are almost completely unenforced and

[118] S. J. Gould and R. Lewontin, 'The Spandrels of San Marco and the Panglossian Paradigm: A Critique of the Adaptationist Programme', 205 *Proceedings of the Royal Society*, ser. B, 581, 581–2 (1979).

ignored, but which do not evoke enough negative pressure to motivate their repeal.

It follows from 'natural selection' within Darwinian theory that one cannot speak of individual animals (or whole species) trying to attain or obtain a certain adaptive advantage. Selection works upon the random variations that result from genetic mutation and recombination. So a Darwinian talking about an organism's attribute, unlike someone discussing a human social institution or social practice, cannot speak of its point or purpose in terms of what the originator's intention was, for no conscious intention is at work. The Darwinian can only talk of point or purpose in terms of a theory of the larger context (in the case of Darwinian theory, that larger context is natural selection and sexual selection).

How do Dworkin's discussions of purpose compare to these discussions from evolutionary theory? When Dworkin wrote that '[o]ur discussions about law by and large assume . . . that the most abstract and fundamental point of legal practice is to guide and constrain the power of government,'[119] what is the nature of that claim? Assuming that this is the purpose of law (and leaving aside for the moment the questions of incommensurability raised by the phrases '*most* abstract' and '*most* fundamental'), within the dichotomy just mentioned it seems less likely to be an explanation for why legal systems were introduced[120] than to be an explanation of how some politicians and legal theorists later came to think of (or 'use') legal systems.

Further, here Dworkin's own phrasing is confusing: given the general argument, in which nearly all interesting aspects of legal analysis turn out to be interpretative, one would think that he was making an interpretative claim here as well ('seeing law in its best light requires us to see its purpose as being . . .'). However, the wording strongly ties the claim to the actual perceptions of participants ('[o]ur discussions about law by and large assume . . .'). On the other hand, little by way of historical, sociological, or anthropological analysis was then forthcoming.

[119] Dworkin, *Law's Empire*, 93. In other places in the same text, Dworkin described law not as a *constraint* on government power, but as a *justification* of government power: ibid. 109, 127. The differences are subtle, but important; however, the issue is beyond the scope of my present discussion.

[120] This is one area where I think analysis in terms of *particular* legal systems, especially ones as relatively 'new' as the American legal system, would be unhelpful.

An interpretative argument could side-step all historical questions regarding why certain practices were introduced, what intentions various officials had, and what had been the perceptions of officials and non-officials at various times. However, it remains to be proved whether an ahistorical approach, without further theoretical supplementation, can sensibly discuss *the* point or purpose of a complex institution. One can only imagine an interpretative approach advancing all the morally good effects that a legal system does have (or, with slight modification, might have) as jointly being the 'purposes' of that legal system. As discussed below, without further stage-setting, I do not know any basis on which Dworkin could justify selecting one such consequence from among the many as 'the' purpose or point of the legal system.

In 'Law as a Functional Kind',[121] Michael Moore surveyed the broad range of attributes which various theorists have offered as the (necessary or essential) 'features' of law, and the even broader range of goals or purposes theorists have attributed to law.[122] In trying to reach his own conclusion regarding what the function or purpose of law might be, he rejected the idea that an object's purposes could be equivalent to a list of its effects.[123] In any event, law, a large and complex institution (or institutional process) within an even larger and more complex society, has a vast number of effects on the society, so it would get us nowhere to equate law's purposes with its effects.

Moore argued that a function or purpose is a particular kind of effect, defined in terms of some larger context: when the entity is part of some larger system, the entity's function is defined by how it serves one (or more) of the entity's overall goals.[124] This is the method by which one can select among an institution's myriad goals and crown one a 'function'. However, it implies that the conclusion that (something) is the function or purpose of law can only be made after one has shown (or assumed for the purpose of argument) a moral-political theory about human goods within society. Moore summarized the steps one would have to take before discussing the function or purpose of law:

[121] M. Moore, in *Natural Law Theories*, 188–242 (R. George, ed., Oxford: Oxford University Press, 1992).
[122] Ibid. 213–17. [123] Ibid. 208–9. [124] Ibid. 209–10.

> Suppose one has a full theory of the good and the right. And suppose that one has enough of an idea of the structural characteristics of a legal system to sort through that full moral theory and isolate which good(s) are those uniquely achievable through law. One could then hypothesize which of the suggested goals of law is in fact its goal.[125]

Dworkin has not done any of this kind of stage-setting. He has not shown why it would be sensible, and not misleading, to speak of law having a defining purpose.

I have heard it argued that Dworkin need not work that hard for his conclusion; that he could argue as follows: 'As an interpretative matter (though not necessarily as a historical matter) our legal system serves these (say) dozen purposes, each to a varying degree and through varying aspects of the system. Though the necessary calculations, reshaping the pre-interpretative data in line with the collection of purposes, would be difficult even for a Herculean judge, there is no reason to think it impossible. Therefore, the criticisms offered above do not rebut the interpretative approach to law.'

There are two problems with this approach. The first is the problem of incommensurability. If there are a variety of 'purposes', they might reflect incommensurable values, and then, if one accepts the Mackie/Finnis/Raz approach to incommensurability discussed earlier in the chapter, there would not be a unique correct reshaping of the pre-interpretative data in light of the multiple purposes. Of course, if, by contrast, one accepts Dworkins arguments on the subject, incommensurability would not be a problem (at least until the interlocutor had met the burden of providing a substantive theory proving incommensurability in the particular situation).

The second problem is that I am not convinced that it is intelligible to speak of an activity with a dozen or more purposes, such that descriptions of the activity should be responsive to those many purposes. (I fear that this is only an intuitive judgement, and I am not sure how the argument could be advanced by either side, either for the position that such a notion *is* intelligible, or for the contrary position.)

A different attack on the practice/purpose disaggregation of law can be found in Gerald Postema's writings. Postema argued that

[125] Ibid. 216.

law is a social practice not only in the sense that many people are involved, but also in the sense that it is 'a collective meaningful activity', that is, 'an activity collectively understood'.[126] The point can be discussed at a number of levels. First, and most obviously, a legislator, a judge, or an advocate cannot be concerned only with his or her own interpretation of the law. Even when the legislator need not worry about convincing colleagues, or the judge need not worry about a reviewing court, they must concern themselves with how their statements of the law or about the law will be interpreted by other legal actors in the future. In terms of Dworkin's image of the chain novel, each author must be concerned not only that his or her understanding is consistent with the themes and plot subtleties of past authors, but also that the author's own intentions and devices will be clear to the future authors that continue the task; otherwise, the author's efforts will be without consequence.[127] Law is social in much the same way that language is social: without certain shared understandings, the enterprise would fail.

A different perspective on the same argument can be seen through an analysis of Dworkin's idea of the 'pre-interpretative' data which are the subject of interpretation. Dworkin does not claim that these data are completely value-neutral:[128] 'I enclose "preinterpretive" in quotes because some kind of interpretation is necessary even at this stage. Social rules do not carry identifying labels.'[129] The question is how much he actually gave away with that concession, whether his theory can even survive it. When he wrote that 'some kind of interpretation' was necessary even at the pre-interpretative stage, this interpretation must be different from the interpretation of those 'data' at the second stage, or else no second stage would be needed (or possible). If the data come already 'fully interpreted', then Dworkinian judges would not—indeed, could not—disagree about their content.

The focus on the interpretation that has gone on in 'creating' the

[126] G. Postema, ' "Protestant" Interpretation and Social Practices', 6 *Law and Philosophy* 283 (1987).

[127] See ibid. 310–12; see also Cover, 'Violence and the Word', 1612.

[128] As Charles Taylor pointed out, the problem in talking about 'uninterpreted data' can be traced back at least as far as Kant's critique of Humean empiricism: C. Taylor, 'Overcoming Epistemology', in *After Philosophy*, 476 (K. Baynes, J. Bohman, and T. McCarthy, eds., London: MIT Press, 1987).

[129] Dworkin, *Law's Empire*, 66; see also 422, n. 14.

pre-interpretative data fits well with Postema's critique. Postema had pointed out that any discussion of a complex social practice like law will be heavily theory-laden, even at a 'pre-interpretative' level. For example, to describe someone as 'voting' rather than merely as putting a marked scrap of paper in a box, or as 'writing a judicial opinion' rather than merely as scribbling marks on a series of pages, already assumes knowledge of (or a theory about) what rules and social practices are being followed.[130]

Postema wrote:

> A regularity of behavior is a regularity only relative to some rule, and for different rules, different regularities. Similarly, practice behavior and its consensus rules are meaningful, i.e., are the actions or rules they are only within the web of the practice as a whole . . . [D]ifferent theories of [a] practice as a whole [will] yield different actions.[131]

From Postema we should learn that the value in the already-value-laden ('pre-interpretative') legal data derives from the community practices which constitute a particular legal system and its immediate background context. Most of the work transforming 'mere behaviour' into legally significant actions seems to occur at the so-called 'pre-interpretative' level, before Dworkin's judicial procedures even occur. According to Postema, in trying to understand law our focus should be on social practices and shared understandings, not on individual (and potentially idiosyncratic) impositions of meaning on 'mere data'.

Dworkin might respond that if one believes that all the important work is already done at the 'pre-interpretative' stage where everyone is in agreement, then one would face an unpleasant dilemma that his approach had avoided. Either we all perceive the material with the same theoretical colouring, in which case our descriptions of law should converge and the theoretical disagreements that actually occur within and about law could not be explained; or that theoretical disagreement is not true disagreement at all. If theoretical disagreement implies that the participants' understandings are based on differing sets of rules and perceptions, these would not be substantive disagreements

[130] Hans Kelsen made a similar point: that people's use of legal terminology to describe events involves an interpretation of events *as normative*. See Kelsen, *Pure Theory of Law*, 2–4.

[131] Postema, ' "Protestant" Interpretation and Social Practices', 306.

(that is, disagreements about some common matter) and there would not any obvious basis for resolving such disputes.[132]

The challenge for Postema was the same as it was for Dworkin (and for Hart before him): to explain disagreements within the law and about the law; and part of this explanation involves describing the area(s) of agreement underlying the substantive disagreements.[133] Without some amount of underlying agreement, all disagreements within law would be (as some Critical Legal Studies theorists might have it) political arguments for how society should be run, as opposed to arguments about the correct way to interpret or apply past decisions.

Postema offered two alternative explanations of substantive disagreement in law. First, the disagreement may only mean that the subject of the disagreement is complex and/or difficult to know fully. Postema wrote:

> [Interpretations of social practices] are formulations, or successive reformulations, of shared understandings, proposals for a better understanding of our common activity. This does not entail that all participants must agree about how to understand their practice, but it does imply that one's own understanding be addressed to other participants and be sensitive to their understanding of it.[134]

Secondly, within a common practice, within 'a matrix of collectively meaningful participation',[135] there is always room to 'disagree about how best to articulate, formulate, or express this common meaning', disagreements which often come down to questions of emphasis and priority.[136]

In summary, Postema's approach to law can be seen as a closely related alternative to Dworkin's holistic approach to law. Dworkin's approach to law and legal theory is 'holistic' in that no claims within or about law are 'foundational': the truth of any particular claim depends on the truth of other claims within the theory, and all such claims, including 'paradigmatic' instances, are

[132] See Dworkin, *Law's Empire*, 3–15, 31–53.

[133] See Postema, ' "Protestant" Interpretation and Social Practices', 297–9 (Dworkin's view), 315–19 (Postema's view).

[134] Ibid. 312.

[135] Ibid. 315.

[136] Ibid. 317. The Wittgensteinian nature of Postema's critique and alternative position is clear, and there are a number of direct references to Wittgenstein's work in the article: ibid. 304 and n. 31, 307, n. 34, 316, n. 49, 318, n. 56.

potentially open to challenge.[137] Dworkin's 'concession' that the 'pre-interpretative' data also have theoretical content could also be seen as evidence of the holistic nature of his approach (or as an argument for such an approach). However, as Dworkin realized, for a holistic approach to offer any constraint on what we claim to be true or correct, there must be some 'functional distinctions, within that system, among the various kinds and levels of belief'.[138] In Dworkin's approach, these functional distinctions occur through the 'pre-interpretative' data and the defining purpose, through the way the first is recharacterized in the light of the second.

Postema's argument was that all of the work in understanding or describing law is already done by the time we have the 'pre-interpretative data'. This is because even our most basic understanding of events derives from community practices (with equal emphasis on 'community' and on 'practices'). Discussions based on Moore and on Gould and Lewontin struck at the other aspect of Dworkin's approach: the problem of understanding purpose in the context of social practices. I believe that the arguments raised show deep, and perhaps insuperable, difficulties in the mechanism through which the approach works. The final section in this chapter will criticize a different integral aspect of that approach.

INTENTION AND INTERPRETATION

An integral part of Dworkin's approach was his rejection of an 'conversational interpretation' for social practices, in particular his rejection of giving priority in interpreting laws to the rule-makers' meaning (intention).[139] Interpretation is to be constructive, making the object of interpretation the best it can be (though, on occasion, making the object the best it can be may require reference to intentions; still, the 'constructive' aspect of interpretation has priority, not the 'conversational' aspect).[140] It is part

[137] See e.g. R. Dworkin, 'My Reply to Stanley Fish (and Walter Benn Michaels)', 292–5; Marmor, *Interpretation and Legal Theory*, 78–82.

[138] Dworkin, 'My Reply to Stanley Fish (and Walter Benn Michaels)', 293.

[139] See Dworkin, *Law's Empire*, 50–68, 313–54.

[140] See ibid., 49–53; Marmor, *Interpretation and Legal Theory*, 36–9.

of Dworkin's holism about law; particular rules are interpreted in the light of other rules, not merely in the usual sense that rules should not be interpreted in such a way that they create contradictory imperatives, or even that similar terms in similar pieces of legislation should be interpreted in similar ways. The holism here is much stronger: that all past legal texts and decisions should be interpreted to be the best they can be, and as though they were the product of a single voice. However, as a number of theorists have pointed out, it is difficult to square this approach with the importance of authority to law, an importance implicitly accepted elsewhere in Dworkin's approach.[141]

Dworkinian judges are to make constitutional clauses, statutes, and past judicial decisions the best they can be. The question is, why choose these texts rather than randomly selected others, and why worry about how close one's reading is to the usual reading? Why not read the United States Constitution as *Hamlet*?[142] Better yet, why not just read *Hamlet*? The ready answer would be that to act in that way—either in the choice of texts or their interpretation—would not 'fit' past practices; it would deviate too far from how 'law' was practised in the past and how it is understood by officials and lay persons today.

The problem is that to see that much, but no more, in past practices is to read those practices too superficially. As Dworkin would readily admit, people do not merely act; they act *for reasons* and *according to rules*. The reason that American judges refer (and defer) to the Constitution is that they believe that the writers of that document (once the document was duly approved) had authority to set standards for the nation. For a similar reason, the Constitution is not read as *Hamlet*: those writers did not intend the document to be read that way.

As Larry Alexander noted: 'Abandoning conversational standards for interpreting the words of canonical rules is morally undesirable because it is morally desirable that legislative bodies have the ability to settle moral controversies through the enactment of canonical rules.'[143] Legislators are not like the oracle at

[141] See e.g. L. Alexander, 'Striking Back at the Empire: A Brief Survey of Problems in Dworkin's Theory of Law', 6 *Law and Philosophy* 419, 424–5 and 425–6, n. 14 (1987); Raz, 'Dworkin: A New Link in the Chain', 1112–14, 1118–19.

[142] See Raz, 'Dworkin: A New Link in the Chain', 1119.

[143] Alexander, 'Striking Back at the Empire', 424.

Delphi, such that only the words spoken are important and there are doubts that the speakers themselves actually know the meaning and significance of those words.[144] The words are important *as* embodying the rule-makers' intentions: whether as resolutions of disputes or as choices among possible co-ordination schemes. It is true, as Alexander conceded, that following the (relatively) concrete intentions of rule-makers may mean ignoring their most abstract intentions (for example, 'to make the morally best choice'), intentions which might approximate to the result of a Dworkinian constructive interpretation of the texts. However, at that abstract level of intention—and with the variety of different readings it would inspire in different judges[145]—the authorities (and the authoritative sources) would then fail in their function of making (largely) determinate and (largely) settled choices.[146]

It may at first appear that my criticisms of Dworkin are inconsistent. After first arguing that it is a mistake to claim that law has a particular purpose to which its practices are responsive, I am now arguing that *another* problem with his approach is that it undermines one of law's purposes. However, it is important to see the difference between my claim and Dworkin's. He claimed that law has a particular purpose, and our understanding of what the law requires may have to be re-formed in order to keep that understanding in line with the purpose. My claim is far weaker: that law is generally understood (in many societies) to serve a number of functions (for example, resolving moral questions, co-ordinating behaviour, and resolving disputes), and that we should have severe doubts about a theory of law that would disable the legal system from performing any of those functions.

Conclusion

As the past few sections have argued, Dworkin's interpretative (holistic) approach fails, even on its own terms. It fails to 'fit' our

[144] See L. Alexander, 'Of Two Minds about Law and Minds', 88 *Michigan Law Review* 2444, 2446–7 (1990).

[145] As discussed earlier in this chapter.

[146] See Alexander, 'Striking Back at the Empire', 426, n. 14; 'Of Two Minds about Law and Minds', 2447–8. For a slightly different and far more detailed critique, see Marmor, *Interpretation and Legal Theory*, 155–84. I return to the subject of intention in law in Chap. 6.

practice—for example, the importance of authority and the importance of consensus in our practice; and it fails on the normative level: it would disable law from doing many of the tasks we want and expect that institution to perform.

5
Michael Moore's Metaphysical Realism

'When I use a word,' Humpty Dumpty said, in a rather scornful tone, 'it means just what I choose it to mean — neither more nor less.'

'The question is,' Alice said, 'whether you *can* make words mean so many different things.'

'The question is,' said Humpty Dumpty, 'which is to be the master—that's all.'[1]

INTRODUCTION

Michael Moore has written a number of lengthy articles defending metaphysical realism[2] and urging that legal theory and legal practice be reformed consistent with that philosophical position. He argued against much of what had been considered common sense, obvious, settled, and beyond question, and offered a global challenge to jurisprudence with regard both to thinking about the law and thinking within the law.

Moore's challenge is aimed at legal thinking, but its roots run much deeper and its repercussions are, potentially, much broader. His one-man crusade is premised on the notion that most of us are terribly misguided. In general, we are said to be fundamentally mistaken about the nature of law, the nature of language, the nature of morality, and even the nature of reality. Within law, we are said to be badly misinformed regarding statutory interpretation and constitutional interpretation, common-law reasoning, and judicial reasoning.

For those of us who think Moore may be a false prophet, the

[1] L. Carroll, *The Annotated Alice: Alice's Adventures in Wonderland and Through the Looking Glass*, 269 (M. Gardner, annot., New York: Meridian, 1960).

[2] Though Moore usually referred to his position as 'realism', to prevent confusing his position with the various (and quite different) theories and movements in law, politics, literature, and art which carry that label, I will refer to his approach as 'metaphysical realism'.

best strategy to rebut his arguments is to fight them at their source: metaphysical realism. Yet the arguments for and against this position constitute a substantial category in the philosophical literature. It would be far too ambitious to try to refute metaphysical realism in a single book, let alone a single chapter. I have set my sights on what I hope to be a more attainable objective.

Moore offers his own (slightly unusual) version of metaphysical realism, and the power of his argument comes from his prima-facie showing that approaches to language other than his own cannot adequately deal with certain fundamental matters (such as changing scientific beliefs). If I can show that Moore has underestimated the alternatives to his approach (in particular, approaches based on the work of the later Wittgenstein) and if I can show that his approach has problems of its own, then perhaps we need not, after all, rethink everything we thought we knew about law and legal theory.

This chapter will be concerned primarily with the appropriate theory of language, and with arguing that Moore's approach is not the correct one (or, at the least, that he has not proved that it is superior to other approaches). However, the chapter includes arguments in the alternative: in later sections, I argue (briefly) that even if Moore was correct about metaphysical realism, it may make no difference in how we think about or do law; and even if it would make some difference, that difference is quite small and would usually be swamped by other factors that (as Moore admitted) judges should take into account.

In the course of discussing Moore's work, I will also find it helpful to consider some recent work by David Brink, who, like Moore, has tried to apply the 'lessons' of metaphysical realism to legal theory.

METAPHYSICAL REALISM

It is worth taking a moment to try to give an overview of the contrasts between metaphysical realism and its alternatives. A difficulty with this task is that many theorists in their attempts to give such an overview have divided up the range of opinion in many different ways. The labels 'realist', 'Platonist', and 'metaphysical realist' have been given very different boundaries both by supporters and by opponents. I will offer a small sample of these different overviews in order to give the reader a sense of where the battle lines have been drawn.

In lamenting the lack of clear boundaries in the debate about metaphysical realism, Crispin Wright went so far as to describe realism as 'a syndrome, a loose weave of separable presuppositions and attitudes'.[3] Wright offered a series of foci around which to consider the realist–anti-realist disputes, though emphasizing the 'three distinct species of objectivity':[4] (1) the objectivity of truth—that a class of statements may be intelligible even though determining the statements' truth-values is beyond our powers of rational appraisal; (2) the objectivity of meaning—that statements have a truth-value independently of our opinion about their truth-value (that is, they can be 'undetectably true'); and (3) the objectivity of judgement—that the statements have a ' "genuinely factual" subject-matter'.[5] Wright argued that both the objectivity of meaning and the objectivity of judgement would follow from the objectivity of truth, but that the converse implication probably did not hold.[6]

Wright argued that many of the debates over metaphysical realism have been not about the objectivity of truth but about the objectivity of judgement. Beyond questions of objectivity, Wright discussed two other sets of questions regularly involved in disputes over metaphysical realism: questions of the irreducibility of a class of statements, and questions of ontology (for example, the reality of mathematical objects).[7]

A somewhat different description of the debates about metaphysical realism was given by Simon Blackburn, who described a metaphysical realist's approach to an area of discourse as follows: (1) the commitments in the area 'are capable of strict and literal truth'; (2) 'they describe the world'; (3) 'they answer to (independent) facts of a particular kind'; and (4) '[t]hese facts are discovered, not created, and they make ontological and metaphysical

[3] C. Wright, *Realism, Meaning and Truth*, 3–4 (Oxford: Basil Blackwell, 1987).

[4] Ibid. 5–8.

[5] Wright commented on his own description: 'this is a largely unhelpful characterization, [but] notoriously difficult to improve on', ibid. 6.

[6] Ibid. 5–7.

[7] Ibid. 8–9.

demands.'[8] He added that in most, but not all, areas of discourse, a metaphysical realist would also believe that (5) the facts that make the commitments true or false are 'mind-independent'; and (6) the commitments in the area are irreducible.[9] (An example of an area in which a metaphysical realist would not cling to the fifth requirement would be metaphysical realism about psychological ascriptions, which would not include claims of mind-independence for those statements.)[10]

For a third perspective on the realist–anti-realist debate, I return to the main subject of this chapter. Michael Moore offered the following belief-checklist for being a 'full-blooded' metaphysical realist about some class of entities: (1) the entities in question exist and this existence is independent of individual minds and community conventions; (2) a correspondence theory of truth; (3) a classical theory of logic; (4) a truth-conditional theory of the meaning of sentences; and (5) a causal theory of meaning (the Kripke–Putnam theory of reference) for natural-kind words.[11]

In the above summaries one can already see the complications and confusions that accompany most discussion within or about the realism–anti-realism debate.[12] First, arguments put forward to support a particular approach seem to imply global claims, that this approach is appropriate (superior to other approaches) for all areas of discourse, when the evidence offered rarely warrants more than a claim about a single area of discourse. (Among the areas of discourse that often receive special attention in the philosophical literature, because they involve special problems regarding truth, meaning, or ontology, are mathematical propositions, modal terms, generalizations of natural science, statements concerning the past, statements concerning the future, ethical

[8] S. Blackburn, 'Options for the World', 4 (unpublished manuscript).

[9] Ibid.

[10] Ibid.

[11] Moore, 'The Interpretive Turn in Modern Theory', 878–9.

[12] 'Anti-realism' is used in the literature in two different senses. In the broader sense, it means any position opposed to metaphysical realism. In the narrower sense, it is a particular non-realist position (sometimes associated with the work of Michael Dummett). It is in the light of the narrower use of the term that a commentator could suggest that Wittgenstein's work was neither realist nor anti-realist. See P. M. S. Hacker, *Insight and Illusion*, 62–5, 322–35 and *Wittgenstein: Meaning and Mind*, 545–6 (Oxford: Basil Blackwell, 1990). However, I will be using the term in the first, broader sense.

propositions, subjunctive conditionals (counter-factuals), and descriptions of other people's mental states.)

Secondly, there is often a deep ambiguity about the focus of the theorists' claims: whether they are claims about language (what certain words mean), psychology (what people mean when they use certain words), or the world (whether certain kinds of entities exist or not). One can even see the different approaches in the summaries: while Crispin Wright focused on beliefs about 'class[es] of statements' and Simon Blackburn wrote about attitudes towards 'areas of discourse', Michael Moore's discussion focused on beliefs about 'some class of entities'.[13] Similarly, purported metaphysically realistic approaches to law sometimes seem to be about language (for example, that 'malice' means one thing rather than another), sometimes about psychology (for example, that by using a particular term, speakers (or legislators) meant to defer to (future) experts' opinions about that entity), and sometimes about the world (for example, that certain 'moral kinds' or 'natural kinds' exist). Obviously, there are many connections between these three categories, and claims of one kind often blur into claims of another kind. (For example, a metaphysical realist's claim that 'cruelty' refers to a particular 'moral kind' entails the claim that such 'moral kinds' exist.) Still, the possibilities for ambiguity and confusion remain, and part of my task will be to clarify the nature of the claims the theorists have made (and those I make in response).

SUMMARY OF MOORE'S POSITION

Moore's discussions about language can be summed up in two related assertions: (1) whether we know it or not (and however much some of us may deny it), we intend our words to be understood in a metaphysically realist way; and (2) definitions offered in dictionaries, statutes, and elsewhere are merely 'conventional glosses on the meaning of words'.[14] As for the

[13] Wright, *Realism, Meaning and Truth*, 5; Blackburn, 'Options for the World', 2; Moore, 'The Interpretive Turn in Modern Theory', 878.

[14] M. Moore, 'A Natural Law Theory of Interpretation', 58 *Southern Californian Law Review* 277, 331 (1985).

role of language in legal theory, he would probably respond that while language may be ambiguous or have uncertain boundaries, it should not be our focus. For Moore, language is only an imperfect tool for describing reality. We should be concerned with discovering the true nature of (for example) virtue, equality, and death, not with the changing and uncertain usage patterns of the words 'virtue', 'equality', and 'death'.

In discussing Moore, I will focus on one article, 'A Natural Law Theory of Interpretation',[15] because in that article he came closest to putting forward a full theory of legal interpretation and judicial reasoning. He characterized his 'natural law theory of interpretation' as follows: (1) 'there is a right answer to moral questions, a moral reality if you like', and (2) judges should rely on that moral reality in interpreting and applying the law.[16] He also argued that a metaphysically realist theory of meaning extended to evaluative terms (for example, 'responsible' and 'justice') and natural-kind words (for example, 'bird'), and that a metaphysically realist analysis should be used even for terms that are specifically defined within a statute.[17] My focus in this chapter will be on metaphysical realism about meaning (in particular, regarding the meaning of simple descriptive terms) and Wittgenstein's critique of that position. Metaphysical realism regarding other areas of discourse—for example, science, mathematics, modal terms, and morality—involves other issues and its consideration is outside the scope of this book (though my discussion may touch upon those issues, and, of course, arguments about metaphysical realism regarding one area of discourse, even though not conclusive, have some relevance to the arguments about metaphysical realism in other areas of discourse).[18]

Moore's metaphysically realist theory of meaning is based on the idea that a word 'refers to a natural kind of event that occurs in the world and that it is not arbitrary that we possess some symbol to name this thing'.[19] Under this approach, our use of a word, and the definition we offer for it, will not necessarily be static, but will

[15] M. Moore, 'A Natural Law Theory of Interpretation'.

[16] Ibid. 286; see also M. Moore, 'Moral Reality', 1982 *Wisconsin Law Review* 1061.

[17] Moore, 'A Natural Law Theory of Interpretation', 300–1.

[18] See Blackburn, *Spreading the Word*, 145–7.

[19] Moore, 'A Natural Law Theory of Interpretation', 294.

change as our understanding of the object, event, or idea to which the term refers changes.[20] Moore offered 'conventionalism' as the (disfavoured) alternative to a metaphysically realist theory of meaning: in contrast to metaphysical realism, '[a] conventionalist theory . . . regards the relationships between symbols and things to be essentially arbitrary'.[21]

(Moore's division of theoretical space into only metaphysical realism and conventionalism is contentious and probably, strictly speaking, untenable. Wittgenstein's approach to the philosophy of language, which I will bring forward at various points, rejected both options.[22] To be fair, though, Moore was left in a dilemma. In order to have an alternative to metaphysical realism specific enough to be summarized and evaluated, he had to present an approach to which not all opponents of metaphysical realism would agree.)

One would have thought that one instance in which a judge should not need recourse to any theory of meaning is when the judge must explicate a term that the legislature has explicitly defined within a statute. However, Moore gave metaphysical realism a prominent role even here. He gave an example of how a close (in fact, somewhat myopic) reading of a hypothetical statute's definition clause could allow a judge to conclude that a horse with a downy pillow on its back should be considered a bird for the purpose of the statute.[23] The statute defined a 'bird' as an animal, with two legs, covered with feathers; the horse was an animal, it was covered with feathers, and it had (at least) two legs.[24] Moore's point was that we are vulnerable both to absurd results and to missing the legislature's intention if we treat the statute's stipulative definition on its own. Instead, we must understand that the ordinary meaning and usage of a term and our beliefs about the world provide a background, a context within which we interpret statutory definitions. For Moore, legislative definitions, like conventional definitions, are merely 'conventional glosses on the [real or realist] meaning of words' and it may be

[20] Ibid.

[21] Ibid. 291–2.

[22] See Pears, *The False Prison*, ii. 486–9; cf. Blackburn, 'Options for the World', 1–16 (describing and discussing four separate approaches to an area of discourse).

[23] Moore, 'A Natural Law Theory of Interpretation', 329–32 (paraphrasing H. Pomerantz and S. Breslin, 'Judicial Humour—Construction of a Statute', 8 *Criminal Law Quarterly* 137 (1965)).

[24] Ibid. 329.

necessary for judges sometimes 'to ignore the [legislative] definition when it runs counter to the true nature of the thing the definition was attempting to pick out'.[25]

THE PROBLEM ABOUT 'DEATH'

According to Moore, one major advantage of metaphysical realism over 'conventionalism' in the legal context is the relative inflexibility and immobility of the latter. Moore argued that as our understanding of objects and processes in the world changes and improves, 'conventionalism' offers neither processes nor justifications for modifying our definitions of words to keep up. 'Meaning will "run out" in our attempt to describe the world.'[26] According to Moore, under 'conventionalism' any attempt to apply an old term to new circumstances must be characterized as a change of that term's meaning.[27] His favourite example to explain and justify his realist theory of meaning was the word 'death'.[28] People once equated death with the cessation of heart and lung function. Such definitions were occasionally incorporated into statutes (for example, determining when a person's organs could be removed for use in transplant surgery).[29] More recently, doctors have gained the ability to revive some persons whose heart and lungs had stopped (for a short period of time). Moore pointed out that doctors and legislators now tend to equate death with the cessation of brain function or with non-revivability; however, he argued that, contrary to what he claimed that a 'conventionalist' must believe, the meaning of 'death' has not changed. 'Whether a person is really dead or not will be ascertained by applying the best scientific theory we have about what death really is . . . A realist . . . believes that there is more to what death is (and thus what "death" means) than is captured by our current conventions.'[30]

Within this area, Moore's argument for his theory of statutory interpretation has some initial plausibility. If the statute authorizing transplants explicitly used the old definition of 'death', we would still think it ghastly for a judge to rely on that definition to allow

[25] Moore, 'A Natural Law Theory of Interpretation', 331.
[26] Ibid. 293.
[27] Ibid.
[28] See ibid. 293–4, 297–300, 308–9, 322–8, 382.
[29] Ibid. 293, 322–8.
[30] Ibid. 294.

the removal of an organ from a person who could still be revived.[31] For Moore, statutory definitions in such cases are not stipulations so much as initial estimations subject to change. The legislature 'should be held to have the same linguistic intentions as other language users, namely, [metaphysically] realist ones'.[32]

However, I do not think that the word 'death'—and the concept of it—is as helpful to Moore's metaphysically realist theory of meaning as he implied. There are two different kinds of challenges that can be brought against his analysis: first, that 'death' may not be a single 'kind' or a sufficiently unitary 'kind' to fit into his analysis;[33] and secondly, that contrary to Moore's analysis, a 'conventionalist' about 'death' would *not* be troubled about the increased ability to resuscitate. I will discuss these two challenges in turn.

The advances in medical knowledge in the past generation have not created a consensual change in the way we think about death. On the contrary, the advances have only led to unending debate and controversy in many realms: politics, medicine, ethics, theology, and law. Though more and more persons may now equate death with the complete cessation of brain function (or 'higher brain function'), there are still sensible, intelligent observers who insist that those whose brain has ceased to function but who retain heart, lung, and metabolic function (perhaps with the help of 'life-support' systems) are still alive. The consensus Moore assumed and implied does not exist. Medical advances have also left us with a series of intermediate cases: patients in permanent comas, patients in permanent vegetative states, and patients whose brains retain some minimal functioning and who may or may not be able to feel pain or pleasure (doctors cannot tell in many cases). The very active debate in the courts, the legislature, and the academic journals as to when medical treatment for such patients can (or should) be discontinued and who should make such decisions indicates that scientific advances

[31] Ibid. 322–5.

[32] Ibid. 323.

[33] Compare the medical term 'shock', which as used by British doctors during the First World War was thought to name a single type, a single kind of injury. Medical research during the Second World War (in which Wittgenstein played a minor role) seemed to show that the term had been used to describe a variety of (probably unrelated) problems. See R. Monk, *Ludwig Wittgenstein: The Duty of Genius*, 444–7, 451–2 (London: Jonathan Cape, 1990).

have muddled rather than clarified the issue of what death—and life—mean.[34]

(I did not mean to claim that consensus is important to Moore. As a metaphysical realist, he would not rely on consensus in determining meaning or ontology. However, in this particular discussion, he implied that there was a popular consensus about 'death', which reflects the current scientific 'best theory' about it. The absence of a consensus on this matter does not by itself disprove metaphysical realism about 'death'; it may only mean that our perception of a unified category is partial or flawed, but it *may* mean that there is no unified category to perceive. The absence of consensus is not inconsistent with metaphysical realism, but it is *more* consistent with alternative approaches, and it is part of an argument that an approach other than metaphysical realism would be appropriate here.)

One could argue that the way we have reacted to these medical advances supports not a metaphysically realist interpretation of 'death', but one based on a criteriological-conventionalist theory of meaning. That is, we associate a list of criteria with a term, and when some of those criteria apply but others do not, then there will no longer be a consensus as to whether the term should apply to the new situation.[35] One listing of criteria for life might be: systemic function, lower brain function, higher brain function ('consciousness'), and ability to feel pain and pleasure. In earlier times, these criteria were always present ('life') or absent ('death') together. Advances in medical science have led to there being patients who show almost every possible permutation of these criteria; the absolute terms 'life' and 'death' thus become less and less helpful, and there is no consensus regarding what alternative characterizations might be appropriate.[36]

Future scientific advances—ones that are foreseeable, though

[34] For an overview of some of the issues in the 'right to die' area, see e.g. *Cruzan* v. *Director, Missouri Department of Health*, 497 U.S. 261 (1990); N. Cantor, *Legal Frontiers of Death and Dying* (Bloomington, Ind.: Indiana University Press, 1987); B. Bix, book review, 18 *Seton Hall Law Review* 523 (1988).

[35] See Moore, 'A Natural Law Theory of Interpretation', 296; Hart, *The Concept of Law*, 123–4.

[36] cf. *Severns* v. *Wilmington Medical Center*, 421 A.2d 1334, 1344 (Del. 1980) ('the penumbra where death begins but life, in some form, continues'); *In re L.H.R.*, 321 S.E.2d 716, 722 (Ga. 1984) ('Under these circumstances, we find that the life support system was prolonging her death rather than her life').

still far away—will probably further decrease our ability to think (in the way Moore would prefer) about life and death as simple and separate. The possibility of transplanting one person's brain (and thus that person's consciousness as well?) into another person's body or of cloning persons undermines our traditional ideas about (continuous and unique) personal identity and about death (*qua* the cessation of one person's identity).[37] As our confidence diminishes that 'life' and 'death' represent two unitary areas which are clearly demarcated, Moore's argument that we are (and should be) metaphysical realists about the term 'death' becomes less persuasive.

(Moore claimed not to be troubled by 'more radical . . . thought experiments', arguing that they would only serve to refute 'deep conventionalism' while supporting metaphysical realism. Regarding a hypothetical situation where the body could die but the mind live on, he responded: 'Would we say that no one dies, that there is no such event as death? Or would we say that death has a very different nature than we had thought?'[38] I cannot concur with Moore's response; my reactions certainly do not suddenly become metaphysically realist when I consider his thought experiment. I would have concluded from the hypothetical facts, (1) that the term 'death' was becoming increasingly inadequate (overburdened and overstretched), (2) that at the least it has come to describe a family-resemblance group of phenomena rather than a unitary 'natural kind of event', and (3) that 'conventionalist' responses of language running out and arbitrary language-choices being required (do we call that phenomenon 'death' or not?) seem appropriate here. These are hardly metaphysically realist responses—though I cannot be sure how widely shared such responses would be.)

Moore might argue that underlying the disagreement between the person who believes that life ends when higher brain functions cease and the person who believes that life ends only when all brain functions cease, there is (must be) an underlying agreement. The underlying agreement is that there is a fact of the matter regarding when 'death' (the event) occurs, and the only disagreement could be regarding this fact, this truth. The metaphysical

[37] See D. Parfit, *Reasons and Persons*, 199–320 (Oxford: Clarendon Press, 1986).

[38] Moore, 'A Natural Law Theory of Interpretation', 299–300.

realist's response to disagreement is to point out that it is disagreement *about some object or entity*. That is why metaphysical realism is as compatible with substantial disagreement as it is with consensus, and that is why it can explain conceptual change.

However, an alternative characterization of the dispute is possible. When the argument in newspaper editorials and at the meetings of hospital ethics committees is put in terms of 'Is this patient really still alive?', the various terms used ('alive', 'really alive', 'delayed death', 'limbo between life and death', and so on) are often only place-markers for positions on difficult ethical questions (for example, 'Should the patient continue to receive certain forms of treatment despite the fact that she is in a permanent vegetative state?'). The discussion is in terms of 'life' and 'death' not because of any underlying metaphysical or ontological agreement, but because these are the only terms available and generally understood (at this point) in public discourse. The fact that these terms are used in unconventional ways in the dispute (for example, 'the penumbra where death begins but life . . . continues') indicates a dissatisfaction with, not an acceptance of, the usual semantics and metaphysics.

This analysis need not be confined to Moore's example about 'death'. It is often useful to consider whether labels are being used (in part or in whole) as markers for legal or moral conclusions. For example, disputes regarding whether a particular agreement constitutes a 'contract' can often profitably be seen as arguments about whether agreements of this kind should be validated and enforced by the legal system.

This type of analysis is close to that offered by H. L. A. Hart in his earliest work.[39] I would only note that this type of analysis does not require that one go as far as some have read Hart's article as having done, that is, to see legal terms as *only* being performative utterances. There is conceptual room in the analysis to see terms as also being (at least in part) descriptions (or interpretations) of past legal actions. (Wittgenstein often warned against 'one of the great sources of philosophical bewilderment: a substantive makes us look for a thing that corresponds to it.')[40] The agreement underlying substantive disagreement need not be a

[39] See H. L. A. Hart, 'The Ascription of Responsibility and Rights', 49 *Proceedings of the Aristotelian Society* 171 (1948–9).

[40] L. Wittgenstein, *The Blue and Brown Books*, 2nd edn., 1(New York: Harper Torchbooks, 1972).

thing to be described; it can be a question of how people should act or of what should be done.

Regarding my second set of responses to Moore, his criticism of a conventionalist approach to 'death' depends on whether the greater ability to revive patients in certain circumstances has changed the meaning of the term 'death'. Moore, the metaphysical realist, does not think so, but I do not see why someone who was not a metaphysical realist would think so either. The disagreement between the legislators of a hundred years ago and those of today is not regarding what death is, but when (by what criteria) one could be certain that life has ended.

Moore complicated matters by focusing not on death *qua* property of an entity that once was alive but is not now, but rather on death as an event, as the moment of transition between an entity's living and non-living state.[41] One problem this focus leaves Moore is how to describe those people whose heart has stopped, who could still be revived, but if resuscitation techniques are not applied quickly will become unable-to-be-revived. Is such a person alive during this 'transition period', even though none of the normal signs of life (for example, breathing and pulse) are present? Moore might say that the person is still alive (or, at least, 'not dead'), because resuscitation is still possible; death—the event—occurs at the point when resuscitation is *no longer possible*. However, if the final conclusion is that 'death (the event) occurs at the point where resuscitation is no longer possible', there is no reason why 'conventionalists' past or present would ever have disagreed; nor need they believe that because that dividing line has changed with medical progress the meaning (or even the definition) of 'death' has changed.

The discovery that some cessations of breathing are only short-term or are reversible is nothing more or less than that. There is a flexibility to language and to meaning which allows it to adopt to minor changes in circumstances without forcing us to come up with wholly new concepts (or to become metaphysical realists). We are allowed to judge whether a slight increase in revivability changes the concept of 'death' (either as event or as state of being).[42] We

[41] See e.g. Moore, 'A Natural Law Theory of Interpretation', 294: ' "death" refers to a natural kind *of event* that occurs in the world' (emphasis added).

[42] At the least, we seem to have added the concept 'clinically dead' for those whose breathing stops but who are later revived.

have not yet concluded that the concept has changed (or needs to be changed), but we might well judge differently in the future if we discover (for example) that people could be revived after having been frozen for a hundred years, or that bodily functions could be maintained indefinitely after all brain functioning had ceased permanently.

CHANGING BELIEFS AND CHANGED CONCEPTS

Moore insisted that 'conventionalism' could not justify such flexibility in the use of language, that under approaches other than metaphysical realism any modification in criteria must constitute a change in the concept. Though there may be theorists who believe that the only alternative to Platonism about meanings is equating a term rigidly with certain sufficient and necessary conditions, this is certainly not true for most theorists in the literature, and specifically not true of the later Wittgenstein.[43]

In his discussions of family resemblance, ostensive definitions, and rule-following, Wittgenstein emphasized that how we apply terms depends as much on judgements—common, shared judgements that can be traced to a common 'form of life'—as it does on reference to set criteria[44] or paradigms.[45] For example even though scientific beliefs about these concepts have changed in the last hundred years, a Wittgensteinian need not say that 'momentum' or 'simultaneity' either refers to something different or has a different meaning now than it did before Einstein's work caused us to rethink those notions. In Hilary Putnam's words, it is a matter of recognizing that a word can have a new sense (and new applications) without having a new meaning, and it all depends on people (whether scientists or laymen) 'knowing how to go on'.[46]

[43] See e.g. Wittgenstein, *Philosophical Investigations*, secs. 65–88; Baker and Hacker, *Wittgenstein: Understanding and Meaning*, 315–450.

[44] As Stephen Mulhall has pointed out to me, one should not overstate the distinction between judgements and criteria, as judgements ultimately refer to or are grounded in criteria.

[45] See Wittgenstein, *Philosophical Investigations*, secs. 65–74, 208–9, 212–17, 224–7; Baker and Hacker, *Wittgenstein: Understanding and Meaning*, 178–84, 320–43; and *Wittgenstein: Rules, Grammar and Necessity*, 165–81.

[46] See H. Putnam, 'Experience and Mathematical Necessity', 19 (unpublished manuscript); S. Cavell, *The Claim of Reason*, 120–2 (New York: Oxford University Press, 1979).

Whether a particular novel set of circumstances is sufficiently similar to other events we have called 'death' to also carry that label is like the decision whether a particular activity is sufficiently similar to other activities we know as 'games' to be called a game.[47] As we saw in Chapter 2, these decisions cannot be ascribed to Platonic entities or described as arbitrary choices. They come from people reacting in a certain way, 'doing what comes naturally'.

The starting-point for analysis is that in the contexts of changing beliefs over time or disagreement in beliefs between persons at a particular time, we often assume that, believe that, or act as if the subject of the changing beliefs or the disagreement in beliefs was constant. For example, we do not think that we are speaking about something different from what our eighteenth-century forebears spoke of when we talk about 'gravity', even though our beliefs about gravity differ sharply from theirs. Moore argued that this underlying assumption entails metaphysical realism, and that the 'constant subject' that anchors changing beliefs must be a Platonic entity.

I do not agree. First, because of the complex nature of many concepts, a significant change or divergence in beliefs about an object or change in application of a term can occur without there being any change or divergence in the meaning(s) of that term.[48] For example, we might agree about the definition of a term, but disagree about—have differing judgements regarding—how to apply the relevant criteria; the term may be a 'family resemblance' concept (as discussed elsewhere in this chapter); or there may be uncertainties in applying a term in a new and unexpected context where the relevant criteria no longer seem to 'hang together' (the problem of 'open texture' discussed in Chapter 1).

Secondly, there is no sharp divide between a change of beliefs about a concept and a change of concepts. The idea of 'same concept' is not itself transparent and self-evident. In much the same way that Wittgenstein argued that the idea of 'the same' could not be analysed separately from the idea of a 'rule',[49] one could argue that the idea of 'same concept' cannot be analysed

[47] See Wittgenstein, *Philosophical Investigations*, secs. 65–77 (discussing 'game' as a family-resemblance concept).

[48] This point is based on comments made to me by Stephen Mulhall.

[49] See Wittgenstein, *Philosophical Investigations*, secs. 208, 224, 225.

separately from the way concepts are actually used (at a particular time as well as over time). We are often willing to describe slightly different objects or slightly different situations as 'the same'. How much leeway there is in the expression 'the same' (that is, how different objects or situations have to be before we feel compelled to describe them as 'different') can thus be seen to be itself responsive to, and reflective of, our usages and practices.

These points might be easier to see in discussions about the nature of 'justice', 'democracy', 'equality', or 'the Christian way of life', than they are in Moore's hypothetical situations involving 'death'. In political and moral discourse, it is equally hard to show either that the disputants are definitely talking about the same thing or that they are definitely *not* talking about the same thing (for example, when they disagree about the nature of 'justice' or 'democracy').[50] As discussed in Chapter 2, attempts to find an agreement about an entity or a paradigm which underlies the disagreement often come up empty. At the same time, we do not then immediately conclude that the disagreement was based only on a misunderstanding.

As the line between change in beliefs and change in concepts in many areas seems to blur upon close inspection, one can be sceptical about the ability to use substantive disagreement as a base for proving (or disproving) metaphysical realism.

WITTGENSTEIN'S CRITIQUE OF METAPHYSICAL REALISM

In earlier sections, I argued that Moore overstated the difficulties of approaches to language and meaning other than metaphysical realism. In this section, I will suggest that he has also overstated the strengths of metaphysical realism. The argument will proceed by summarizing and adapting Ludwig Wittgenstein's criticism of one form of metaphysical realism about meaning.[51]

The metaphysical realist Wittgenstein takes as his interlocutor

[50] A matter which may have been (indirectly) shown by W. B. Gallie's and Ronald Dworkin's discussions about substantive disagreement, discussions summarized in Chap. 2.

[51] My discussion of Wittgenstein's critique follows Pears, *The False Prison*, ii. chaps. 16–18; see also D. Pears, 'Rule-Following in *Philosophical Investigations*', in *Wittgenstein in Focus*, 249–61 (B. McGuinness and R. Haller, eds., Amsterdam: Rodopi, 1989).

claims that the meaning of terms exists out in the world somehow, and our minds are able to grasp the meaning in some way. Understanding a term's meaning is thus equivalent to grasping the Platonic entity, which in turn somehow guides our application of the term in a potentially infinite number of circumstances.

The metaphysical realist is looking for something *in the world* which determines what the meanings of particular terms are and how those terms should be applied. Placing meanings out in the world seems to solve many problems: meaning is now constant even in the face of scientific progress or lack of consensus; and evaluations of correctness of meaning and correctness in application seem to be independent of people's beliefs about the object.

Wittgenstein offered the following image for the idea that the rule for applying a term already exists in the world:

> we might imagine rails instead of a rule. And infinitely long rails correspond to the unlimited application of a rule.
>
> . . . I no longer have any choice. The rule, once stamped with a particular meaning, traces the lines along which it is to be followed through the whole of space.[52]

Wittgenstein then added: 'But if something of this sort really were the case, how would it help?'[53]

Having meanings 'in the world' would only help us if there were some way for us to have cognition of, to grasp somehow, those meanings. 'Rails laid out to infinity would be useless unless the traveller were locked on to them, and, similarly, complete guidance by rules already laid down in reality would be useless unless there were something in the rule-follower's mind that latched him on to them infallibly.'[54]

Even if our minds did internalize some magic image or formula that was said to contain somehow all the applications of a term, it would not be enough. For that image or formula would still need to be interpreted.[55] Images (and the related ostensive definitions), like rule-formulations, are not self-interpreting. Their connections to objects, to actual applications, are explained by the way people

[52] Wittgenstein, *Philosophical Investigations*, secs. 218–19.
[53] Ibid., sec. 219.
[54] Pears, *The False Prison*, ii. 466.
[55] See Wittgenstein, *Philosophical Investigations*, secs. 139–41; Pears, *The False Prison*, ii. 469–73.

act and react. The place of natural reactions is illustrated in the following passage from Wittgenstein's lectures:

For instance: you say to someone 'This is red' (pointing); then you tell him 'Fetch me a red book'—and he will behave in a particular way. This is an immensely important fact about us human beings . . .

Another such fact is that pointing is used and understood in a particular way—that people react to it in a particular way.

If you have learned a technique of language, and I point to this coat and say to you, 'The tailors now call this colour "Boo" ' then you will buy me a coat of this colour . . . The point is that one only has to point to something and say, 'This is so-and-so', and everyone who has been through a certain preliminary training will react in the same way.[56]

Metaphysical realism of the full-blooded type (with meanings equated with Platonic entities) is thus shown not to help—indeed, not to affect—the language-user. Even if we posit the existence of these strange Platonic entities, meaning and usage still come down to human judgements and human reactions, not to abstract entities. Moore seemed to avoid Wittgenstein's criticisms by joining his metaphysical realist ontology with a coherence epistemology,[57] but he can do so only at the cost of removing the significance of his approach. Once one rejects the claim that we have some direct cognition of the 'real', the advantage of metaphysical realism—in explaining how we actually behave or in prescribing how we should approach problems of meaning—seems to disappear. If what we are to seek are beliefs that fit in well with our other beliefs and observations, and our sole criterion for accepting a belief is its fit with our other beliefs and observations, then the Platonist notions about truth and meaning are empty concepts that do no work. If a theorist writes about judges searching for 'the best scientific theory of what death *really* is like' or 'what vehicles *really* are', the implied reference to 'reality' and '[metaphysical] realism' does not affect what the judge should do or think; the term 'real' here is a disconnected wheel in the machinery: it spins but it does no work.[58]

[56] L. Wittgenstein, *Wittgenstein's Lectures on the Foundations of Mathematics*, 182 (C. Diamond, ed., Sussex: Harvester Press, 1976).

[57] See Moore, 'A Natural Law Theory of Interpretation', 312, and 'Precedent, Induction, and Ethical Generalization', 197–8.

[58] See D. Patterson, 'What Was Realism?', 2 *Canadian Journal of Law and Jurisprudence* 193, 194–5 (1989) (discussing Brink); S. Fish, 'Dennis Martinez and the Uses of Theory', 96 *Yale Law Journal* 1773, 1782–5 (1987) (discussing Moore).

MOORE'S PROJECT: A SECOND LOOK

Perhaps Moore's metaphysical realism is *not supposed* to help us. It is not always clear from Moore's articles how he saw his project, whether as reform or as merely revisionist description. On the one hand, he was emphatic that beliefs regarding metaphysical realism make a difference, in the sense that whatever position one takes on metaphysical matters, he claimed, has an effect on practical matters:

> I aim . . . to rescue the [metaphysical] debate . . . from the criticisms of those who proclaim it either meaningless or irrelevant to any practical concern . . . The metaphysical debate over realism is both meaningful and relevant to practical concerns, in law as elsewhere.[59]

More specifically, he argued that metaphysical realist views will 'lead [the believer] to practice law in quite a distinctive way':[60] interpreting statutes, applying precedents, interpreting the United States Constitution, and even doing legal theory in a way different from the way a 'conventionalist' would.[61]

Regarding my chosen focus, metaphysical realism about meanings,[62] Moore was clear that adherence to it would entail a change of practice and would lead to changes in the outcome of cases:

> Judges should guide their judgments about the ordinary meanings of words by the real nature of the things to which the words refer and not by the conventions governing the ordinary usage of those words.[63]

> [J]udges should use the realist theory of meaning [rather than a 'conventionalist' theory] whenever the ordinary meaning of a legal text is relevant.[64]

> [T]he realist theory of meaning also seems likely to produce better results in the long run [than a 'conventionalist' approach would].[65]

[59] Moore, 'The Interpretive Turn in Modern Theory', 873.

[60] Ibid. 883.

[61] Ibid. 882–8.

[62] As in other discussions in this chapter, I am bypassing questions about the realism–anti-realism debate regarding other areas of discourse. Moore had a great deal to say, for example, about a metaphysically realist approach to morality and moral terms, and how that approach might (or might not) require a change in how judges decide cases. However, such questions are beyond the scope of my project.

[63] Moore, 'A Natural Law Theory of Interpretation', 287.

[64] Ibid. 301.

[65] Ibid. 325.

Against this theme of 'mend your ways', and 'seek truth, not error'—the idea that changing our beliefs to conform to metaphysical realism will lead to a change in practice—there are also times when Moore's articles seem to follow a different theme, as though all Moore was trying to do was to inform us that we were *already* metaphysical realists: no change in practice is necessary. Like the character who was surprised to learn that he had been 'speaking prose all along', all of the purported 'conventionalists' will be surprised to learn that they have been metaphysical realists all along:

> The respective legislatures using the word 'death' in the above statutes should be held to have the same linguistic intentions as other language users, namely, realist ones.[66]

> [Most people] fairly expect their courts to give 'death' the meaning they themselves would give it: as the name of a natural kind of event about which we can learn all sorts of surprising facts without changing the meaning of the word at all.[67]

> [O]ur interpretive practices reveal us to be . . . metaphysical realists . . . [T]he way we use language in both ordinary speech and in statutes presupposes a realist metaphysics about the hidden nature of natural kinds.[68]

Finally, there is a third theme: that while reforming one's actions and thoughts to Moore's requirements would get one the right answer, it might be that one would be as likely to get there by a different path, perhaps even by intuition.[69] Moore wrote that his thesis aimed 'at telling us what is the correct interpretation of a legal text, not what psychological steps judges should go through to reach it'.[70]

This is all rather confusing, and probably not entirely consistent. And there is, after all, something strange, something paradoxical, about the whole project. Moore purported to tell us how to understand language, though his project was not the same as the usual theme of such articles, that there is some *special way* in which *legal* texts should be understood and interpreted (for example, always to view enactments in the light of the problems to which they were responding, to treat judgments as if they were

[66] Moore, 'A Natural Law Theory of Interpretation', 323. [67] Ibid. 324.
[68] Ibid. 397. [69] Ibid. 396, n. 218. [70] Ibid.

part of chain novels, or to remember that 'it is a *constitution* we are interpreting'). Moore's prescription was (primarily) not of that form: in fact, he often emphasized how the interpretation of legal texts should *not* differ from that of ordinary texts.[71] However, surely we understand normal words and sentences (in our own language) well enough, and if we sometimes need assistance, it would be from a dictionary, not a philosophical treatise.

I would venture that Moore's work took this possible response into account, implicitly if not explicitly. It is what accounts for the theme of non-reform—revisionary description—in the articles. What remains to be explained then are the prescriptive elements of the articles. One possible explanation for the prescriptive elements is the view, which sometimes surfaced in the articles, that judges, though metaphysical realists in 'real life' like the rest of us, are as a group under the delusion that they should follow awkward conventionalist theories when they interpret statutes.[72] Another possible explanation: Moore's arguments had a prescriptive force for those occasions when we (as interpreters and appliers of norms) have to choose between speakers' meaning and words' meaning, and when we have to decide how to treat either after the passage of time (for example how to treat a rule-maker's comments about entities if popular or expert opinion about those entities has since changed). While these are difficult questions of policy, the notion that a philosophical theory about meaning could settle the matter does not seem tenable.

Moore tried to transform difficult questions of authority and interpretation into a more direct question about semantic content, removing the whole question of speaker's intent by reducing it to a simple function of semantic content. He sought to prevent the chasm between speakers' meaning and words' meaning from coming about by talking about speakers' 'linguistic intentions' for how their words should be understood, and then positing that everyone's 'linguistic intentions' were (a priori?) the same.[73] However, all of this analysis seems powerless to make the chasm disappear: for example, when due to my ignorance of botany I say 'lady's slipper' when I wish to refer to tulips, I would still want to

[71] See e.g. ibid. 323 ('legislatures . . . should be held to have the same linguistic intentions as other users').

[72] See e.g. ibid. 326, n. 86, 333–6, 353–8.

[73] See ibid. 323–4.

be understood as referring to tulips, even though the reference of the term 'lady's slipper' itself is different. Our 'linguistic intentions' are often to be understood according to what we meant, even when this seems to disagree with what we said. With authority subsumed by semantic content in Moore's analysis, it was then open to him to claim that a term within a rule should be interpreted as being equivalent to our best current theory about the entity named. For reasons discussed in the last chapter as well as in this one, it should be clear that the independent claim of authority in law (and the problems it poses for judicial interpretation) cannot be so easily overcome.

Perhaps the reason why it is so unclear whether Moore's metaphysically realist positions are supposed to make a difference is that the whole theoretical machinery worked largely as a diversion or a disguise. The theory was there as an excuse to focus on semantic content and to discount or ignore authoritative intentions.

TWO ADDITIONAL CRITICISMS

Before going on to other topics, I want to mention briefly two criticisms that have been made of Moore's work. First, Frederick Schauer has recently argued that Moore's writings should be understood as having been not so much about meaning or metaphysics as about rule application. In applying a nineteenth-century statute which contained the words 'death' or 'vehicle', Schauer argued, the decision to interpret those words in terms of our current understanding of them rather than the drafters' understanding is simply a choice to interpret the rule according to its purpose rather than according to the meaning of a rule-formulation.[74] Throughout his book, Schauer referred to this as particularistic decision-making, as contrasted with rule-based decision-making. The rule-based approach, accepting the drafters' notions about what the words meant, may lead to some absurd or sub-optimal results, as is the case with all rule-based decision-making (consider the usual hypothetical example: the statues, emergency vehicles, and cleaning vehicles that seem to be within

[74] Schauer, *Playing by the Rules*, 215–18.

the scope of the rule 'no vehicles in the park'). However, there are here, as elsewhere, all the benefits of staying with rule-based decision-making: predictability, stability, separation of powers, and so on. The 'metaphysically realist' approach thus may be better as a matter of policy, but should not be seen as required as a matter of the nature of language or the nature of rules.[75]

At one point, Moore briefly considered and brushed aside an argument similar to Schauer's. He described a 'conventionalist' arguing that a judge would not allow the removal of organs from a patient who was revivable (but 'dead' by the criteria of an old authorizing statute) 'because all judges check ordinary meaning against the *purpose* of a rule'. However, Moore argued, this would require 'us[ing] a realist notion of death in formulating the purpose behind the rule'.[76] At best, this takes the argument too quickly.

A judge in the above hypothetical situation could argue as follows: at the time the statute was enacted, the rule-makers thought that 'death' (the event) was a simple boundary between life and 'death' (the state of being). Now we know that some patients go through not one, but two 'events' before they are dead: first, a point at which most bodily functions cease, but the patient could still (in principle) be revived; and second, the point at which the patient could no longer be revived. Whether we call the first event 'death' (as in the original statute) or 'clinical death' or something else, it would clearly be contrary to the purpose of the original enactment to allow organ removals before the second event (non-revivability) is reached. Contrary to Moore, this account does not require a metaphysically realist view of 'death' (the event), and as there has been no change in beliefs about 'death' (the state of being), the question of metaphysical realism about that term does not arise.

Whatever the merits of Schauer's argument as a reading of Moore, it hinted at a basic problem with many recent articles on law and interpretation (and law and rhetoric, law and hermeneutics, and law and Wittgenstein). The question of how judges should decide cases cannot be conclusively decided—it probably cannot be more than slightly furthered—by a (new and better) theory about meaning or understanding. All the important

[75] See ibid.

[76] Moore, 'A Natural Law Theory of Interpretation', 328.

questions require a political theory about the appropriate relationships among the rule-makers, the rule-interpreters, and the general public.

This conclusion is supported by the way the same judicial action can be characterized in many different ways. For example, the refusal to allow an outdated statute to justify the removal of organs (for transfer) from a patient who could still be revived could be seen as following the (metaphysically) real meaning of 'death' rather than the legislative definition, or as the judge refusing to follow the plain meaning of the statute because it would create an extremely unjust or absurd result, or as interpreting the rule's words in terms of the rule's purpose, or as applying the statute in a way which reflects how the rule-makers would have reacted to the situation had they known about it. Also one's political theory might value above all other things either (1) that a rule's interpretation should be consistent with the general public's understanding of the rule, or (2) that the rule-maker's wishes should be followed. In either case, it would be appropriate to follow the general public/rule-maker's understanding of what a particular term in the rule-formulation meant (in terms of the distinction made earlier, what they did mean/would have meant in using the term), even if that understanding was wrong or misguided according to one's philosophical (and scientific) theories regarding what the term 'actually' means.

(I do not claim that the authors discussed in this section would necessarily disagree with my position. To the contrary, I think their articles tend to support (explicitly or implicitly) what I am saying. For example, Brink explicitly stated that a proper semantic theory is only one part of a theory of legal interpretation and that the 'semantic content' of a statute might be bypassed if it was clear that the rule-makers meant something else by those words.)[77]

The second criticism was that Moore's arguments sometimes seemed to confuse causes with effects, or at least labels with explanations. In one place, he wrote that the legal term 'malice' is a 'functional kind' whose nature is 'whatever makes one properly liable for the punishment fixed for murder' (defined as a killing performed with malice).[78] In discussing the idea of right answers to

[77] D. Brink, 'Semantics and Legal Interpretation (Further Thoughts)', 2 *Canadian Journal of Law and Jurisprudence* 181, 186–7 (1989).

[78] Moore, 'The Interpretive Turn in Modern Theory', 886, 884.

legal problems, he wrote that for a metaphysical realist, 'an answer is right when it corresponds to a complex moral fact (which in law includes the institutional facts that further moral facts make important)',[79] which seems to translate to nothing more than saying that the 'right answer' is what a judge gets after properly applying the appropriate standards and balancing techniques. As with the 'functional kind' 'malice', the metaphysical entity posited ('a complex moral fact') does not guide the reasoning process, it merely decorates it. (Ronald Dworkin's discussions of 'right answers' may be subject to a similar criticism, but Dworkin was less insistent that ideas of the kind proposed by his theory about 'right answers', by themselves, were either guiding judges in their actions or explaining those actions after the fact.)

SUMMARY OF BRINK'S POSITION

> If, say a chicken began to lay perfectly ordinary walnuts which were planted and grew into walnut trees, I would not wish to refer to this result as the production of a grove of chickens.[80]

There are many parallels between the writings of Michael Moore and those of David Brink, though it is hard to find reference to either in the other's work. Moore has written extensively in law journals, his primary theme often being the defence and application of metaphysical realism. Brink has written primarily in philosophy journals, where he has defended his own version of metaphysical realism,[81] but he has also written a handful of articles about legal theory and law. His articles about law have not directly promoted a metaphysical realist approach, but have centred on an approach to reference and meaning which is often associated with metaphysical realism.[82] (I will consider this connection later in this chapter.) Finally, his criticism of legal positivism as having been

[79] Moore, 'Metaphysics, Epistemology and Legal Theory', 480.

[80] J. Dupré, 'Natural Kinds and Biological Taxa', 90 *Philosophical Review* 66, 88 (1981).

[83] See D. Brink, *Moral Realism and the Foundations of Ethics* (Cambridge: Cambridge University Press, 1989).

[82] See D. Brink, 'Legal Theory, Legal Interpretation, and Judicial Review', 17 *Philosophy and Public Affairs* 105 (1988); 'Semantics and Legal Interpretation (Further Thoughts)'.

based on 'empiricist' semantics is analogous to Moore's criticism of legal positivism as having been based on 'conventionalism'.

Brink began by arguing that every legal theory explicitly or implicitly relies on a semantic theory, and that the theory upon which most forms of legal positivism rely is wrong.[83] He characterized legal positivism as basing the argument for judicial discretion on the open texture of general terms, which in turn was based on a semantic theory which tied a term's meaning and reference to the properties speakers associated with the term.[84] According to Brink's characterization of legal positivism, if people with legal training disagree about the application of a term to a particular case, then the term's meaning and reference are uncertain in that area and a judge must use discretion in deciding whether the term (and its statute) should apply.[85]

As Brink argued, there are at least two (related) problems with this semantic theory. First, it has trouble explaining disagreement: if two people have different ideas about 'mass' or about 'due process', the theory would be forced to conclude that these people were in fact talking about different things.[86] Secondly, the theory cannot distinguish changes in belief from changes in subject-matter: that someone's (or some community's) beliefs about 'gold' or about 'cruelty' can change without the object of those beliefs being different.[87]

As an alternative semantic theory, Brink proffered one which asserts that 'the way the world is', rather than our own beliefs, determines the reference of our words.[88] He argued that a correct theory of semantics would show that meaning—or at least reference—does not depend on users' beliefs about the term, but only on the properties of the object or class of objects to which the term corresponds. Since mere disagreement would no longer justify judicial discretion, he argued, the level of legal indeterminacy would be much smaller if one followed a legal theory based on a correct semantic theory.[89] Our beliefs about particular objects could be mistaken, though the beliefs of authorities and experts will be 'our best evidence about what the nature of these referents is'.[90] The fact that disagreement would continue means

[83] Brink, 'Legal Theory, Legal Interpretation, and Judicial Review', 111–16.
[84] Ibid. 112–13.
[85] Ibid. 112.
[86] Ibid. 114–16.
[87] Ibid. 115–16.
[88] Ibid. 117.
[89] See ibid. 120–1.
[90] Ibid.

only that there was a risk that judges would occasionally get the matter wrong; it would not justify judges choosing as they liked, assured that any choice they made would be acceptable. A semantic theory of this kind has no difficulty dealing with disagreements about the meaning of words or with the evolution of a term's meaning over time.[91] Our disagreement with our colleagues (and our forebears) about what constitutes 'due process' or 'cruel punishment' does not come about because we and they are (were) talking about different things, but because we disagree about the ('real') 'nature' of the matter in question, and (at least) one of us is (was) wrong about that nature.[92]

Brink does allow for one type of situation where judicial discretion would be required: where there is agreement about what criteria should be used to determine whether a term applies, but there is disagreement in the application of the criteria to a particular case.[93] He gives the example of whether an extremely dark charcoal shade should be considered grey or black. He called such cases 'borderline' or 'fuzzy' cases, though they are far closer to Dworkin's idea of 'weak discretion' ('the standards an official must apply cannot be applied mechanically but demand the use of judgment') than they are to Hart's ideas about discretion in borderline cases.[94]

Brink was careful in his claims about and for his alternative semantic theory. First, the theory was said to be derived from the writings of Saul Kripke and Hilary Putnam, but not identical to those writers' theories.[95] Secondly, he allowed that other semantic theories, perhaps even certain forms of empiricist semantics, might be able to meet his criteria for a proper semantic theory.[96] Thirdly, he allowed that his semantic theory (and the theories of Kripke and Putnam) probably did not entail metaphysical realism.[97]

[91] Ibid. 116–19.

[92] cf. Dworkin, *Law's Empire*, 11–44 (on the nature of disagreements in law).

[93] Brink, 'Semantics and Legal Interpretation', 189.

[94] cf. ibid. with Dworkin, *Taking Rights Seriously*, 31–2, and with Hart, *The Concept of Law*, 123–6.

[95] Brink, 'Legal Theory, Legal Interpretation, and Judicial Review', 117–19 and nn. 17–18.

[96] Ibid. 118–19 and n. 19; Brink, 'Semantics and Legal Interpretation', 182, 185.

[97] 'Semantics and Legal Interpretation', 182–5.

CRITICISM OF BRINK

The major problem with Brink's argument is that it attacked a non-existent adversary. No legal theorist I know advocated either the view of semantics or the view of judicial discretion Brink described. The theorist he used as an example, H. L. A. Hart,[98] had a very different view, as I discussed in detail in Chapter 1. In brief, for Hart, judges have discretion in part because rules embody choices made relative to particular situations and circumstances; when the rule must be applied to other situations and circumstances, a fresh choice must be made. This model has its own difficulties, but they are not those described by Brink.

Brink's approach would not help us if we believed that judicial interpretation was largely a matter of implementing (or being 'guided by') the choices made by people in authority. That we now use certain words differently from the way the rule-makers did is interesting, but why should it be relevant to implementing the earlier choices?[99] Brink's response might be that the rule-makers first and foremost wanted to refer to a type or group, and if we now know more about the boundaries and the nature of that type or group, the rule-makers would have wanted the implementation of their choices to take that additional knowledge into consideration.[100]

Brink does not deny, however, that a rule-maker's 'specific intent' may diverge over time with the 'semantic content' of the rule, or that sometimes the former should override the latter in implementing the rule.[101] In fact, it appears that Brink has solved little—other than the rebuttal of a position that no one claimed to hold. At the end of his primary discussion of interpretation, he casually admitted that 'meaning and purpose can conflict, and this gives rise to certain interpretive difficulties'.[102] We have not travelled very far at all from Hart's picture of rule-application and judicial discretion in *The Concept of Law*.

[98] Brink described his argument as being against the view given in Hart's *The Concept of Law*: e.g. Brink, 'Legal Theory, Legal Interpretation, and Judicial Review', 106–7. However, at times, he was less sure that his characterization fitted that text. See Brink, 'Semantics and Legal Interpretation', 189, n. 8.

[99] See Alexander, 'Of Two Minds about Law and Minds', 2446–7.

[100] See Brink, 'Legal Theory, Legal Interpretation, and Judicial Review', 121–4.

[101] See ibid. 122–9; Brink, 'Semantics and Legal Interpretation', 186–8.

[102] Brink, 'Legal Theory, Legal Interpretation, and Judicial Review', 128–9.

A similar point could be made about Moore's approach. Even if one agreed that judicial practices should be reformed in line with Moore's suggestions and one allowed that metaphysical realism requires us to change radically our ideas about meaning in some cases, it still might be the case that adopting Moore's metaphysically realist programme would not substantially change the results the courts reach. His prescribed four-step interpretative scheme for judges was as follows: (1) determine the ordinary meaning of the text; (2) determine 'what interpretation is suggested' by precedent; (3) 'check' ordinary meaning and precedent against 'what the judge takes to be the purpose of the provision'; and (4) 'check' ordinary meaning, precedent, and purpose against 'an "all things considered" value judgment about the best result in this case'.[103]

Moore considered but then rejected the idea that his approach to meaning and morality would entail giving precedent no weight. 'Even a [metaphysical] realist, who thinks that all interpretation should aim at describing the nature of the moral natural quality named by legal texts, can and should admit that the rule of law virtues are real values too and that, accordingly, how prior courts have decided like cases has some moral force behind it.'[104] According to Moore, how much moral force a precedent will have will vary among different areas of law, for predictability and reliance are more important in some areas of law (for example, criminal law) than in others.[105]

Thus, for a Moorean judge, in common-law cases as well as in statutory interpretation cases, the lessons of metaphysical realism must often yield to, or at least be modified by, consistency with past decisions. Moore recognized that within a legal system, the value of getting the meaning of the words right is often balanced against values of consistency, acceptability, and justice. The fact that a judge with proper metaphysically realist credentials would interpret (understand) a sentence one way under normal circumstances does not indicate that this judge would (or should) interpret that sentence the same way if the sentence was part of a legal rule the judge was applying. Within Moore's own suggestions about judicial reasoning, metaphysical realism about meanings is

[103] Moore, 'A Natural Law Theory of Interpretation', 376.
[104] Ibid. 372.
[105] Ibid. 363.

only one factor among many in determining how *this* statute should be applied to *this particular* fact situation.

THE KRIPKE–PUTNAM THEORY OF REFERENCE

> On those remote pages [of a certain Chinese encyclopedia] it is written that animals are divided into (a) those that belong to the emperor, (b) embalmed ones, (c) those that are trained, (d) suckling pigs, (e) mermaids, (f) fabulous ones, (g) stray dogs, (h) those that are included in this classification, (i) those that tremble as if they were mad, (j) innumerable ones, (k) those drawn with a very fine camel's-hair brush, (l) others, (m) those that have just broken a flower vase, (n) those that resemble flies from a distance.[106]

In the remaining sections of this chapter, I want to consider the Kripke/Putnam approach to semantics and reference more closely (considering general applications as well as possible applications to law and legal theory), in order to see whether that approach entails (or is entailed by) metaphysical realism, as Moore believed,[107] or whether it is compatible with other views (in particular, whether it is compatible with a Wittgensteinian view). I want to explore, if briefly, not only the arguments put forward, but also the 'status' of those arguments: for example, to what extent the claims are conceptual or metaphysical.

Putnam's argument had been that meanings were not in the mind.[108] What a person means by a word is not some summation of that person's beliefs about the term, or even some consensus within the community about the term. Within an analysis of meaning, according to Putnam, the use of a term acts primarily as a pointing, an act of ostension. 'What I mean by "water" is the group/category/kind of thing of which that [pointing to a liquid] is a member.'[109] It may then be left to others in the community to

[106] J. L. Borges, 'The Analytical Language of John Wilkins', in *Borges: A Reader*, 142 (E. R. Monegal and A. Reid, eds., New York: E. P. Dutton, 1981).

[107] See Moore, 'A Natural Law Theory of Interpretation', 292, n. 25; see also Moore, 'The Interpretive Turn in Modern Theory', 876. As I noted earlier, Brink did not claim a necessary (logical) connection between a Kripke/Putnam approach and metaphysical realism.

[108] See H. Putnam, 'The Meaning of "Meaning" ', 227.

[109] See P. Pettit and J. McDowell, 'Introduction', in *Subject, Thought, and Context* 4 (P. Pettit and J. McDowell, eds., Oxford: Clarendon Press, 1986).

discover (and then report) the nature of that kind. The ostension, the connection of this term with that natural kind, is done by the community. Any particular individual within the community could of course be mistaken as to which liquid 'water' was meant to refer to.

We associate a word with an object, and by that word we mean to refer to that object and all other objects of the same nature.[110] To say that objects are of the same nature is to say that they 'have the same composition, or obey the same rules—indeed, what makes composition important, when it is, is its connection with laws of behavior'.[111]

Putnam's purpose had been to attack a theory of meaning which stated: (1) knowing the meaning of a term consists of having a particular psychological state, and (2) meaning, in the sense of intension, determines a term's extension.[112] In particular, he wanted to emphasize the contribution of society and the contribution of the real world to both the intension and the extension of a term. The contribution of society derives from the linguistic division of labour, the contribution of the world from the idea of natural kinds.[113]

After arguing that one could not defend the notion that 'meanings were in the head' or that a term's intension determines its extension, Putnam went on to offer an alternative analysis of 'meaning', which centred on the term's extension, but which included other elements.[114] I believe this part of Putnam's article should be seen as having a different status from the earlier part (the claims about reference and about the linguistic division of labour), that it should be seen as an optional recommendation rather than a proven conclusion. It is open to someone to agree with Putnam that a term's intension does not determine its extension, yet still believe that meaning should be equated with intension.[115] As long as one is consistent, it would seem that what aspect(s) of language and language use one delimits as 'meaning' is

[110] See H. Putnam, 'Reference and Truth', in *Realism and Reason*, 71 (Cambridge: Cambridge University Press, 1983).

[111] Ibid. 74.

[112] Putnam, 'The Meaning of "Meaning" ', 215–19.

[113] See ibid. 223–47.

[114] Ibid. 269.

[115] See Brink, 'Legal Theory, Legal Interpretation, and Judicial Review', 117; Katz, *The Metaphysics of Meaning*, 216–24.

a matter of stipulation, though this stipulation should be explained or justified.

There is some doubt about the status of even the core elements of Putnam's article. For example, when Putnam argued that a substance in an alternative world which had the same properties as water but a different composition would not be part of the extension of 'water', is he making a conceptual point about language, reference, or meaning, or is he merely describing a contingent truth about our intuitions and our choices in moments of linguistic uncertainty?[116] (A Wittgensteinian might argue that the former type of claims always reduce to or are functions of the latter.) The question is what Putnam (or Kripke or any other theorist who takes a similar position) would say to someone who disagreed with their claims, for example, with the claim that the alternative substance that has all the properties of water but a different chemical composition should not be called 'water'.[117] What would it mean to say that Putnam's position is right and his interlocutor is wrong?

Another example comes from Jerrold Katz. He referred to Putnam's hypothetical example, where we discover that all cats are in fact Martian robots, an example that allegedly challenges equating the meaning of 'cats' with the 'belief' that 'cats are feline animals'.[118] Katz asked why we would not conclude in these circumstances that 'there were no such things as "cats" after all', rather than 'cats have a different nature than we at first thought' (just as we conclude that 'there were no such things as "witches",' rather than that 'witches have different properties than the people in the sixteenth century thought they had').[119]

The Wittgensteinian approach offers its particular analysis of meaning because, within its approach to language in general, meaning is part of an interlocking complex of training, understanding, and use:

[116] See Dupré, 'Natural Kinds and Biological Taxa', 70–1.

[117] See ibid.; Katz, *The Metaphysics of Meaning*, 225–6.

[118] H. Putnam, 'It Ain't Necessarily So', in *Mathematics, Matter and Method*, 237–9 (Cambridge: Cambridge University Press, 1975). Putnam's discussion in that article was directed mostly at the question of analytic versus synthetic statements, but the discussion is consistent with and similar to his later discussions about 'natural kinds' analysis.

[119] Katz, *The Metaphysics of Meaning*, 216–21.

The meaning of an expression is what one understands when one understands the expression. It is what is explained by an explanation of meaning. An explanation of meaning provides a standard or rule for the correct use of an expression. For one's use of a word is correct, makes sense, when it accords with an appropriate explanation of meaning. A person's understanding of an expression is manifest in his use of it (i.e. whether he does use it in accord with the correct explanation) and in his giving correct explanations of it on appropriate occasions. And also, of course, in his responding appropriately to the use of the expression by others.[120]

A similar point was made by Michael Dummett. He wrote that the reason we want (contrary to Putnam's position) to maintain a concept of meaning that is connected with knowledge is that 'precisely what we want a notion of meaning for is to give an account of what knowledge of a language consists in, of what it is that someone knows when he knows a language or knows some word or fragment of a language'.[121] Also, Dummett argued, to tie meaning to reference in the way Putnam did would entail the claim 'that only chemists, jewellers, etc., fully understood the word "gold"; and this claim would be resisted by most English speakers'.[122]

A recent comment by Putnam might be seen as a reply to his critics:

The impossibility of a notion of 'meaning' which agrees at all with our preanalytic intuitions about sameness and difference of meaning *and* which is invariant under belief-fixation dooms the notion to be exactly what it is: a vague but useful way of speaking when (by intuition and by experience) we correlate words and phrases in different languages and discourses.[123]

I believe that one can agree both with Putnam's approach to meaning and the Wittgensteinian approach to meaning, though I am not in a position to demonstrate that (nor am I entirely sure what such a demonstration would look like).[124] However, it is at

[120] Hacker, *Insight and Illusion*, 247–8; cf. Baker and Hacker, *Language, Sense and Nonsense*, 221 n. 19 (the Putnam/Kripke approach 'ignor[es] the internal relations between meanings and explanations of meaning').

[121] M. Dummett, 'The Social Character of Meaning', in *Truth and Other Enigmas*, 420 (London: Duckworth, 1978).

[122] Ibid. 426.

[123] H. Putnam, 'Meaning Holism', in *Realism with a Human Face*, 291 (London: Harvard University Press, 1990).

[124] An argument that may approximate to such a demonstration appeared in Dummett, 'The Social Character of Meaning', 424–30.

least worth remembering that the target of Putnam's attack, semantic theories which see meaning as a state of mind, is quite different from Wittgenstein's approach to meaning (which centred on usage).[125]

Another way to approach the idea of 'natural kinds' is through the related concept of 'the linguistic division of labour'.[126] The notion involves (roughly) the idea that we defer to other persons, as part of our competence in a language, in our understanding of particular terms. For example, part of the nature of gold is its chemical composition and the way it reacts with other chemicals. However, most speakers of the language, though they are (and are said to be) competent users of the language and (are said to) know the meaning of the word 'gold', do not know (amongst other things) these chemical facts. Putnam summarized the linguistic division of labour as follows: 'the fact that confirmation procedures for *being gold* or *being aluminum*, or *being an elm tree*, or *being David* are not the property of every speaker—the speakers defer to experts for the fixing of reference in a huge number of cases.'[127] Simon Blackburn offered the following example: 'As a group we defer to medical authority in defining what does and does not count as arthritis, and [in using the term "arthritis"] I will be held to have said whatever it tells me I said . . . And this is so regardless of my own understanding of what I was doing.'[128]

One can see how Putnam's approach is consistent with a Wittgensteinian (or other non-metaphysically realist) approach to language: as long as the Wittgensteinian allows that for some terms part of understanding the term's meaning involves knowing that under certain circumstances one must defer to the opinions of others (experts), the Wittgensteinian has no reason to reject Putnam's approach (adding only that some criteria for application must remain available to ordinary speakers as well).[129] That it is a scientist in our society who makes the final judgement regarding which one-celled organisms are 'plants' and which are 'animals' or that it is an elder of a certain community who makes the final

[125] Marmor, *Interpretation and Legal Theory*, 144, n. 11.

[226] See Putnam, 'The Meaning of "Meaning" ', 227–9.

[127] H. Putnam, *Meaning and the Moral Sciences*, 114 (London: Routledge & Kegan Paul, 1978).

[128] Blackburn, *Spreading the Word*, 131.

[129] I am grateful to Stephen Mulhall for this point.

judgement regarding whether a particular form of discipline is 'cruel' (and therefore prohibited by that community) does not entail that 'animal' or 'cruel' refer to Platonic entities. This deference within language is, of course, consistent with metaphysical realism, but it is also consistent with a wide range of approaches other than metaphysical realism. Putnam's approach is thus seen as a matter of language use and not (at least not necessarily or primarily) a matter of (metaphysically realist) ontology.

One might object that I am ignoring the point of 'natural kinds' analysis, that part of what a word means is determined by the 'contribution of the world'. The problem with 'the contribution of the world' is that the world does not speak to us directly. The 'contribution of the world' turns out to be, in day-to-day life, deference to what experts (often scientists) tell us about the object. Such experts do not—because they cannot—tell us what the 'real nature' of the object is. All they can tell us is that *relative* to our current conceptual categories and our current (scientific) procedures and practices, this object seems to be a member of this unitary group which appears to have this nature.[130] Deference to experts, though certainly consistent with the belief that 'real natures' of unitary kinds exist independent of us (that is, independent of human attitudes, observations, and needs), is also consistent with a variety of non-metaphysically realist approaches (including Wittgensteinian approaches and Putnam's 'internal realism').

Finally, I think it worth noting that Putnam has come to reject metaphysical realism even while still advocating 'natural kinds' analysis.[131] While it is of course true that it is open to other theorists not only to agree with both 'natural kinds' analysis and metaphysical realism, but also to claim that the first requires or entails the second, I think it at least worth noting that the person who did the most to develop the 'natural kinds' analysis now thinks otherwise (especially in the context of evaluating a theorist like Moore, who is not a specialist in philosophy of language, but only

[130] See H. Putnam, 'Realism with a Human Face', in *Realism with a Human Face*, 3–29.

[131] See ibid; Putnam, 'A Defense of Internal Realism' and 'Is Water Necessarily H_2O?', ibid. 330–42, 54–9, and *Reason, Truth and History*, 22–48 (Cambridge: Cambridge University Press, 1981).

a legal theorist who uses ideas from philosophy of language to promote a certain view of the law).

A FURTHER LOOK AT NATURAL KINDS

The idea of natural kinds has played an important role in the writings of both Moore and Brink. It is used both as an argument against 'conventionalist' or 'empiricist' approaches to language, and as a bridge between the semantic and ontological claims of metaphysical realism. In the articles on law under consideration, the idea of natural kinds is a central part of arguments about why judges should not defer to rule-makers' specific intent or to the terms of statutory definitions.[132] In this section, I will offer a brief critical review of the use of natural-kinds analysis in these articles.

A natural-kind term is one whose extension is answerable to the outside world. The same point can be put in a different way: a natural-kind term refers to a class of objects, where the boundaries of the class are defined by facts which are independent of us. Objects that are members of a particular natural kind share a single essence or nature. The idea that a term's extension is the group of objects which has the same essence, an essence based on 'objective laws' 'fixed by the world',[133] seems strongest when discussing terms which refer to chemical elements or chemical compounds. Our experience in science, and our knowledge of the history of science, lead us to believe that the dividing up of the chemical world is not very vulnerable to ideologies and subjective interests, and that different chemists working at different times under different circumstances are likely to reach similar conclusions (that is, the relevant data seem to be 'objective'). The contrast is not only with topics of study in subjects whose status as 'sciences' is under dispute, like sociology and psychology, but even with some of the 'harder' sciences, like biology. For terms referring to plants and animals, it is actually quite rare for common language to correspond to a non-arbitrary grouping in scientific taxonomy.[134]

[132] See e.g. Moore, 'A Natural Law Theory of Interpretation', 322–58; Brink, 'Legal Theory, Legal Interpretation, and Judicial Review', 120–9.

[133] Putnam, 'Reference and Truth ', 71.

[134] See Dupré, 'Natural Kinds and Biological Taxa', 73–83.

It would be an unobvious, and perhaps unwarranted, extension of the natural-kinds analysis to apply it to human artefacts. What reason do we have to believe that human creations divide up into clear categories in the same way that the objects of chemistry and biology seem to do? Despite the apparent difficulties, in an early article Putnam applied natural-kinds analysis to pencils.[135] Pencils, tables, and other objects of human creation seem less resistant than chemicals or animals to the idea that the term's intension (for example, the criteria thought necessary and sufficient for the term's application) determine the term's extension. Let us say that 'pencil' is defined as 'a thin, cylindrical object, which contains graphite to allow it to make marks on paper or similar substances'. Putnam would then query: 'What would happen if we discovered that all the objects we thought of as pencils turned out to be alive?'[136] The discovery would affect our beliefs about pencils and it might cause us to introduce further terms with different criteria (if not all pencils were living, terms like 'live pencils' and 'inert pencils' might enter the language to label the subcategories), but I do not see how that could be seen to change the 'meaning'—either the intension or the extension—of the term 'pencil'.[137]

The problem with Putnam's approach may not be evident if we consider a situation where all pencils turn out to be 'alive' (as he pointed out, such an example seems to strengthen his argument). The questions come if we consider a situation where only one or a few of the pencils are 'alive'. The reason such a situation causes problems for a natural-kinds analysis is that then the group described no longer shares an essence, and the description of the group as 'a single kind', a category defined independent of human observations and human needs, is undermined.

It is interesting to contrast Putnam's example with the type of example Friedrich Waismann used in discussing 'open texture'.[138] What if, instead of discovering that *all* pencils were living organisms, we discovered that only one—or only a small number—were? I do not think that anything Putnam argued would affect

[135] Putnam, 'The Meaning of "Meaning" ', 242–4.

[136] Ibid.

[137] In his later work, Putnam seemed to pull back from the idea that natural kinds analysis should be applied to artefacts. See Putnam, 'Reference and Truth', 74–5.

[138] See Waismann, 'Verifiability', 122–6.

Waismann's conclusion that we would not know what to say here, whether to call these organisms 'pencils' or not.

Also, it may be that the apparently clear categories attached to many concepts are a contingent matter, at least now with the coming of human scientific manipulation. For example, R. M. Sainsbury wrote: 'It may seem that *strawberry* draws boundaries, since there are no borderline cases. But this is just an accident. There could very well be, and no doubt with the advent of genetic engineering soon will be, a series of plants between strawberries and raspberries, many of them borderline for both concepts.'[139] (Here again, we see how speculation about the (near) future creates an overlap between current ideas about vague terms with Waismann's ideas about 'open texture'. In this context, Waismann might have said that when genetic engineering creates a fruit that is like a strawberry, but has properties distinct from other fruits, we will not know whether to call that entity a 'strawberry' or not.)

It is of some importance that a natural-kinds theorist should be able to state what is meant by the 'same essence' and 'same nature' that the different members of the group are said to share. Putnam emphasized composition—chemical composition for chemical objects, and underlying genetic code for living organisms. Whatever the difficulties with this analysis in these cases (for example, for living organisms, Dupré has pointed out that the genetic variability within a species is sometimes larger than it is between two related species),[140] the problems are far greater when no source can be immediately identified which assigns objects to their respective categories.

Someone might merely assert that the boundaries of various groups are clear to us, and seem clearly to be independent of linguistic conventions, even though what constitutes the group members' shared essence cannot (yet) be determined. However, it would then be open to an interlocutor to cite Wittgenstein's discussion of family-resemblance concepts.[141] With family-resemblance concepts, the category borders seem to be independent of us, but the delimiting of the category one way rather than

[139] Sainsbury, *Concepts Without Boundaries*, 22; see also id., 'Is there Higher Order Vagueness?', 182.

[140] Dupré, 'Natural Kinds and Biological Taxa', 84–5.

[141] See Wittgenstein, *Philosophical Investigations*, secs. 65–77; Baker and Hacker, *Wittgenstein: Understanding and Meaning*, 320–43.

another may in fact be due to our 'form of life' (common human nature or common training): this is just the way we react (the way we 'go on'); this is just the way the objects seem *to us* to group.

One point to keep in mind is that even if one accepts that meaning something often primarily involves 'pointing' to some group or category, the community (as well as nature) sometimes plays a part in how 'reality' is divided into groups.[142] For example, the fact that the term 'arthritis' includes only rheumatoid complaints that affect the joints rather than all rheumatoid complaints is contingent, it could have been otherwise.[143] How our concepts divide up reality is arbitrary, in the sense that one cannot speak about it as 'true' or 'justified' (or as 'more true' or 'more justified' than some alternative division). This is Wittgenstein's idea of 'the autonomy of grammar'.[144]

(There is also a sense in which grammar is not arbitrary. 'The claim that it is arbitrary does not mean that it is capricious, unimportant, or a matter of individual whim. Nor does it mean that we cannot ever give *reasons* why such-and-such grammatical rules are useful, or that there cannot be reasons why, for rather specialized purposes, we choose to adopt new grammatical structures.')[145]

ALTERNATIVES TO NATURAL-KINDS ANALYSIS

In a recent article, Moore distinguished 'nominal kinds', where items in a category are connected only by a common label (the items share no common nature), not only from 'natural kinds' ('a thing exists in nature as a kind without human contrivance')[146] but also from 'functional kinds'. Items within the same 'functional kind' share the same nature, but that shared nature 'is a function and not a structure'.[147] Moore cited the example of mowers: 'It is not very plausible to think that mowers have some essential structural features, features without which they would not be

142 Pettit and McDowell, 'Introduction', 6–10. For the importance of social interests and arbitrary community choices even in biological classifications, see Dupré, 'Natural Kinds and Biological Taxa', 73–83.

143 Pettit and McDowell, 'Introduction', 7–8.

144 See Hacker, *Insight and Illusion*, 185–206.

145 Ibid. 193; see Wittgenstein, *Zettel*, sec. 358.

146 Moore, 'Law as a Functional Kind', 206.

147 Ibid. 208.

mowers . . . Anything that mows hay is a mower, whatever its structural features turn out to be.'[148]

The point of talking about 'functional kinds' is that it justifies study of the object in question. Moore wrote: 'If law were [only] a nominal kind . . . then there would be no unified nature to seek in descriptive general jurisprudence.'[149] Calling something a functional kind may respond to an academic worry, but it does not seem to have any metaphysical or ontological implications.

Moore cited a Seventh Circuit case where the court defined 'mower' as covering the class of things which do what a mower does.[150] In other words, the court treated 'mower' as a functional kind. However, that some terms are defined by objects' functions is as consistent with 'conventionalism' as it is with metaphysical realism, and we do not need a radical change in our theories of language or judicial reasoning to justify judges sometimes interpreting statutory terms in that way.

If I do not give Moore's analysis of 'functional kinds' more time in my argument, it is not because I think it either uninteresting or obviously wrong. I shrug off his position because I do not believe that he has claimed (let alone proved) anything with which critics of metaphysical realism need disagree. Unlike other aspects of Moore's metaphysical realist approach to law, the discussion of 'functional kinds' seems to make no ontological or epistemological claims (or to require any special ontological or epistemological assumptions). The closest Moore came to making such a claim was when he wrote, 'Unlike nominal kinds, items making up a functional kind have a nature that they share that is richer than the "nature" of merely sharing a common name in some language.'[151] Unless and until a much stronger claim is made about the (ontological and epistemological) consequences of the ambiguous phrase 'shared nature', I do not believe that critics of metaphysical realism have any case to answer from Moore's discussion of 'functional kinds'.

Brink tried to get around the limitations of traditional natural

[148] Moore, 'Law as a Functional Kind', 207; cf. Moore, 'The Interpretive Turn in Modern Theory', 885 (listing 'lawyer', 'knife', 'vehicle', and 'paperweight' as 'functional kinds').

[149] Moore, 'Law as a Functional Kind', 206.

[150] *Matter of Erickson*, 815 F.2d 1090, 1092–4 (7th Cir. 1987), cited in Moore, 'Law as a Functional Kind', 207.

[151] Moore, 'Law as a Functional Kind', 208.

kinds analysis by offering a broader notion of 'natural kinds'. His use of the concept would include any 'property or universal that figures in laws and explanatory generalizations'.[152] The central idea in Brink's modified analysis is that there is a difference between the 'real nature' of some object (where such objects could include 'institutions, practices, and relations') and 'descriptions conventionally associated' with those objects or people's beliefs about them.[153]

In the end, it seems like the lesson Brink learned from Kripke and Putnam that he wanted to pass on to judges and legal theorists is that our theory of meaning must be such that people (whether individually or collectively) can intelligibly be said to be wrong about *anything*, including aspects of social institutions. To some extent, this is also the foundation of, and strongest argument for, most forms of metaphysical realism: that we can be justified in distinguishing 'being justified in claiming *x*' and '*x* being true'. This type of analysis, which one associates both with the Kripke/Putnam theory of reference and with metaphysical realism, contrasts with forms of analysis under which whatever everyone believes about some matter or associates with some term would be, by definition, 'correct'.

However, one need not become a metaphysical realist to be able to distinguish 'truth' from consensus or from justified belief. If this kind of weak conceptual separation is all that is required by metaphysical realism or natural kinds analysis, then such approaches would be compatible with all sorts of sceptical, nominalist, and anti-realist approaches. Consider the following example: a position often attributed to American legal realism is that 'law is whatever the judges say it is'. However, even under this extreme position, Brink's requirements would still be met: people (individually or collectively) could be wrong in their descriptions of what law is. If a realist perspective is to be something more than a mere recharacterization of various anti-realist descriptions, if it is going to have *metaphysical* implications, then the realist philosopher will have to make some ontological claims regarding the meaning of 'nature', 'real nature', or 'kind'.

152 Brink, 'Semantics and Legal Interpretation', 185.
153 Ibid.

RESPONSE TO MOORE

Michael Moore recently wrote an article which included an extended reply to critics. The reply focused on the argument that metaphysical realism about morality does not make any difference (either in general or in a legal context);[154] an earlier version of this chapter that had been published separately was one of the pieces discussed. I cannot give Moore's reply the attention it warrants, in part because of limitations of space and in part because Moore's focus was metaphysical realism about morality, a topic beyond the scope of this book. However, as the debate is too interesting to walk away from and as Moore's comments about metaphysical realism about morality may have some application to metaphysical realism about meaning, I will at least discuss one argument from the many subtle ones presented.

The problem Moore saw with non-metaphysically realist approaches to morality, including the Wittgensteinian approach I describe, was that though they could account for (or justify) some leeway in the way applications of terms seem to change over time, they have limits. They could not justify a truly radical change in the application of a term the way a metaphysically realist approach could. Something that was 'clearly unjust' or 'the paradigm of injustice' today, one could not say tomorrow was 'just' without changing the meaning of the term.[155]

This argument has a strong initial power. However, upon deeper consideration, I have doubts about the intelligibility of a change of meaning sufficiently 'radical' (whether regarding moral terms or descriptive terms) for Moore's argument to apply. One can certainly imagine someone saying: 'We once thought that justice—"treating other people as equals" involved giving to each according to their ability but we now think it means giving the same to everyone'. However, that would only be a change in the application of more general agreed criteria (in an example of what Moore would refer to as 'deep conventionalism'). What would a truly radical change in beliefs, not just a change in the second-level application of criteria, look like (or feel like)?

[154] M. Moore, 'Moral Reality Revisited', 90 *Michigan Law Review* 2424 (1992).
[155] Ibid. 2487–8.

It clearly would not look like the following: 'We no longer think justice involves treating other people fairly; we now think it is a kind of plush sofa.' This seems absurd to the point of mockery, but there is an interesting point hidden here. We should consider: why is it that such a response is immediately seen as non-serious?

The answer would obviously be along the lines that one cannot be talking about 'justice' one minute and plush sofas the next. The metaphysical realist would say that there are categories (which include natural kinds and moral kinds) whose existence and boundaries are independent of us. One of those categories corresponds (in some way) to what most people call 'justice', even though most, or even all, persons could be wrong about its nature. One would respond to the person who thought that the real nature of 'justice' had something to do with sofas, not that she has an interesting if implausible view of what justice really is, but that she was not really talking about justice at all. She must be thinking about a different category (which may or may not be independent of our thoughts and interests), one corresponding with sofas.

How did we reach this conclusion? How are we so sure that she has not simply discovered the 'true nature' of justice, a matter about which the rest of us have been badly wrong for a long time? The point is that the metaphysical realist must face the same problem as the 'conventionalist': how to tell the difference in a disagreement between there being different beliefs about/analysis of/interpretation of a concept and there simply being different concepts.

A Wittgensteinian might say that there is something in our usage of a term (and our reaction to other people's usage of the term) which allows us to tell when we are considering a new application (or 'interpretation') of the concept rather than a different concept altogether. What alternative can a metaphysical realist offer? References to our practices, reactions, conventions, or stipulations are the tools of non-metaphysically realist approaches; and the problems of positing intuition or other forms of direct perception of Platonic essences were discussed earlier in this chapter (in discussion of Wittgenstein's critique of metaphysical realism).

There is one other way out for Moore in this context. He could explain radical change in the concept of 'justice' in terms of justice being a 'functional kind'. However, as I have explained earlier in this chapter, I do not think that a non-metaphysical realist need object to a 'functional kinds' analysis, at least as Moore has presented it.

CONCLUSION

The greatest benefit of theories like those of Michael Moore and David Brink is that they remind us of how dependent thinking about the law and thinking within the law are on unstated beliefs about metaphysics, semantics, and morality. Not only are these foundational assumptions usually unstated, they are also usually unquestioned, and any theorist who can uncover and challenge these assumptions is well worth our time and consideration.

Moore showed us how much may be at stake if we are persuaded to think differently about philosophical issues; these are not mere parlour games for legal theorists. Our day-to-day practices as lawyers and law teachers might be radically changed if we were to accept Moore's approach to statutory interpretation, constitutional interpretation, precedent, and legal reasoning.

However, I do not think that Moore has yet met his burden of proof in his attempt to show that the way most of us currently think about language or the way most of us currently do (and teach) law is incorrect. In particular, I do not think that he has shown that approaches to language other than metaphysical realism are, as he claimed, inadequate for scientific, moral, and legal discourse.

Metaphysical realism is a response to an insecurity that arises from pondering the foundations of thought and action. A series of anxious questions can come to mind: If language is not directly connected with some set of stable objects independent of us (and our interests), what grounds its day-to-day operation? How can we know whether a term applies or not in a novel situation? How can we understand current disagreements—or the changes of meanings of terms over time—as anything other than people talking about different things and only deluding themselves into thinking that they are discussing a common matter? Metaphysical realists doubt alternatively the ability to ground language simply in human practices and tendencies, and the legitimacy of doing so even if it were possible. They seek solace in a complicated ontology and epistemology, which they hope will both justify and make sense of the way we actually speak.

The problems and insecurities to which metaphysical realism seems to respond become even greater when it is brought into the context of legal thought. Here we are also worried about the divergence between what rule-makers intended and what the words in their enactment (seem to) mean, and about the problem of applying texts written long ago to current situations. Metaphysical realists hint that they might be able to give us simple solutions even to these problems, by making the answer to *all* interpretative questions depend on current expert opinion. Difficulties of institutional competence, institutional legitimacy, and political theory seem to dissolve in the mixture of ontological and epistemological claims in the underlying theory. Like most panaceas, I suspect that metaphysical realist approaches to law are more fraud than cure.

What Wittgenstein in his later writings and other sophisticated critics of metaphysical realism have been trying to persuade us of is that the way we actually use language is grounded in our practices and inclinations and *is* adequate to our needs. No further buttressing is necessary, or even possible. In the context of law, one need add only that we cannot escape difficult moral and political questions by seeking ever more sophisticated theories of meaning and metaphysics. Wittgenstein's work offers no miraculous solutions: it leaves us where we began, though less anxious about language in general, and, one hopes, also less likely to try to use theories of language to solve questions belonging to an entirely different realm.

6

A Summing-Up

INTRODUCTION

In this final chapter, I wish to try to bring together some of the disparate pieces of the previous chapters. The first section of this chapter will summarize the book's themes; the subsequent sections will discuss some topics of general importance raised but not fully explored in earlier chapters: intention, the possibility of general jurisprudence, and the temptation of relativism.

THREADS IN THE ROPE

The book has had three overlapping themes: the role of language in law, Wittgenstein's philosophy of language, and the problems of legal determinacy. Taking them one at a time, I believe that language has, for the most part, been a false focus for legal theory. Language and theories of language have been used as an excuse for decisions that are more properly attributable to political—or at least policy—decisions about how we want the various institutions in our legal system to interact: When do we want judges to ignore or override legislative intent? Are there times when rules should be overruled, altered, or ignored due to the apparent absurdity or injustice of their application? And how much attention should be given to the more abstract aspects of the rule-maker's intentions? I believe that it is at best misleading to claim that the problems of resolving disputes in the context of a legal system would be resolved if only we had a better theory of language, or if only judges would follow the proper theory of language that we already have.

A theory about language and communication is likely to consider various elements: what ideas the speaker meant to convey, how words are conventionally understood, how context affects intention, meaning, or understanding, and the role of dialects and idiolects. However one arranges these elements in constructing a theory of meaning, it could still be argued that different factors should be emphasized in the special context of drafting, interpreting, and enforcing legal rules (the argument emphasizing the special features of rule-application or the special features of law, or both).

As for the second theme, I tried to emphasize the importance of understanding that Wittgenstein's rule-following considerations assume rather than prove the (short-term) determinacy of language. Wittgenstein's primary interest was in understanding and explaining why it was that language had the determinacy that it did (at least in the more mundane cases). This is a harder and more paradoxical problem than it at first appears, and the rule-following considerations devote a great deal of time to showing that the answers to which philosophers might first turn—Platonic ideas, counterfactuals, and dispositions—were inadequate. Wittgenstein's final answer, to the extent that he gave a final answer, was that the determinacy of language depends on shared judgements, which in turn are probably based on some combination of shared training, shared culture, and a shared biological nature.

As I stated earlier, I am sceptical of claims that Wittgenstein's rule-following considerations, or any other theory of or about language, can resolve the difficult questions of jurisprudence. It is worth remembering that Wittgenstein characterized his own writings not as telling us something new about language, but as untangling the philosophical difficulties into which our thinking had brought us. He wrote: 'Philosophy may in no way interfere with the actual use of language; it can in the end only describe it. For it cannot give it any foundation either. It leaves everything as it is.'[1] Philosophy's task is only to describe; no explanation beyond offering a clear overview of matters we already know is necessary.[2]

Therefore, I think it inconsistent with Wittgenstein's view of his own work to believe that his rule-following considerations will solve difficult interpretative questions in law. On the other hand, it is quite consistent with Wittgenstein's view about how his writings could and should be used, for the rule-following considerations to be applied in order to counter positions justified on the basis of

[1] Wittgenstein, *Philosophical Investigations*, sec. 124.

[2] For a more detailed discussion of Wittgenstein's attitude, see Hacker, *Insight and Illusion*, 151–65.

other, more complex theories of reality and language. Wittgenstein's fear was that philosophical thinking causes the tangles in our understanding; so it must be for (a different kind of) philosophy to untangle our thinking and to show us that no problem actually existed.[3] That is why though I did not approve of Langille's and Patterson's uses of the rule-following considerations (discussed in Chapter 2), where those ideas were presented as offering magical new insights into how law does or should work, I thought the rule-following considerations appropriate and helpful in the critique of Michael Moore's metaphysically realist approach to law (discussed in Chapter 5).

Regarding the third theme, the issue of legal determinacy, like the question of language within law, often seems better understood as a marker for questions of political or social theory (that is, not what the nature of law *is*, but how we *should* organize our particular legal system). Before we can make any progress in understanding the problems of the area, we must separate off political questions posing as conceptual and empirical questions from whatever truly conceptual or empirical questions may be present.

One difficulty in the area of 'legal determinacy' is that the underlying concepts are deceptively complex or ambiguous. As I tried to indicate at the beginning of Chapter 4, simply to clarify what we mean by saying that there is a 'right answer' to a legal question leads us to ponder problems of 'legal mistake', the line between 'legal' and 'extra-legal' standards, the meaning of judicial review, and the nature and workings of precedent. As indicated elsewhere in the same chapter, understanding Ronald Dworkin's approach to legal determinacy also requires attention to problems of holistic or coherence approaches to law, incommensurability, and the dynamics of multi-person decision-making.

Discussions of legal determinacy often bring up the topic of 'easy cases' (the primary subject of Chapter 3), but this topic sometimes seems to confuse the issue more than it clarifies it. The phrase 'easy case' or 'clear case' is used to refer to any problem for which there is no significant disagreement or doubt within the relevant community regarding the correct solution (keeping in mind that the factors of disagreement and doubt—consensus and

[3] See e.g. Wittgenstein, *Philosophical Investigations*, sec. 133.

conviction—can be separated: for example, we might all agree about a conclusion at the same time that many of us are less than certain about that conclusion).

Agreement, like disagreement, can be the result of a variety of factors, individually or working in tandem. One should usually not ascribe certainty or consensus to one factor rather than another. Calling a single factor '*the* reason' for a case being 'easy' is much like the way we talk about causation. We tend to label as '*the* cause' of an event the factor that was least expected in the situation or most important for our purposes, even though a number of other factors were also necessary for that event to have occurred. Singling out one factor among many may suit our immediate purposes, but it can also cause us to forget that other factors were equally 'responsible'.

A result may seem to be 'required' by the wording of the relevant rule; the facts of the case may seem identical to a previous case; or it may seem that any result other than the one chosen would be too absurd or too unjust to tolerate. However, there is only likely to be consensus on the result if there are no complicating factors: for example, it may not be enough that the wording of a statute seems to require a particular result, if that result is unjust or contrary to the apparent purpose of the act or in tension with other prior decisions. The role of language in 'easy cases' is thus at best as one factor among many, for the clarity of a legal rule's application to some case *as a matter of language* is neither sufficient nor necessary for the case to be an easy one. The language may seem clearly to indicate one result, but the judge reaches (or at least seriously considers reaching) a different result because the result indicated by language alone seems absurd or unjust. On the other hand, the language of the rule may be ambiguous, but interpretation guide-lines may indicate that in situations of uncertainty (say, in criminal cases), all ambiguities should be interpreted against the State, and thus the result of the case may nonetheless be clear.[4]

[4] See Dworkin, 'No Right Answer?', 68. In a different context in Chap. 1, I rejected Dworkin's argument based on this presumption. The basis of my argument then was that there is no reason to believe that there are clear boundaries between clear applications of a term and borderline cases. However, that analysis does not deny (in fact it probably assumes) that there are cases where an application is clearly a borderline case, and where the presumption would clearly apply.

Decision-makers may claim that they are talking about matters of language when they say that the rule 'no vehicles in the park' does not apply to emergency vehicles, and they may even believe this to be the case. There is no point to getting tied up in questions about labels here. Even if we say that these *are* questions of language, they are still *different in kind* from questions in a normal (non-normative) context about whether 'vehicles' applies to normal pieces of fruit. The latter question of application is *merely* a matter of language—that is, unlike the former situation, it is not even within the reasonable extension of the term to apply that word to that object—while in the former case, the definition or usage of the word alone does not (clearly) exclude the application of the term in that way; some reference to the *purpose* of the rule, the absurdity or injustice of applying it to this particular case, is added to justify not applying the term to that object *in this context.*

The dependence of legal determinacy questions on matters that seem to be simply language-based but are not, is due to the nature of normative discourse. In saying what must or must not be done (whether in law, morals, or even a sporting contest), we need clear lines, clear limits. In normal circumstances, say, talking with a friend while walking through the park, it matters little whether we call a moped a 'vehicle' or not. Heated arguments are unlikely to break out, not because we all agree about how a term should be used, but because nothing important is at stake; the natural flexibility of language does not threaten. We are therefore willing to tolerate another person's applying a term somewhat differently from the way we would have done, as long as her use is close enough to the way we use the term that we can understand what is being said. However, in the context of a moral or legal imperative, it is important to know the limits of a term's application, because it is important to know whether an action is included or excluded from a prohibition or authorization.

Additionally, there are factors that come from legal discourse being a special kind of normative discourse: unlike in (say) most moral discourse, in law there are often questions about to what extent to defer to other people's intentions, and how to understand texts that were written at a much earlier time, and with significantly different circumstances in mind. The topic of intention will be the focus of the next section.

ON INTENTION IN LAW

My discussions about the relationship between language and law (especially those in Chapter 4) occasionally relied on the position, sometimes expressed, sometimes implied, that authority is basic to the nature of law. Part of my argument against Ronald Dworkin's approach to law was that it misses or discounts that point. Statutes and judicial decisions are not mere Delphic pronouncements from which we should try to construct the most coherent or most just picture that we can. Our reason for considering such official actions at all is the authority those officials have (or had) within the system; their authority is not merely to pronounce something that would be reshaped by others, but an authority to make choices for the common good. The argument is that these choices should therefore be shown deference.

First, I should clarify what my position *does* not entail. While I argue for the importance of authority and, implicitly, of some notion of rule-maker's intention, for understanding the nature of law, I do not want my position to be confused with a particular disfavoured position within American constitutional theory, which sometimes goes under the label of 'intentionalist' or 'original intention' theory. That approach argues that an interpretation of the United States Constitution is legitimate only if it is consistent with the specific intentions of the people who drafted the language being interpreted.

I distance my views from that approach, first, because it is a theory about interpreting a particular document within a particular legal system, while my discussion attempts to be at the level of understanding legal systems in general, and second, because the extreme view of 'original intent' theorists uses a concept of 'intention' that I think is far too narrow, for their purposes as well as for my own. While there may be theorists who seriously claim that the application of *every* clause in the United States Constitution should *always* derive from the drafters' specific intentions, most writers who favour an intention-based approach to constitutional interpretation use a much broader concept of intention: allowing intentions about intentions and intentions to defer to other decision-makers, as well as allowing that there are situations (for example, where circumstances have changed significantly since the drafting) where the 'original intent' should be ignored or overruled.[5]

It is a commonplace in the literature that there are difficulties with discussing intentions in the law. Some theorists have justified or shaped their theories in large part on those difficulties: for example, Heidi Hurd and (to some extent) Ronald Dworkin have put forward non-authority-based, non-intentionalist theories of law and judicial reasoning, justified in part by the difficulty of making straightforward sense of intention in the context of group decision-making.[6] I believe that the difficulties in this matter are often overestimated: the differences between applying notions of 'intention' in individual and group contexts are overstated, and the possibility of related but different notions in the two contexts is rarely explored.

Let us begin at an earlier point in the analysis. The concept of 'intention' takes on different aspects in different contexts. While the concept may be uncomplicated enough when considering the orders of a dictator or an employer, the problems arise when we ponder the nature of authority in most modern Western legal systems. When the courts ask: 'What did Parliament intend by this enactment?' one may wonder what is meant by claiming that a group of persons acting in an institutional context collectively intended anything. We understand—or at least we think we understand—intention in an individual context: an individual who makes a statement usually has thoughts or desires regarding what she wants her listeners to think or what she wants them to do.

In normal discourse, we may give even more emphasis to intention than we do in a legal context: for the point is to figure out what the other person is trying to communicate to us. (Perhaps it would be clearer to say that we look for a different type of intention, or look to intention for a different reason.) The fact that the person may be using a dialect or an idiolect, or falling victim to a malapropism or a standard mistake in word choice, may make it harder for us to understand what the person meant, but (to the extent we are aware of the difference) we will continue to concentrate on what the person was trying to communicate rather than on what the words she used (conventionally) mean.

[5] See e.g. R. Posner, *Law and Literature*, 220–68.

[6] See e.g. H. Hurd, 'Sovereignty in Silence', 99 *Yale Law Journal* 945 (1990); Dworkin, *Law's Empire*, 313–54 (discussing statutory interpretation).

The unique and somewhat paradoxical nature of law is summarized well by a passage from J. B. White:

> It is . . . the genius of law that it is not a set of 'commands', but a set of texts meant to be read across circumstances that are in principle incompletely foreseeable. This is what it means to pass a piece of legislation, or to decide a case—or even to draft a contract—at one point in time, with the knowledge that it will in the future be brought to bear by others (or ourselves) in contexts, and with meanings, that we cannot wholly imagine.[7]

Because legislation is often applied long after it is enacted, the rule-maker's intentions, at least those which the interpreters of the rules are likely to consider important, will be more abstract. When we are speaking to a person we know, we keep in consideration how we think that particular person would respond to what we say. To the extent that our audience is unknown to us, that more specific type of intention (and the extra clarity that may come from knowing how the listener will understand a comment) will largely be absent. I do not want to overstate the differences. Rule-makers will know *some* things about their audience, and may alter their formulations accordingly. At least as to the judicial 'audience', the drafters know the canons and conventions of statutory interpretation and they will keep them in mind when drafting statutes.

Intention in normal discourse has its own complications, for we may not have thought out matters of purpose before speaking or acting. In such situations, intention is usually thought of in terms of counter-factuals: for example, how would we have answered particular questions if we had been asked at the time. A standard example of this aspect of individual intention is given by Wittgenstein: 'Someone says to me: "Shew the children a game." I teach them gaming with dice, and the other says, "I didn't mean that sort of game." Must the exclusion of the game with dice have come before his mind when he gave the order?'[8] The way we use the term 'intention' and the way we understand the concept do not require the thought actually to have been in someone's mind while speaking for the idea to be ascribed as that person's intention at the time.

[7] J. B. White, 'What Can a Lawyer Learn from Literature?' (book review), 102 *Harvard Law Review* 2014, 2035 (1989).

[8] Wittgenstein, *Philosophical Investigations*, 33.

Compared to the situation with individuals, the problems seem to become far greater when we consider the intentions of a group, a collective, or a legal construct (for example, a corporation), either because there are many individuals involved, or because we are not sure with which individuals we should be concerned. The problems of determining legislative intention have been repeated often enough: for example, do we focus on the draftsman or the legislators who voted on the statute (even if they did so without reading the text)? Should we consider committee reports and legislative debates even if many of those voting on the statute have not read or heard those materials? Do we consider what those who voted against the legislation thought of it? How do we 'sum' different intentions if those intentions vary among the relevant legislators? How do we choose between different 'levels' of intention (for example, belief that a statutory term refers to *x*, as against belief that the term should be held to refer to whatever most scientists think it refers to, as against belief that judges should be the final interpreters of what the term means)? These are real difficulties, though it is not clear why they should make us abandon talk of 'intention' in the legal context.

One alternative for understanding intention in the context of group decision-making is the traditional one of adapting as best we can the way we think about intention for individuals. Andrei Marmor's recent discussion is an excellent example of this: in brief summary, the focus remains on individuals not on the corporate entity, 'legislative intention' exists where the legislators had a *shared* intention about some matter (where no such consensus prevailed, there simply was no legislative intention), and (shared) intentions as to the purpose of legislation should be given priority over (shared) intentions as to the application or interpretation of the text.[9]

Along with this traditional approach, I would like to suggest that different approaches might be possible and that different characterizations of our current practices are possible. I begin with the views of Joseph Raz, who summarized his position as follows:

> [T]he intention thesis errs in isolating each act of lawmaking and regarding the law made by it as determined by that episode in isolation, once and for all. This is an unsustainable view. What we need is a way of

[9] Marmor, *Interpretation and Legal Theory*, 155–72.

regarding the law as the function of the activities of legal authorities in general, that is, a way of seeing how its content is a function of various activities, and layers of activities, in continuous interaction, rather than as a function of a single act, fixed once and for all. This authority-based view of the law will avoid the pitfalls of the intention thesis, while preserving its ability to explain the institutional nature of the law.[10]

Raz's approach, as roughly outlined, can be seen as one of deriving intention from a series of acts, emphasizing context and plans.

There are similarities as well as differences between individuals and groups when we think of intention in terms of plans. One can ask of an individual: 'What was she trying to accomplish?' or 'What piece of information was she trying to get us to learn?' The application to collective bodies or to artificial entities tends to be more constructive. Not 'What was the corporation trying to do?', as it becomes ever more bizarre to ascribe thoughts and plans to entities (as distinct from ascribing thoughts and plans to the individuals that constitute or lead them) at a particular time, but: 'Of what type of plan would this action be a reasonable first step?'

One can see constructions of a similar sort in the approach to statutory interpretation associated with the English courts (discussed briefly in Chapter 3). The English courts try to 'discover Parliamentary intent' by focusing almost exclusively on the text of the statute itself. Though the prohibition on looking at the records of Parliamentary debate (partially lifted in 1992)[11] had specific policy underpinnings,[12] it had the effect of circumventing many of the problems of summing the intentions of individual legislators.[13]

There is also an argument for putting great emphasis on the text as the basis for discovering intention, even as against supplementary records that purport to record intention. One could argue that it does not matter what legislators in debates and committee reports *say* that they are trying to do, if the legislation that results

[10] J. Raz, 'The Relevance of Coherence', 72 *Boston University Law Review* 273, 296 (1992).

[11] *Pepper* v. *Hart* [1992] 2 W.L.R. 1032.

[12] One sometimes stated was that statutes should not be interpreted one way rather than another on the basis of records to which the public does not have easy access.

[13] This problem still is not present in English law even after *Pepper* v. *Hart*, as (other than in exceptional circumstances) only statements of the government minister or other promoter of a Bill will be considered. See *Pepper* v. *Hart*, at 1055, 1061 (per Lord Browne-Wilkinson).

in fact does something significantly different. There may be purposes that the legislators are hiding for one reason or another, and there may be purposes of which the legislators are not entirely aware. In the context of a modern understanding of the unconscious, it is not absurd to say that a person may mean something by a statement or by an action that the person herself would not have given as part of her intention if she had been asked about it. This is not necessarily a question of lying about one's intentions; rather it is a matter of people sometimes having intentions of which they themselves are not fully aware.

It may be that the problems of applying 'intention' to collective bodies are not as great as is sometimes claimed. What I mean is not that we can apply the term to such entities in the same way that we do to individuals, but that we should not react so strongly to the fact that the 'grammar' of the term is occasionally different in the two contexts. Many of the 'rules' for talking about intention are identical, or at least similar. For example, for individuals, we speak of intention by using counter-factuals, even when the person had no thoughts on the matter at the time she spoke or wrote. To the extent that intention is about counter-factuals ('What would she have said had you asked her about *that* at the time?'), it applies as well to collective bodies (for example: 'would Congress at the time of the relevant Antitrust Act have been likely to have wanted maximum resale price maintenance prohibited?'). Those who reject counter-factuals in a legislative context as not 'really' about intention forget how often this is all we *can* mean by intention when talking about individuals.

There are problems with counter-factuals that come not from the difference between individual and collective bodies, but from the passage of time. As James Boyd White (among others) pointed out, simple counter-factuals will not allow us to 'discover' the intentions of legislators who wrote long ago, regarding matters about which they could not have been aware.[14] Consider the counter-factual for the (eighteenth-century) drafters of the Fourth Amendment to the United States Constitution regarding whether the reference to 'searches and seizures' in that amendment includes or excludes electronic wire-tapping. For the drafters even to understand the question they must be assumed to have

[14] See White, 'What Can a Lawyer Learn from Literature?', 2022, 2034–5.

knowledge, not only about modern electonics, but also about organized crime, modern policing, the role the telephone plays in our lives, and so on. As we keeping adding hypothetical knowledge to the drafters, it becomes less like asking *them*, because all this extra knowledge about our world would inevitably change them, making them more like us.[15]

While I certainly would not say that 'intention' is the same in the contexts of individuals and groups, this concession by no means concludes the discussion. The usual analysis is that collective bodies are different from individuals for the purposes of 'intention', and therefore the application of that concept to collective bodies is inappropriate or illegitimate. But is this radical conclusion warranted? Given that we use 'intention' in both contexts, we usually understand what other people mean when they refer to 'intention' in both contexts, and that there are set criteria that govern our use of 'intention' in both contexts, why should we not just accept that the use of the term is equally legitimate—even if slightly different—in both contexts? Also, the use of the term in the two contexts is sufficiently similar that we should not think of the term referring to different concepts in the different contexts (this is not far different from pointing out that the word 'game' has different criteria without being a different concept, in its application to board games and to team sports.)

In summary, while there are problems with 'intention' in a legislative context, these problems are probably not as daunting as is sometimes claimed, and they need not make the reference to 'intention' unintelligible or unusable. Also, the view that the concept is workable in talking about individuals but not in talking about collective bodies is not justified either by our practices or by an analysis of the concept's application in both contexts. I certainly do not claim that these brief comments have resolved the problems in the area of intention and authority, nor am I trying to say that the doubts raised in this area are fictional or insignificant. I only hope to suggest both that we should not overestimate the differences between applying notions of intention in the context of individuals and in the context of groups, and that we should consider the possibility that we can (and in fact do) use slightly different concepts in the two contexts, and that this is legitimate.

[15] Ibid. 2034–5.

THE MEANING OF 'LAW'

One problem in jurisprudential discussions is to distinguish claims which are true only for particular legal systems and those which derive from the nature of law itself, and therefore would be true of all legal systems. Underlying this comment is the assumption that it is intelligible to speak of the nature of law as such, a matter which some theorists have questioned.

On what basis can we talk about 'the nature of law'? Ronald Dworkin has argued that a significant legal theory must be an interpretation of *a particular* legal system. While not denying that one could speak of (have an interpretation of) legal systems as a class, he asserted that there was sufficient variance within the group that any interpretation we could offer of all legal systems would be at so high a level of generality as to be uninteresting.[16] To the argument, like the one I offered earlier, that authority is central to the nature of law, Dworkin might answer: 'there is no such thing as "the nature of law", there are only individual legal systems; it may be that a proper interpretation of a particular legal system requires great deference to intention and authority, but that says nothing about the correct approach to (the interpretation of) other legal systems'.

Michael Moore denied that we could speak of different legal systems sharing the same nature in terms of sharing the same structure, institutions, or processes. However, he thought that the study of law in general could go forward, since different legal systems could be said to be examples of a single 'functional kind'; that is, that they all serve the same functions within their societies.[17]

In Chapter 5, I briefly discussed Moore's ideas about the 'functional kind' law, but only long enough to note that it was not clear that the concept 'functional kind' made any significant epistemological or ontological claims (though it was likely that Moore thought that it did), such that critics of metaphysical realism need object to his discussion. The concept of 'functional kinds' need mean nothing more than that we can divide up the

[16] Lecture at Oxford University, 16 Jan. 1990; see Dworkin, 'Legal Theory and the Problem of Sense', 16 and *Law's Empire*, 102–3.

[17] Moore, 'Law as a Functional Kind', 206–8.

world according to functions. In a non-metaphysically realist use of that concept, there may be overlapping and inconsistent ways of dividing the world; one assumes that the same would not be true under a metaphysically realist version of the concept.

Different approaches to 'functional kind' analysis might have different consequences in an attempt to justify general jurisprudence. Under a non-metaphysically realist approach, studying 'law in general' would still be possible, and would probably be justified, but the project would seem to be less ambitious and the results less important than would be the case under a metaphysically realist approach. As with the discussion of 'natural kinds', the question between a metaphysically realist and a non-metaphysically realist approach turns on the extent to which we think the category of 'law' is contingent (perhaps relative to our short-term or long-term interests) as opposed to being necessary and independent of us. The idea is that it is less significant to investigate a category we created ourselves, but this may well be unwarranted prejudice. Even if the category of things which serve particular, significant functions is an artificial one, any knowledge we could have about that category would be useful and important.

H. L. A. Hart is one writer who continued to advocate the more traditional position on this issue: that one can—and should—have a legal theory which attempts to describe 'a form of social institution . . . which in its recurrence in different societies and periods exhibits many common features of form, structure, and content'.[18] Hart did not attempt to explain why this 'form of social institution' *does* recur so often in different societies and at different times. One might imagine explanations based on anthropology/psychology (for example, in terms of a basic human need for a particular kind of order), morality (for example, that a legal system is the best way to respond to certain requirements of justice), ontology (for example, that law is a 'natural kind' or a Platonic Idea), or history (for example, that it fulfilled a need for a particular kind of institution in the progress from a feudal society to a capitalist society).

In some ways, it might not be important to determine the

[18] H. L. A. Hart, 'Comment [on Dworkin]', in *Issues in Contemporary Legal Philosophy*, 36 (R. Gavison, ed., Oxford: Clarendon Press, 1987).

'correct' delimitation of which social institutions warrant the label 'law'. Perhaps all attempts to divide up social reality are arbitrary: A could be grouped with B, excluding C, in one way of dividing up social reality; but it may be equally legitimate to group A with C, excluding B. Perhaps the only basis for preferring one way of dividing up reality to another is that it suits our immediate (analytical) needs better. There would then be no a priori objection to choosing one division over another (if one thought that this division served one's purposes or was interesting for other reasons), as long as one's analysis was clear and accurate for whatever group (however arbitrary the grouping) one was studying.

One can derive from Lon Fuller's work one way in which a division of social institutions might be criticized. Fuller had argued that some combination of having the wrong legal theory to begin with and focusing too much on modern Western legal systems had encouraged a view of law as essentially a 'one-way projection of authority'. According to Fuller, this basic misunderstanding of known legal systems encouraged misunderstandings of tribal systems of law that were later investigated, systems where customary law and other collaborative aspects of law are more prevalent than they are in Western systems.[19] However, this objection was less to which systems were included in the grouping 'law', and more to the accuracy of the analysis offered (as Fuller thought that the 'one-way projection of authority' was inappropriate for Western legal systems as well, even if the lack of fit is not as obvious as it is for the tribal systems). While the selection of institutions to study can affect the misreadings one is tempted to make, no argument has yet been made that negative consequences can follow a particular selection even when the theories of those institutions are not in error.

At first, there may seem to be a danger of circularity when talking about 'the nature of law'. For the delimitation of the group (the social institutions that will be held to warrant the label 'law') will depend, at least in part, on what we think distinctive of legal systems. At the same time, what we think distinctive of legal systems is likely to be a function of which social institutions we thought should be included in the group. If we delimit the social

[19] Fuller, *The Morality of Law*, 232–7.

institutions that we consider the proper subjects of legal theory to those which give prominence to pronouncements by authoritative institutions, then it is neither surprising nor interesting when we discover that authority or claims to authority are integral to our theory about such institutions and processes.

However, it may be that this 'circularity', to the extent that it is present, need not trouble us. Joseph Raz[20] suggested an approach which is similar in structure, if not purpose, to Gallie's discussion of 'essentially contested concepts' (which I analysed in Chapter 2, as part of my attempt to understand the nature of disagreement in hard cases). Gallie had offered an explanation of substantive disagreement, of how people who disagree about the meaning or application of (evaluative) terms could be offering different views about a common subject rather than simply talking past one another. According to Gallie, the differing views were to be seen as different interpretations of paradigms. For example, people who disagree about the nature of 'democracy' arguably could be seen to be disagreeing about what was most significant about the political system of ancient Athens.

Similarly, disagreements not only about the nature of law, but also about whether particular systems warrant the title 'law', could be seen as disagreements based on contrary interpretations of the speakers' own legal system (which fulfils a role analogous to the role of the paradigm in Gallie's analysis). Our analysis of the concept of 'law', under this approach, neither presupposes a metaphysical entity nor tries to discover one. What we are seeking is a better understanding of our own legal system, and part of the process of investigation involves looking at similar social institutions from other societies (again, 'similar' is defined by reference to one's own legal system). One therefore selects a group of legal systems to help one understand what is important about one's own local system. It is not surprising (or illegitimate) that the criteria for inclusion in the group refer to one's (initial, tentative) conclusions about importance. It is a kind of reflective equilibrium: by (conscious or unconscious) assumptions of what is significant about our own legal system, we delimit the group of social institutions which are sufficiently similar to carry the same label ('law'). Deeper reflection about these institutions may make us

[20] In conversation, 13 Mar. 1992.

reconsider what is most significant about our own legal system, which in turn may make us adjust our judgements about whether particular other social institutions should have been included in the group.

As mentioned in Chapter 2, one problem with Gallie's use of 'essentially contested concepts' to explain substantive disagreement had been that one can legitimately wonder why we should use (for example) the governmental system of ancient Athens as the paradigm of 'democracy'. To be sure, there may be historical reasons for why one example has been used as the paradigm for a particular concept, but it is always open to someone to argue for a revision of the practice: for example, that the inequalities of ancient Athens actually make it a poor exemplar of the values we today associate with 'democracy'. As a historical matter, ancient Athens might have been the origin of a way of thinking, but it is now that way of thinking that matters, not its origin.

These questions and problems need not arise with the approach to law that I have been discussing. The social institutions chosen to be included in the group that we call 'law' for the purposes of general jurisprudence are brought together for a particular objective, and that objective is what justifies the selection. Legal theory can be seen as an exercise in self-understanding.

Admittedly, what is 'important' or 'significant' about one's legal system is not a matter that can be demonstrated, and it is not surprising that different theorists have come to significantly different conclusions. Consider some of the recent work in legal theory: Joseph Raz treats as the most significant aspect of law its role in practical reasoning, regulating behaviour and co-ordinating action'[21]; John Finnis makes reference to similar aspects of practical reasoning, but in the context of seeing them (and seeing law) as means to promoting basic human goods; and Ronald Dworkin takes a completely different perspective in seeing law as being primarily about the justification of state coercion by reference to past official action. Consider the following situation: a discussion is set up between theorists who believe that the most basic aspect of law is justifying coercion, and those who believe that the most basic aspect of law is regulating and co-ordinating behaviour. What kinds of arguments could a participant in this

[21] See e.g. Raz, 'The Relevance of Coherence', 296, n. 35.

discussion use to argue that her approach was the correct one and that the alternative approach was wrong? Judgements about importance and significance are, if not the most fundamental steps in the argument, at least closely related to them. What we think important and significant is usually tied to basic judgements either about the purpose of social organizations or the purpose of studying social organizations. Such assertions are not usually thought to be subject to criticism and revision on the basis of more fundamental shared criteria. The effects of this situation on the status of the claims in legal theory are discussed in the next section.

THE STATUS OF THE CLAIMS AND THE TEMPTATION OF RELATIVISM

In this book, I have tried to put forward certain positions about the role of language in law and the problem of legal determinacy. The arguments have occasionally depended upon, or led me to make, certain claims about the nature of law. However, I do not purport to have offered a new approach to law or to legal theory in this book that could be placed in competition with those of Hart, Finnis, Fuller, Raz, and Dworkin. My claims for this work are nowhere near so grand.

Regarding my attitude to the theories I have criticized, my effort has usually been to quiet—though usually not to silence—their claims. My argument has not been that theorists who make use of Wittgenstein, coherence theory, interpretation, or the like, have brought no important insights to legal theory, but that they have sometimes claimed too much or pushed their points too far.

In the course of this book, inevitably I have stated (or implied) that certain theorists were wrong about certain matters, and that they should have taken my position or approach rather their own. There is nothing unusual here; this is what philosophical debate is all about: analysing arguments and trying to distinguish the successful from the unsuccessful. However, in legal theory I think there is a particularly strong temptation to relativism.

The argument begins as follows: legal systems, and people's experiences of them, are extremely complex. Inevitably, a theory about law will capture only a portion of the relevant facts. So far these claims are neither new nor surprising. H. L. A. Hart's discussion of the internal aspect of rules and of law, and John Finnis's discussion (based on Max Weber's work) of central case analysis, are both based on the insight that social theories must select among the available data.[22]

Once one accepts the importance of selection in constructing social theories, the focus then turns to the basis on which selection or evaluation occurs. If the criterion is one of 'importance' or 'analytical insight', then we should not be surprised when fair-minded persons (including fair-minded theorists) disagree or even when an individual oscillates between competing positions over time.

(As in the various discussions on 'right answers' in Chapter 4, the point is not to claim that all answers would be equally right or acceptable, but to consider the possibility that a number of answers might be equally correct or acceptable. While there may be more than one tenable argument regarding what is (most) important or significant about our legal system, there are wrong answers: for example, 'that it gives business to various printing and publishing companies connected with the legal reporters and reference books' would not be a tenable answer.)

The temptation to relativism is encouraged in a different way, in that different legal theorists often seem to be answering different questions and responding to different concerns. 'Debates' in the jurisprudential literature are often nothing more than theorists talking past one another. For example, I sometimes wonder if one can choose between a legal positivist, Hart-like approach to law and legal theory and a Dworkinian approach. There is no easy or obvious way to choose between characterizing law in a 'descriptive' way, as a core of clearly present norms which are added to or modified on the margin by judicial legislation (holding to a strong version of the analytical separation between what law is and what it ought to be), and characterizing it as an interpretative matter, a matter where what the law requires can always be answered and determining what the law requires is partly a function of what the law ought to be. Any judicial decision could in principle be characterized in either way. (Both sides can bring arguments to support their characterization: for the interpretative theorist it is

[22] See Hart, *The Concept of Law*, 79–88; Finnis, *Natural Law and Natural Rights*, 1–11.

the way lawyers and judges write in terms of what the law requires even in the most difficult cases[23], while for the descriptive theorist it is the distinction, deeply ingrained in both legal and public discourse, between 'the law the court finds and the law it creates'.)[24] However, I believe that both of these vastly different methods of characterization remain tenable.

For another example, Fuller argued that it is important to understand that law is a particular way of guiding and controlling group behaviour, and that a full understanding would consist in part of knowing what factors contribute to or detract from the effectiveness of this method ('the internal morality of law').[25] However, it is far from clear why this claim must be seen, as it traditionally has been, as inconsistent with the legal positivists' argument that it is useful for most analytical purposes to distinguish a law's validity from its moral value, and to distinguish rules which are identified by their sources from those that require further moral argument or deliberation.

The possibility that claims in legal theory may sometimes be relative to a particular purpose or a particular viewpoint does not empty legal theory of all significance or interest. I think quite the contrary; at most it means that the arguments offered must be more subtly made. However, the possibility of relativism should make us a bit more careful and a bit more modest in the way we put forward our own claims about law and legal theory, as well as the way we discuss other theorists' claims.

[23] See e.g. R. Dworkin, *Law's Empire*, 37–43.
[24] J. Raz, 'Dworkin: A New Link in the Chain', 1117.
[25] See e.g. Fuller, *The Morality of Law*, 33–94.

Bibliography

ALEXANDER, L., 'Constrained by Precedent', 63 *Southern California Law Review* 1 (1989).

—— 'Law and Exclusionary Reasons', 18 *Philosophical Topics* 5 (1990).

—— 'Of Two Minds about Law and Minds', 88 *Michigan Law Review* 2444 (1990).

—— 'Striking Back at the Empire: A Brief Survey of Problems in Dworkin's Theory of Law', 6 *Law and Philosophy* 419 (1987).

ALEXY, R., *A Theory of Legal Argumentation* (R. Adler and N. MacCormick, trans., Oxford: Clarendon Press, 1989).

ALTMAN, S., 'Beyond Candor', 89 *Michigan Law Review* 296 (1990).

ANSCOMBE, G. E. M., 'Wittgenstein on Rules and Private Language' (book review), 95 *Ethics* 342 (1985).

AUSTIN, J., *The Province of Jurisprudence Determined* (London: Weidenfeld and Nicolson, 1955).

BAILEY, S. H. and GUNN, M. J., *Smith and Bailey on The Modern English Legal System*, 2nd edn. (London: Sweet & Maxwell, 1991).

BAKER, G. P., 'Criteria: A New Foundation for Semantics', 16 *Ratio* 156 (1974).

—— 'Defeasibility and Meaning', in *Law, Morality, and Society*, 26–57 (P. M. S. Hacker and J. Raz, eds., Oxford: Clarendon Press, 1977).

—— 'Following Wittgenstein: Some Signposts for *Philosophical Investigations* sections 143–242', in *Wittgenstein: To Follow a Rule*, 31–71 (S. Holtzman and C. Leich, eds., London: Routledge & Kegan Paul, 1981).

—— '*Philosophical Investigations* Section 122: Neglected Aspects', in *Wittgenstein's Philosophical Investigations: Text and Context*, 35–68 (R. Arrington and H.-J. Glock, eds., London: Routledge, 1991).

BAKER, G. P. AND HACKER, P. M. S., 'The Grammar of Psychology: Wittgenstein's *Bemerkungen Ueber die Philosophie der Psychologie*', 2 *Language and Communication* 227 (1982).

—— *Language, Sense and Nonsense* (Oxford: Basil Blackwell, 1984).

—— *Scepticism, Rules and Language* (Oxford: Basil Blackwell, 1984).

—— 'Wittgenstein and the Vienna Circle: The Exaltation and Deposition of Ostensive Definition', 2 *Teoria* 5 (1985).

—— *Wittgenstein: Rules, Grammar and Necessity* (Oxford: Basil Blackwell, 1985).

—— *Wittgenstein: Understanding and Meaning* (Oxford: Basil Blackwell, 1980).

BALKIN, J. M., 'Deconstructive Practice and Legal Theory', 96 *Yale Law Journal* 743 (1987).

—— 'Taking Ideology Seriously: Ronald Dworkin and the CLS Critique', 55 *UMKC Law Review* 392 (1987).

BEARDSMORE, R. W., 'The Theory of Family Resemblances', 15 *Philosophical Investigations* 131 (1992).

BELL, J., 'The Acceptability of Legal Arguments', in *The Legal Mind* 45–65 (N. MacCormick and P. Birks, eds., Oxford: Clarendon Press, 1986).

—— *Policy Arguments in Judicial Decisions* (Oxford: Clarendon Press, 1983).

BIX, B., 'A. D. Woozley and the Concept of Right Answers in Law', 5 *Ratio Juris* 58 (1992).

—— 'The Application (and Mis-Application) of Wittgenstein's Rule-Following Considerations to Legal Theory', 3 *Canadian Journal of Law and Jurisprudence* 107 (1990), reprinted in *Wittgenstein and Legal Theory* 208–23 (D. Patterson, ed., Boulder, Col.: Westview Press, 1992).

—— book review, 18 *Seton Hall Law Review* 523 (1988).

—— 'Dancing in the Dark: The Philosophical Moves of Ronald Dworkin' (book review), 23 *Harvard Journal on Legislation* 307 (1986).

—— 'H. L. A. Hart and the "Open Texture" of Language', 10 *Law and Philosophy* 51 (1991).

—— 'Michael Moore's Realist Approach to Law', 140 *University of Pennsylvania Law Review* 1293 (1992).

BJARUP, J., 'Kripke's Case', 19 *Rechtstheorie* 39 (1988).

BLACKBURN, S., 'How Can We Tell Whether a Commitment Has a Truth Condition?', in *Meaning and Interpretation*, 201–32 (C. Travis, ed., Oxford: Basil Blackwell, 1986).

—— 'The Individual Strikes Back', 58 *Synthese* 281 (1984).

—— 'Options for the World' (unpublished manuscript).

—— 'Rule-Following and Moral Realism', in *Wittgenstein: To Follow a Rule*, 163–87 (S. Holtzman and C. Leich, eds., London: Routledge & Kegan Paul, 1981).

—— *Spreading the Word* (Oxford: Clarendon Press, 1984).

BOBBIT, P., *Constitutional Fate* (Oxford: Oxford University Press, 1982).

BOGHOSSIAN, R., 'The Rule-Following Considerations', 98 *Mind* 507 (1989).

BORGES, J. L., 'The Analytical Language of John Wilkins', in *Borges: A Reader*, 141–3 (E. R. Monegal and A. Reid, eds., New York: E. P. Dutton, 1981).

BRAINERD, S., 'The Groundless Assault: A Wittgensteinian Look at Language, Structuralism, and Critical Legal Theory', 34 *American University Law Review* 1231 (1985).

BRINK, D., 'Legal Theory, Legal Interpretation, and Judicial Review', 17 *Philosophy and Public Affairs* 105 (1988).
—— *Moral Realism and the Foundations of Ethics* (Cambridge: Cambridge University Press, 1989).
—— 'Semantics and Legal Interpretation (Further Thoughts)', 2 *Canadian Journal of Law and Jurisprudence* 181 (1989).
BUDD, M., 'Wittgenstein on Meaning, Interpretation and Rules', 58 *Synthese* 303 (1984).
—— *Wittgenstein's Philosophy of Psychology* (London: Routledge, 1989).
BURGE, T., 'Philosophy of Language and Mind: 1950–1990', 101 *Philosophical Review* 3 (1992).
CANDLISH, S., critical notice, 99 *Mind* 467 (1990).
CANTOR, N., *Legal Frontiers of Death and Dying* (Bloomington, Ind.: Indiana University Press, 1987).
CARROLL, L., *The Annotated Alice: Alice's Adventures in Wonderland and Through the Looking Glass* (M. Gardner, annot., New York: Meridian, 1960).
CAVELL, S., 'The Availability of Wittgenstein's Later Philosophy', 71 *Philosophical Review* 67 (1962).
—— *The Claim of Reason* (New York: Oxford University Press, 1979).
—— *Must we Mean what we Say?* (Cambridge: Cambridge University Press, 1976).
—— 'The Uncanniness of the Ordinary', in *The Tanner Lectures on Human Values VIII*, 81–117 (S. M. McMurrin, ed., 1988).
COHEN, F., 'Transcendental Nonsense and the Functional Response', 35 *Columbia Law Review* 809 (1935).
COPPOCK, P., book review, 81 *Journal of Philosophy* 261 (1984).
COVER, R., 'Nomos and Narrative', 97 *Harvard Law Review* 4 (1983).
—— 'Violence and the Word', 95 *Yale Law Journal* 1601 (1986).
CROSS, R., BELL, J., and ENGLE, G., *Statutory Interpretation*, 2nd edn. (London: Butterworths, 1987).
D'AMATO, A., 'Aspects of Deconstruction: The "Easy Case" of the Under-Aged President', 84 *Northwestern University Law Review* 250 (1989).
—— 'Aspects of Deconstruction: The Failure of the Word "Bird" ', 84 *Northwestern University Law Review* 536 (1990).
—— 'Can Legislatures Constrain Judicial Interpretation of Statutes?', 75 *Virginia Law Review* 561 (1989).
—— *Jurisprudence* (Lancaster: Nijhoff, 1984).
—— 'Pragmatic Indeterminacy', 85 *Northwestern University Law Review* 148 (1990).
DAVIDSON, D., 'A Coherence Theory of Truth and Knowledge', in *Truth and Interpretation*, 307–19 (E. LePore, ed., Oxford: Basil Blackwell, 1986).

DAVIDSON, D., 'A Nice Derangement of Epitaphs', in *Truth and Interpretation*, 433–46 (E. LePore, ed., Oxford: Basil Blackwell, 1986).

—— 'On the Very Idea of a Conceptual Scheme', repr. in *Inquiries into Truth and Interpretation*, 183–98 (Oxford: Clarendon Press, 1984).

—— 'The Structure and Content of Truth', 87 *Journal of Philosophy* 279 (1990).

DAVIS, K. C., *Administrative Law Treatise*, 2nd edn., vol. 5 (San Diego: K. C. Davis Publishing Co., 1984).

DEWEY, J., 'Logical Method and the Law', 10 *Cornell Law Quarterly* 17 (1924).

DONATO, J., 'Dworkin and Subjectivity in Legal Interpretation', 40 *Stanford Law Review* 1517 (1988).

DUMMETT, M., 'A Nice Derangement of Epitaphs: Some Comments on Davidson and Hacking', in *Truth and Interpretation*, 459–76 (E. LePore, ed., Oxford: Basil Blackwell, 1986).

—— 'Can Analytic Philosophy Be Systematic, and Ought it to be?', repr. in *Truth and Other Enigmas*, 437–58 (London: Duckworth, 1978).

—— *Frege: Philosophy of Language* (London: Duckworth, 1978).

—— 'Frege's Distinction between Sense and Reference', repr. in *Truth and Other Enigmas*, 116–44 (London: Duckworth, 1978).

—— *The Logical Basis of Metaphysics* (London: Duckworth, 1991).

—— 'Preface', in *Truth and Other Enigmas*, pp. ix–li (London: Duckworth, 1978).

—— 'The Social Character of Meaning', repr. in *Truth and Other Enigmas*, 420–30 (London: Duckworth, 1978).

DUPRÉ, J., 'Natural Kinds and Biological Taxa', 90 *Philosophical Review* 66 (1981).

DWORKIN, R., 'Bork's Jurisprudence' (book review), 57 *University of Chicago Law Review* 657 (1990).

—— *Law's Empire* (Cambridge, Mass.: Harvard University Press, 1986).

—— 'Legal Theory and the Problem of Sense', in *Issues in Contemporary Legal Philosophy*, 9–20 (R. Gavison, ed., Oxford: Clarendon Press, 1987).

—— *A Matter of Principle* (Cambridge, Mass.: Harvard University Press, 1985).

—— 'The Model of Rules', 35 *University of Chicago Law Review* 14 (1967), repr. in modified form in *Taking Rights Seriously*, 14–45 (London: Duckworth, 1978).

—— 'My Reply to Stanley Fish (and Walter Benn Michaels): Please don't Talk about Objectivity Any More', in *The Politics of Interpretation*, 287–313 (W. J. T. Mitchell, ed., London: University of Chicago Press, 1983), repr. in part, in modified form, in *A Matter of Principle*, 167–77 (Cambridge, Mass.: Harvard University Press, 1985).

—— 'No Right Answer?', in *Law, Morality, and Society*, 58–84 (P. M. S.

Hacker and J. Raz, eds., Oxford: Clarendon Press, 1977), repr. in modified form in *A Matter of Principle*, 119–45 (Cambridge, Mass.: Harvard University Press, 1985).

—— 'On Gaps in the Law', in *Controversies about Law's Ontology*, 84–90 (P. Amselek and N. MacCormick, eds., Edinburgh: Edinburgh University Press, 1991).

—— 'A Reply by Ronald Dworkin', in *Ronald Dworkin and Contemporary Jurisprudence*, 247–300 (M. Cohen, ed., London: Duckworth, 1984).

—— *Taking Rights Seriously* (London: Duckworth, 1978).

EISELE, T., 'Hegelian Vanity, Common Law Humility: On Legal Theory, Its Expression and Its Criticism', 10 *Cardozo Law Review* 915 (1989).

—— ' "Our Real Need": Not Explanation, But Education', 3 *Canadian Journal of Law and Jurisprudence* 5 (1990).

EVANS, G., *The Varieties of Reference* (J. McDowell, ed., Oxford: Clarendon Press, 1982).

FALLON, R., 'Reflections on Dworkin and the Two Faces of Law', 67 *Notre Dame Law Review* 553 (1992).

FINNIS, J., 'Allocating Risks and Suffering: Some Hidden Traps', 38 *Cleveland State Law Review* 193 (1990).

—— 'The Authority of Law in the Predicament of Contemporary Social Theory', 1 *Notre Dame Journal of Law, Ethics and Public Policy* 115 (1984).

—— 'Comment [on Sartorius]', in *Issues in Contemporary Legal Philosophy*, 62–75 (R. Gavison, ed., Oxford: Clarendon Press, 1987).

—— 'Concluding Reflections', 38 *Cleveland State Law Review* 231 (1990).

—— *Fundamentals of Ethics* (Oxford: Clarendon Press, 1983).

—— 'Law as Co-ordination', 2 *Ratio Juris* 97 (1989).

—— 'Natural Law and Legal Reasoning', 38 *Cleveland State Law Review* 1 (1990), repr. in modified form in *Natural Law Theory*, 134–57 (R. George, ed., Oxford: Clarendon Press, 1992).

—— *Natural Law and Natural Rights* (Oxford: Clarendon Press, 1980).

—— 'On "Positivism" and "Legal Rational Authority" ', 5 *Oxford Journal of Legal Studies* 74 (1985).

—— 'On Reason and Authority in *Law's Empire*' (book review), 6 *Law and Philosophy* 357 (1987).

—— 'On "The Critical Legal Studies Movement" ', 30 *American Journal of Jurisprudence* 21 (1985), repr. in *Oxford Essays in Jurisprudence*, 3rd ser., 145–65 (J. Eekelaar and J. Bell, eds., Oxford: Clarendon Press, 1987).

FISH, S., 'Almost Pragmatism: Richard Posner's Jurisprudence' (book review), 57 *University of Chicago Law Review* 1447 (1990).

—— 'Dennis Martinez and the Uses of Theory', 96 *Yale Law Journal* 1773 (1987).

FISH, S., *Doing What Comes Naturally* (Oxford, Clarendon Press, 1989).
—— 'Don't Know Much about the Middle Ages: Posner on Law and Literature', 97 *Yale Law Journal* 777 (1988).
—— 'Fish v. Fiss', 36 *Stanford Law Review* 1325 (1984).
—— *Is There a Text in This Class?* (Cambridge, Mass.: Harvard University Press, 1980).
—— 'Still Wrong After All These Years', 6 *Law and Philosophy* 401 (1987).
—— 'Wrong Again', 62 *Texas Law Review* 299 (1983).
FISS, O., 'Conventionalism', 58 *Southern California Law Review* 177 (1985).
—— 'Objectivity and Interpretation', 34 *Stanford Law Review* 739 (1982).
FRUG, G., 'The Ideology of Bureaucracy in American Law', 97 *Harvard Law Review* 1276 (1984).
FULLER, L., 'The Forms and Limits of Adjudication', 92 *Harvard Law Review* 353 (1978).
—— *The Morality of Law*, rev. edn., (New Haven, Conn.: Yale University Press, 1969).
—— 'Positivism and Fidelity to Law—A Reply to Professor Hart', 71 *Harvard Law Review* 630 (1958).
—— *The Principles of Moral Order* (K. I. Winston, ed., Durham: Duke University Press, 1981).
GABEL, P., book review, 91 *Harvard Law Review* 302 (1977).
GALLIE, W. B., 'Essentially Contested Concepts', 56 *Proceedings of the Aristotelian Society* 167 (1955–6).
GARDNER, J., 'Concerning Permissive Sources and Gaps', 8 *Oxford Journal of Legal Studies* 457 (1988).
GAVISON, R., 'Comment [on Dworkin]', in *Issues in Contemporary Legal Philosophy*, 21–34 (R. Gavison, ed., Oxford: Clarendon Press, 1987).
—— 'Positivism, Natural Law and the Limits of Jurisprudence: A Modern Round', 91 *Yale Law Journal* 1250 (1981).
GOLDFARB, W., 'Kripke on Wittgenstein on Rules', 82 *Journal of Philosophy* 471 (1985).
GOLDSWORTHY, J., 'The Self-Destruction of Legal Positivism', 10 *Oxford Journal of Legal Studies* 449 (1990).
GOODRICH, P., 'Law and Modernity', 49 *Modern Law Review* 545 (1986).
GORDON, R., 'Critical Legal Histories', 36 *Stanford Law Review* 57 (1984).
GOULD, S. J., 'A Quahog is a Quahog', repr. in *The Panda's Thumb* 170–77 (Harmondsworth: Penguin Books, 1983).
—— and LEWONTIN, R., 'The Spandrels of San Marco and the Panglossian Paradigm: a Critique of the Adaptationist Programme', 205 *Proceedings of the Royal Society*, ser. B, 581–98 (1979).

GRAFF, G., ' "Keep off the Grass", "Drop Dead", and Other Indeterminacies: A Response to Sanford Levinson', 60 *Texas Law Review* 405 (1982).

GREENAWALT, K., 'How Law Can Be Determinate', 38 *UCLA Law Review* 1 (1990).

—— *Law and Objectivity* (Oxford: Clarendon Press, 1992).

GRICE, H. P., *Studies in the Way of Words* (London: Harvard University Press, 1989).

GRIFFIN, J., 'Are there Incommensurable Values?', 7 *Philosophy and Public Affairs* 39 (1977).

—— 'Mixing Values', *Proceedings of the Aristotelian Society*, supp. vol. 65, 101 (1991).

HACKER, P. M. S., 'Hart's Philosophy of Law', in *Law, Morality, and Society*, 1–25 (P. M. S. Hacker and J. Raz, eds., Oxford: Clarendon Press, 1977).

—— *Insight and Illusion*, rev. edn. (Oxford: Oxford University Press, 1986).

—— 'Language, Rules and Pseudo-Rules', 8 *Language and Communication* 159 (1988).

—— *Wittgenstein: Meaning and Mind* (Oxford: Basil Blackwell, 1990).

HALLER, R., *Questions on Wittgenstein* (Bristol: Routledge, 1988).

HANFLING, O., 'What is Wrong with the Paradigm Case Argument?' 91 *Proceedings of the Aristotelian Society* 21 (1990–1).

HARRIS, J. W., *Law and Legal Science* (Oxford: Clarendon Press, 1979).

—— 'Legal Doctrine and Interests in Land', in *Oxford Essays in Jurisprudence*, 3rd ser., 167–97 (J. Eekelaar and J. Bell, eds., Oxford: Clarendon Press, 1987).

—— *Legal Philosophies* (London: Butterworths, 1980).

—— 'Unger's Critique of Formalism in Legal Reasoning: Hero, Hercules, and Humdrum', 52 *Modern Law Review* 42 (1989).

HART, H. L. A., 'The Ascription of Responsibility and Rights', 49 *Proceedings of the Aristotelian Society* 171 (1948–9).

—— 'Comment [on Dworkin]', in *Issues in Contemporary Legal Philosophy*, 35–42 (R. Gavison, ed., Oxford: Clarendon Press, 1987).

—— *The Concept of Law* (Oxford: Clarendon Press, 1961).

—— *Definition and Theory in Jurisprudence* (Oxford: Clarendon Press, 1953), repr. in 70 *Law Quarterly Review* 37 (1954).

—— 'Introduction', in *Essays in Jurisprudence and Philosophy*, 1–18 (Oxford: Clarendon Press, 1983).

—— 'Positivism and the Separation of Law and Morals', 71 *Harvard Law Review* 593 (1958).

—— 'Problems in the Philosophy of Law', in *Essays in Jurisprudence and Philosophy*, 88–119 (Oxford: Clarendon Press, 1983).

—— *Punishment and Responsibility* (Oxford: Clarendon Press, 1968).

Hart, H. L. A. 'Theory and Definition in Jurisprudence', *Proceedings of the Aristotelian Society*, suppl. vol. 29, 239 (1955).

Heal, J., *Fact and Meaning* (Oxford: Basil Blackwell, 1989).

Hegland, K., 'Goodbye to Deconstruction', 58 *Southern California Law Review* 1203 (1985).

Herzog, D., 'As Many as Six Impossible Things Before Breakfast', 75 *California Law Review* 609 (1987).

Hill, H. H., 'H. L. A. Hart's Hermeneutic Positivism: On Some Methodological Difficulties in *The Concept of Law*', 3 *Canadian Journal of Law and Jurisprudence* 113 (1990).

Holmes, O. W., 'The Path of the Law', 10 *Harvard Law Review* 457 (1897).

Honoré, A. M., *Making Law Bind* (Oxford: Clarendon Press, 1987).

—— 'A Theory of Coercion', 10 *Oxford Journal of Legal Studies* 94 (1990).

Hoy, D., 'Dworkin's Constructive Optimism v. Deconstructive Legal Nihilism', 6 *Law and Philosophy* 321 (1987).

—— 'Interpreting the Law: Hermeneutical and Poststructuralist Perspectives', 58 *Southern California Law Review* 136 (1985).

Hunt, A., 'The Big Fear: Law Confronts Postmodernism', 35 *McGill Law Journal* 507 (1990).

Hurd, H., 'Relativistic Jurisprudence: Skepticism Founded on Confusion', 61 *Southern California Law Review* 1417 (1988).

—— 'Sovereignty in Silence', 99 *Yale Law Journal* 945 (1990).

Hurley, S. L., 'Coherence, Hypothetical Cases, and Precedent', 10 *Oxford Journal of Legal Studies* 221 (1990).

—— *Natural Reasons* (Oxford: Oxford University Press, 1989).

Hutchinson, A., 'Democracy and Determinacy: An Essay on Legal Interpretation', 43 *University of Miami Law Review* 541 (1989).

—— *Dwelling on the Threshold* (London: Sweet & Maxwell, 1988).

—— 'Indiana Dworkin and the Law's Empire' (book review), 96 *Yale Law Journal* 637 (1987).

—— 'Part of an Essay on Power and Interpretation', 60 *New York University Law Review* 850 (1985).

—— 'That's Just the Way it Is: Langille on Law', 34 *McGill Law Journal* 145 (1989).

Janik, A. and Toulmin, S., *Wittgenstein's Vienna* (New York: Touchstone, 1973).

Johnston, P., *Wittgenstein and Moral Philosophy* (London: Routledge, 1989).

Katz, J., *The Metaphysics of Meaning* (Cambridge, Mass.: MIT Press, 1990).

Kelman, M., *A Guide to Critical Legal Studies* (Cambridge, Mass.: Harvard University Press, 1987).

KELSEN, H., *General Theory of Law and State* (New York: Russell & Russell, 1945).

—— *General Theory of Norms* (Oxford: Clarendon Press, 1991).

—— 'On the Theory of Interpretation', 10 *Legal Studies* 127 (1990).

—— *The Pure Theory of Law* (Berkeley, Calif.: University of California Press, 1967).

KENNY, A., *The Legacy of Wittgenstein* (Oxford: Basil Blackwell, 1984).

KING, B. E., 'The Norm in the Bottle', 1961 *Cambridge Law Journal* 103.

KORNHAUSER, L. and SAGER, L., 'Unpacking the Court', 96 *Yale Law Journal* 82 (1986).

KRESS, K., 'The Interpretive Turn', 97 *Ethics* 834 (1987).

—— 'Legal Indeterminacy', 77 *California Law Review* 283 (1989).

—— 'Legal Reasoning and Coherence Theories: Dworkin's Rights Thesis, Retroactivity, and the Linear Order of Decisions', 72 *California Law Review* 369 (1984).

KRIPKE, S., *Naming and Necessity* (Cambridge, Mass.: Harvard University Press, 1972).

—— *Wittgenstein on Rules and Private Language* (Cambridge, Mass.: Harvard University Press, 1982).

LANDERS, S., 'Wittgenstein, Realism, and CLS: Undermining Rule Scepticism', 9 *Law and Philosophy* 177 (1990).

LANGILLE, B., 'The Jurisprudence of Despair, Again', 23 *University of British Columbia Law Review* 549 (1989).

—— 'Political World', 3 *Canadian Journal of Law and Jurisprudence* 139 (1990).

—— 'Revolution Without Foundation: The Grammar of Scepticism and Law', 33 *McGill Law Journal* 451 (1988).

LEAR, J., 'Transcendental Anthropology', in *Subject, Thought and Context*, 267–98 (P. Pettit and J. McDowell, eds., Oxford: Clarendon Press, 1986).

LEE, S., 'Law's British Empire' (book review), 8 *Oxford Journal of Legal Studies* 278 (1988).

LEVINSON, S., 'Law as Literature', 60 *Texas Law Review* 1151 (1985).

—— 'Law: On Dworkin, Kennedy, and Ely: Decoding the Legal Past', 51 *Partisan Review* 248 (1984).

LEWIS, A., 'Wittgenstein and Rule-Scepticism', 38 *Philosophical Quarterly* 280 (1988).

LEWIS, D., 'Putnam's Paradox', 62 *Australasian Journal of Philosophy* 221 (1984).

LIN, P., 'Wittgenstein, Language, and Legal Theorizing: Toward a Non-Reductive Account of Law', 47 *University of Toronto Faculty of Law Review* 939 (1989).

LOVIBOND, S., *Realism and Imagination in Ethics* (Oxford: Basil Blackwell, 1983).

LUBAN, D., '*Fish v. Fish* or, Some Realism about Idealism', 7 *Cardozo Law Review* 693 (1986).
—— 'Legal Traditionalism', 43 *Stanford Law Review* 1035 (1991).
LYONS, D., 'Moral Aspects of Legal Theory', 7 *Midwest Studies in Philosophy* 223 (1982).
—— 'Reconstructing Legal Theory', 16 *Philosophy and Public Affairs* 179 (1987).
MACCORMICK, D. N., 'Doing and Discussing' (book review), *Times Literary Supplement*, 19 July 1991.
—— 'Law as Institutional Fact', 90 *Law Quarterly Review* 102 (1974).
—— *Legal Reasoning and Legal Theory* (Oxford: Clarendon Press, 1978).
—— 'Natural Law and the Separation of Law and Morals', in *Natural Law Theory*, 105–33 (R. George, ed., Oxford: Clarendon Press, 1992).
—— 'Natural Law Reconsidered', 1 *Oxford Journal of Legal Studies* 99 (1981).
—— 'On "Open Texture" in Law', in *Controversies about Law's Ontology*, 73–83 (P. Amselek and N. MacCormick, eds., Edinburgh: Edinburgh University Press, 1991).
—— 'Reconstruction after Deconstruction: A Response to CLS', 10 *Oxford Journal of Legal Studies* 539 (1990).
MACKIE, J., *Ethics: Inventing Right and Wrong* (Harmondsworth: Penguin Books, 1977).
—— 'The Third Theory of Law', repr. in *Ronald Dworkin and Contemporary Jurisprudence*, 161–70 (M. Cohen, ed., London: Duckworth, 1984).
MALCOLM, N., *Nothing is Hidden* (Oxford: Basil Blackwell, 1986).
MARGALIT, A., 'Open Texture', in *Meaning and Use*, 141–52 (A. Margalit, ed., Norwell, Mass.: Kluwer Academic, 1979).
MARMOR, A., *Interpretation and Legal Theory* (Oxford: Clarendon Press, 1992).
—— 'No Easy Cases?', 3 *Canadian Journal of Law and Jurisprudence* 61 (1990).
McDOWELL, J., 'Are Moral Requirements Hypothetical Imperatives?', *Proceedings of the Aristotelian Society*, suppl. vol. 52, 13 (1978).
—— *'Criteria, Defeasibility, and Knowledge'*, 68 *Proceedings of the British Academy* 455 (Oxford: Oxford University Press, 1982).
—— 'Non-Cognitivism and Rule-Following', in *Wittgenstein: To Follow a Rule*, 141–62 (S. Holtzman and C. Leich, eds., London: Routledge & Kegan Paul, 1981).
—— 'Wittgenstein on Following a Rule', 58 *Synthese* 325 (1984).
McGINN, C., *Wittgenstein on Meaning* (Oxford: Basil Blackwell, 1984).
MICHELMAN, F., 'Justification (and Justifiability) of Law in a Contradictory World', in *Justification: NOMOS XXVIII*, 71–99 (J. Pennock and J. Chapman, eds., New York: New York University Press, 1986).

—— 'Politics as Medicine: On Misdiagnosing Legal Scholarship', 90 *Yale Law Journal* 1224 (1981).

MINOW, M., *Making All the Difference* (Ithaca: Cornell University Press, 1990).

—— 'Making All the Difference: Three Lessons in Equality, Neutrality, and Tolerance', 39 *DePaul Law Review* 1 (1989).

—— 'Some Realism about Rulism: A Parable for the Fiftieth Anniversary of the Federal Rules of Civil Procedure', 137 *University of Pennsylvania Law Review* 2249 (1989).

—— 'Words and the Door to the Land of Change: Law, Language, and Family Violence', 43 *Vanderbilt Law Review* 1665 (1990).

MOLES, R., *Definition and Rule in Legal Theory* (Oxford: Basil Blackwell, 1987).

MONK, R., *Ludwig Wittgenstein: The Duty of Genius* (London: Jonathan Cape, 1990).

MOORE, A. W., 'On Saying and Showing', 62 *Philosophy* 473 (1987).

MOORE, M., 'Authority, Law and Razian Reasons', 62 *Southern California Law Review* 827 (1989).

—— 'Do we Have an Unwritten Constitution?', 63 *Southern California Law Review* 107 (1989).

—— 'The Interpretive Turn in Modern Theory: A Turn for the Worse?', 41 *Stanford Law Review* 871 (1989).

—— 'Law as a Functional Kind', in *Natural Law Theories*, 188–242 (R. George, ed., Oxford: Oxford University Press, 1992).

—— 'Metaphysics, Epistemology and Legal Theory' (book review), 60 *Southern California Law Review* 453 (1987).

—— 'Moral Reality', 1982 *Wisconsin Law Review* 1061.

—— 'Moral Reality Revisited', 90 *Michigan Law Review* 2424 (1992).

—— 'The Moral Worth of Retribution', in *Responsibility, Character and the Emotions*, 179–219 (F. Schoeman, ed., Cambridge: Cambridge University Press, 1987).

—— 'A Natural Law Theory of Interpretation', 58 *Southern California Law Review* 277 (1985).

—— 'Originalist Theories of Constitutional Interpretation', 73 *Cornell Law Review* 364 (1988).

—— 'Precedent, Induction, and Ethical Generalization', in *Precedent in Law*, 183–213 (L. Goldstein, ed., Oxford: Clarendon Press, 1987).

—— 'The Semantics of Judging', 54 *Southern California Law Review* 151 (1981).

—— 'Three Concepts of Rules', 14 *Harvard Journal of Law and Public Policy* 771 (1991).

MORAWETZ, T., 'The Epistemology of Judging: Wittgenstein and Deliberative Practices', 3 *Canadian Journal of Law and Jurisprudence* 35 (1990).

MULHALL, S., 'Davidson on Interpretation and Understanding', 37 *Philosophical Quarterly* 319 (1987).
—— *On Being in the World* (London: Routledge, 1990).
NAGEL, T., 'The Fragmentation of Value', in *Mortal Questions*, 128–41 (Cambridge: Cambridge University Press, 1979).
NESSON, C., 'The Evidence or the Event? On Judicial Proof and the Acceptability of Verdicts', 98 *Harvard Law Review* 1357 (1986).
OLSEN, F., 'The Family and the Market: A Study in Ideology and Legal Reform', 96 *Harvard Law Review* 1497 (1983).
PARFIT, D., letter, in *Times Literary Supplement*, 19 July 1991.
—— *Reasons and Persons* (Oxford: Clarendon Press, 1986).
PATTERSON, D., 'Good Faith, Lender Liability, and Discretionary Acceleration: Of Llewellyn, Wittgenstein, and the Uniform Commercial Code', 68 *Texas Law Review* 169 (1989).
—— 'Interpretation in Law—Toward a Reconstruction of the Current Debate', 29 *Villanova Law Review* 671 (1983–4).
—— 'Law's Pragmatism: Law as Practice and Narrative', 76 *Virginia Law Review* 937 (1990).
—— 'Postmodernism/Feminism/Law', 77 *Cornell Law Review* 254 (1992).
—— 'What Was Realism?: A Reply to David Brink', 2 *Canadian Journal of Law and Jurisprudence* 193 (1989).
—— 'Wittgenstein and the Code: A Theory of Good Faith Performance and Enhancement under Article Nine', 137 *University of Pennsylvania Law Review* 335 (1988).
PAULSON, S., 'Kelsen on Legal Interpretation', 10 *Legal Studies* 136 (1990).
PEARS, D., *The False Prison*, 2 vols. (Oxford: Clarendon Press, 1987, 1988).
—— *Ludwig Wittgenstein* (Cambridge, Mass.: Harvard University Press, 1986).
—— 'Rule-Following in *Philosophical Investigations*', in *Wittgenstein in Focus*, 249–61 (B. McGuinness and R. Haller, eds., Amsterdam: Rodopi, 1989).
PELLER, G., 'The Metaphysics of American Law', 73 *California Law Review* 1151 (1985).
PENNER, J., 'The Rules of Law: Wittgenstein, Davidson, and Weinrib's Formalism', 46 *University of Toronto Faculty of Law Review* 488 (1988).
PETTIT, P., 'Affirming the Reality of Rule-Following', 99 *Mind* 433 (1990).
—— 'The Reality of Rule-Following', 99 *Mind* 1 (1990).
—— and MCDOWELL, J., 'Introduction', in *Subject, Thought, and Context*, 1–15 (P. Pettit and J. McDowell, eds., Oxford: Clarendon Press, 1986).
PLATO, 'Euthyphro', in *The Dialogues of Plato*, i. 303–27 (B. Jowett, trans., Oxford: Clarendon Press, 1953).
POMERANTZ, H. and BRESLIN, S., 'Judicial Humour—Construction of a Statute', 8 *Criminal Law Quarterly* 137 (1965).

POSNER, R., 'The Decline of Law as an Autonomous Discipline', 100 *Harvard Law Review* 761 (1987).

—— *Law and Literature* (Cambridge, Mass.: Harvard University Press, 1988).

—— 'Law and Literature: A Relation Reargued', 72 *Virginia Law Review* 1351 (1986).

POSTEMA, G., ' "Protestant" Interpretation and Social Practices', 6 *Law and Philosophy* 283 (1987).

PUTNAM, H., 'A Defense of Internal Realism', in *Realism with a Human Face*, 30–42 (London: Harvard University Press, 1990).

—— 'Experience and Mathematical Necessity' (unpublished manuscript).

—— 'Is Semantics Possible?', repr. in *Mind, Language and Reality*, Philosophical Papers vol. 2, pp. 139–52 (Cambridge: Cambridge University Press, 1975).

—— 'Is the Causal Structure of the Physical Self Itself Something Physical?', repr. in *Realism with a Human Face*, 80–95 (London: Harvard University Press, 1990).

—— 'Is Water Necessarily H_2O?', repr. in *Realism With a Human Face*, 54–79 (London: Harvard University Press, 1990).

—— 'It Ain't Necessarily So', 59 *Journal of Philosophy* 658 (1962), repr. in *Mathematics, Matter and Method*, Philosophical Papers vol. 1, pp. 237–49 (Cambridge: Cambridge University Press, 1975).

—— *The Many Faces of Realism* (LaSalle, Ill.: Open Court, 1987).

—— *Meaning and the Moral Sciences* (London: Routledge & Kegan Paul, 1978).

—— 'Meaning Holism', repr. in *Realism with a Human Face*, 278–302 (London: Harvard University Press, 1990).

—— 'The Meaning of "Meaning" ', repr. in *Mind, Language and Reality*, Philosophical Papers vol. 2, pp. 215–71 (Cambridge: Cambridge University Press, 1975).

—— 'Realism and Reason', repr. in *Meaning and the Moral Sciences*, 123–40 (London: Routledge & Kegan Paul, 1978).

—— *Reason, Truth and History* (Cambridge: Cambridge University Press, 1981).

—— 'Realism with a Human Face', in *Realism with a Human Face*, 3–29 (London: Harvard University Press, 1990).

—— 'Reference and Truth', in *Realism and Reason*, Philosophical Papers vol. 3, pp. 69–86 (Cambridge: Cambridge University Press, 1983).

QUINE, W. V. O., *Theories and Things* (London: Belknap Press, 1981).

—— 'Two Dogmas of Empiricism', in *From a Logical Point of View*, 20–46 (London: Oxford University Press 1953).

—— *Word and Object* (Cambridge, Mass.: MIT Press, 1960).

QUINTON, A., 'Introduction', in F. Waismann, *Philosophical Papers*, pp. ix–xix (B. McGuinness, ed., Holland: D. Reidel, 1977).

Radin, M., 'Reconsidering the Rule of Law', 69 *Boston University Law Review* 781 (1989).

Rawls, J., *A Theory of Justice* (Oxford: Clarendon Press, 1972).

Raz, J., 'Authority and Justification', 14 *Philosophy and Public Affairs* 3 (1985).

—— 'Authority, Law and Morality', 68 *Monist* 295 (1985).

—— *The Authority of Law* (Oxford: Clarendon Press, 1979).

—— *The Concept of a Legal System*, 2nd edn. (Oxford: Clarendon Press, 1980).

—— 'Critical Study: Kelsen's General Theory of Norms', 6 *Philosophia* 495 (1976).

—— 'Dworkin: A New Link in the Chain' (book review), 74 *California Law Review* 1103 (1986).

—— 'Facing Up: A Reply', 62 *Southern California Law Review* 1153 (1989).

—— 'The Inner Logic of the Law', *Rechtstheorie*, Beiheft 10, 101 (1986).

—— 'Legal Principles and the Limits of Law', in *Ronald Dworkin and Contemporary Jurisprudence*, 73–87 (M. Cohen, ed., London: Duckworth, 1984).

—— 'Legal Rights', 4 *Oxford Journal of Legal Studies* 1 (1984).

—— 'Mixing Values', *Proceedings of the Aristotelian Society*, suppl. vol. 65, 83 (1991).

—— *The Morality of Freedom* (Oxford: Clarendon Press, 1986).

—— 'The Morality of Obedience' (book review), 83 *Michigan Law Review* 732 (1985).

—— 'On the Functions of Law, in *Oxford Essays in Jurisprudence*, 2nd ser. 278–304 (A. W. B. Simpson, ed., Oxford: Clarendon Press, 1973), repr. in J. Raz, *The Authority of Law*, 163-79 (Oxford: Clarendon Press, 1979).

—— *Practical Reason and Norms*, 2d edn. (Princeton, NJ: Princeton University Press, 1990).

—— 'The Problem about the Nature of Law', 21 *University of Western Ontario Law Review* 203 (1983).

—— 'The Relevance of Coherence', 72 *Boston University Law Review* 273 (1992).

Redpath, T., *Ludwig Wittgenstein: A Student's Memoir* (London: Duckworth, 1990).

Regan, D., 'Authority and Value: Reflections on Raz's *Morality of Freedom*', 62 *Southern California Law Review* 995 (1989).

Rhees, R., 'Some Developments in Wittgenstein's View of Ethics', 74 *Philosophical Review* 17 (1965).

Robinson, P., 'McDowell Against Criterial Knowledge', 4 *Ratio* (*New Series*) 59 (1991).

RUSSELL, B., 'Vagueness', 1 *Australasian Journal of Psychology and Philosophy* 84 (1923), repr. in *Collected Papers of Bertrand Russell*, ix. 145–54 (J. Slated, ed., London: Unwin Hyman, 1988).

SAINSBURY, R. M., *Concepts Without Boundaries* (London: King's College London, 1991).

—— 'Is There Higher Order Vagueness?', 41 *Philosophical Quarterly* 167 (1991).

—— 'Tolerating Vagueness, 89 *Proceedings of the Aristotelian Society* 33 (1988–9).

SCHAUER, F., 'Easy Cases', 58 *Southern California Law Review* 399 (1985).

—— 'Exceptions', 58 *University of Chicago Law Review* 871 (1991).

—— 'Formalism', 97 *Yale Law Journal* 509 (1988).

—— 'Is the Common Law Law?' (book review), 77 *California Law Review* 455 (1989).

—— *Playing by the Rules* (Oxford: Oxford University Press, 1991).

—— 'The Practice and Problems of Plain Meaning: A Response to Aleinikoff and Shaw', 45 *Vanderbilt Law Review* 715 (1992).

—— 'Rules and the Rule-Following Argument, 3 *Canadian Journal of Law and Jurisprudence* 187 (1990).

—— 'Rules and the Rule of Law', 14 *Harvard Journal of Law and Public Policy* 645 (1991).

—— 'The Rules of Jurisprudence: A Reply', 14 *Harvard Journal of Law and Public Policy* 839 (1991).

—— 'Statutory Construction and the Coordinating Function of Plain Meaning', 1990 *Supreme Court Review* 231.

SEN, A., 'Plural Utility', 81 *Proceedings of the Aristotelian Society* 193 (1980–1).

SHINER, R., 'The Acceptance of a Legal System', 3 *Canadian Journal of Law and Jurisprudence* 81 (1990).

SIMMONDS, N. E., 'Between Positivism and Idealism', 50 *Cambridge Law Journal* 308 (1991).

—— 'Imperial Visions and Mundane Practices', 46 *Cambridge Law Journal* 465 (1987).

—— 'Why Conventionalism Does Not Collapse Into Pragmatism', 49 *Cambridge Law Journal* 63 (1990).

SIMPSON, A. W. B., 'The *Ratio Decidendi* of a Case and the Doctrine of Binding Precedent', in *Oxford Essays in Jurisprudence*, 148–75 (A. G. Guest, ed., Oxford: Oxford University Press, 1961).

SMITH, G. A., 'Wittgenstein and the Sceptical Fallacy', 3 *Canadian Journal of Law and Jurisprudence* 155 (1990).

SOLUM, L., 'On the Indeterminacy Crisis: Critiquing Critical Dogma', 54 *University of Chicago Law Review* 462 (1987).

STAINSBY, J., 'The Possibility of Legal Change: Pragmatism and Legal Theory', 46 *University of Toronto Faculty of Law Review* 456 (1988).

STEWART, I., 'Closure and the Legal Norm: An Essay in Critique of Law', 50 *Modern Law Review* 908 (1987).

STOCKER, M., *Plural and Conflicting Values* (Oxford: Clarendon Press, 1990).

STONE, J., *The Province and Function of Law* (Buffalo, N.Y.: William S. Hein, 1968).

STROUP, D., 'Law and Language: Cardozo's Jurisprudence and Wittgenstein's Philosophy', 18 *Valparaiso University Law Review* 331 (1984).

SUMMERFIELD, D., 'On Taking the Rabbit of Rule-Following out of the Hat of Representation: A Response to Pettit's "The Reality of Rule-Following" ', 99 *Mind* 425 (1990).

TAYLOR, C., 'Overcoming Epistemology', in *After Philosophy*, 464–88 (K. Baynes, J. Bohman, and T. McCarthy, eds., London: MIT Press, 1987).

TRIBE, L., *American Constitutional Law*, 2nd edn. (Mineola, New York: Foundation Press, 1988).

TULLY, J., 'Wittgenstein and Political Philosophy', 17 *Political Theory* 172 (1989).

TUSHNET, M., 'Following the Rules Laid Down: A Critique of Interpretation and Neutral Principles', 96 *Harvard Law Review* 781 (1983).

—— 'Legal Scholarship, Its Causes and Cure', 90 *Yale Law Journal* 1205 (1981).

—— *Red, White, and Blue: A Critical Analysis of Constitutional Law* (Cambridge, Mass.: Harvard University Press, 1988).

URMSON, J. O., 'A Defence of Intuitionism', 75 *Proceedings of the Aristotelian Society* 111 (1974–5).

WAISMANN, F., 'Hypotheses', in *Philosophical Papers*, 38–59 (B. McGuinness, ed., Holland: D. Reidel, 1977).

—— 'Language Strata', in *Logic and Language*, 2nd ser. 11–31 (A. Flew, ed., Oxford: Basil Blackwell, 1961).

—— *Ludwig Wittgenstein and the Vienna Circle* (B. McGuinness, ed., J. Schulte and B. McGuinness, trans., Oxford: Basil Blackwell, 1979).

—— *The Principles of Linguistic Philosophy* (R. Harre, ed., London: Macmillan, 1965).

—— 'Verifiability', *Proceedings of the Aristotelian Society*, suppl. vol 19, 119 (1945), repr. in *Logic and Language*, 1st ser. 117–44 (A. Flew, ed., Oxford: Basil Blackwell, 1963).

WALUCHOW, W. J., 'The Weak Social Thesis', 9 *Oxford Journal of Legal Studies* 23 (1989).

WEINREB, L., 'Law as Order', 91 *Harvard Law Review* 909 (1978).

—— *Natural Law and Justice* (Cambridge, Mass.: Harvard University Press, 1987).

—— 'Natural Law and Rights', in *Natural Law Theory*, 278–305 (R. George, ed., Oxford: Clarendon Press, 1992).

WEST, R., 'Adjudication is not Interpretation: Some Reservations about the Law-as-Literature Movement', 54 *Tennessee Law Review* 203 (1987).

WHITE, J. B., *Justice as Translation* (Chicago: University of Chicago Press, 1990).

—— 'What Can a Lawyer Learn from Literature?' (book review), 102 *Harvard Law Review* 2014 (1989).

WIGGINS, D., 'Truth, Invention and the Meaning of Life', 42 *Proceedings of the British Academy* 331 (1976).

—— 'Weakness of Will, Commensurability, and the Objects of Deliberation and Desire', 79 *Proceedings of the Aristotelian Society* 251 (1978–9).

WILLIAMS, B., 'Conflicts of Values', repr. in *Moral Luck*, 71–82 (Cambridge: Cambridge University Press, 1981).

—— 'Terrestrial Thoughts, Extraterrestrial Science' (book review), *London Review of Books*, 7 Feb. 1991.

WILLIAMSON, T., 'Vagueness and Ignorance', *Proceedings of the Aristotelian Society*, suppl. vol. 66, 145 (1992).

WINCH, P., 'Facts and Super-Facts', 33 *Philosophical Quarterly* 398 (1983).

—— *The Idea of a Social Science* (London: Routledge & Kegan Paul, 1958).

WISEMAN, Z., 'The Limits of Vision: Karl Llewellyn and the Merchant Rules', 100 *Harvard Law Review* 465 (1987).

WITTGENSTEIN, L., *The Blue and Brown Books*, 2nd edn. (New York: Harper Torchbooks, 1960).

—— *Lectures and Conversations on Aesthetics, Psychology and Religious Belief* (C. Barrett, ed., Oxford: Basil Blackwell, 1978).

—— *On Certainty* (G. E. M. Anscombe and G. H. von Wright, eds., D. Paul and G. E. M. Anscombe, trans., New York: Harper Torchbooks, 1972).

—— *Philosophical Grammar* (R. Rhees, ed., A. J. P. Kenny, trans., Oxford: Basil Blackwell, 1974).

—— *Philosophical Investigations*, 3rd edn. (G. E. M. Anscombe, trans., New York: Macmillan, 1968).

—— *Philosophical Remarks* (R. Rhees, ed., R. Hargreaves and R. White, trans., Chicago: University of Chicago Press, 1975).

—— *Remarks on the Foundations of Mathematics*, rev. edn. (G. H. von Wright, R. Rhees and G. E. M. Anscombe, eds., G. E. M. Anscombe, trans., Cambridge, Mass.: MIT Press, 1978).

—— *Tractatus Logico-Philosophicus* (D. F. Pears and B. F. McGuinness, trans., London: Routledge & Kegan Paul, 1961).

—— *Wittgenstein's Lectures: Cambridge 1930–1932* (D. Lee, ed., Chicago: University of Chicago Press, 1980).

—— *Wittgenstein's Lectures on the Foundations of Mathematics* (C. Diamond, ed., Sussex: Harvester Press, 1976).

WITTGENSTEIN, L. *Zettel* (G. E. M. Anscombe and G. H. von Wright, eds., G. E. M. Anscombe, trans., Berkeley, Calif.: University of California Press, 1970).

WOLGAST, E., *The Grammar of Justice* (London: Cornell University Press, 1987).

WOLLHEIM, R., 'A Paradox in the Theory of Democracy', in *Philosophy, Politics and Society*, 2nd ser. 71–87 (P. Laslett and W. G. Runciman, eds., Oxford: Basil Blackwell, 1972).

WOOZLEY, A. D., 'No Right Answer', in *Ronald Dworkin and Contemporary Jurisprudence*, 173–81 (M. Cohen, ed., London: Duckworth, 1984).

WRIGHT, C., critical notice, 98 *Mind* 289 (1989).

—— '*Does Philosophical Investigations* I. 258–60 Suggest a Cogent Argument Against Private Language?', in *Subject, Thought and Context*, 209–66 (P. Pettit and J. McDowell, eds., Oxford: Clarendon Press, 1986).

—— 'Is Higher Order Vagueness Coherent?', 52 *Analysis* 129 (1992).

—— *Realism, Meaning and Truth* (Oxford: Basil Blackwell, 1987).

—— 'Rule Following, Meaning and Constructivism', in *Meaning and Interpretation*, 271–97 (C. Travis, ed., Oxford: Basil Blackwell, 1986).

—— 'Second Thoughts about Criteria', 58 *Synthese* 383 (1984), repr. in *Realism, Meaning and Truth*, 267–86 (Oxford: Basil Blackwell, 1987).

WROBLEWSKI, J., 'Problems Related to the One Right Answer Thesis', 2 *Ratio Juris* 240 (1989).

YABLON, C., 'Are Judges Liars? A Wittgensteinian Critique of *Law's Empire*', 3 *Canadian Journal of Law and Jurisprudence* 123 (1990).

—— 'The Indeterminacy of the Law: Critical Legal Studies and the Problem of Legal Explanation', 6 *Cardozo Law Review* 917 (1985).

—— 'Law and Metaphysics' (book review), 96 *Yale Law Journal* 613 (1987).

Index

The manufacturer's authorised representative in the EU for product safety is Oxford University Press España S.A. of el Parque Empresarial San Fernando de Henares, Avenida de Castilla, 2 – 28830 Madrid (www.oup.es/en or product.safety@oup.com). OUP España S.A. also acts as importer into Spain of products made by the manufacturer.

www.ingramcontent.com/pod-product-compliance
Lightning Source LLC
LaVergne TN
LVHW090355210926
848480LV00002B/350

* 9 7 8 0 1 9 8 2 6 0 5 0 9 *